lonely planet

LOVE JAPAN

A CELEBRATION OF JAPAN'S
CULTURE, CRAFTS AND CUSTOMS
FROM THE PEOPLE WHO LIVE THERE

CONT

ENTS

162

ART, CRAFT AND DESIGN

214

NATURE AND LANDSCAPE

266

MEDIA AND TECHNOLOGY

Takeshita Street
吉野家
YOSHINOYA
WOLFGANG PUCK
WEGO
コインロッカー

Introduction

Teenaged me stood at the entrance of Takeshita St in Tokyo's Harajuku district, peering down the teeming pedestrian alley stuffed with zany fashion boutiques, stands selling strawberry-and-cream-stuffed crepes and street vendors with an array of silver wares tumbling across black velvet. Young people of every stripe jostled along: students in sailor-type school uniforms giggling into their shopping bags, pierced punks with snarls and band T-shirts, and dramatically attired *kawaii* Lolitas in beribboned dresses buoyed by fluffy petticoats. I plunged into the fray, and have been pinballing around the streets of Tokyo ever since.

The number of overseas visitors to Japan has more than doubled in the last decade or so, with almost 20 million arrivals in 2015 and the record figure of over 42 million in 2025. What's more, the Japanese government has a target of 60 million international visitors by 2030. It seems the country's tourism boom is still on the upswing.

Part of the appeal is certainly the weak yen, which has made the formerly relatively expensive destination a bargain, especially compared to countries whose cost of living has spiked in recent years. But many more visitors are drawn to Japan's culture: its clean cities, fantastic transportation infrastructure and its mouthwatering, high-quality food – not to mention its robust arts scene, including the thriving pop-culture worlds of manga, video games and cute characters. Beautiful contradictions abound: ancient and modern; frenetic and meditative; at times rigidly collectivist but with countless thriving subcultures. There are a million entry points to this fascinating place, and something new to learn around every corner.

From anime to Zen, this book leads you around those corners. Each essay or interview shows a different facet of the culture, explaining Japan's *why*. You'll learn about the Shintō, Buddhist and Indigenous beliefs that underpin society; the samurai and shōgun-filled history that informs modern mindsets; the arts and crafts that embody the nation's striking aesthetics.

You'll dive deep into some of the building blocks of Japan's UNESCO Intangible Cultural Heritage–recognised cuisine: miso, sushi, sake, tea and all the ways they fit together. And along the way, you'll meet many stewards of Japanese culture, explaining their calling in

LEFT Prepare for the sensory overload of Takeshita St in Tokyo.

TOP The arrival of the cherry trees' blossom is celebrated by events and parties across Japan.

CENTRE LEFT The torii gate of Shintō's Izumo Taisha shrine in Shimane Prefecture.

BOTTOM A tea bowl repaired in kintsugi-style and a matcha whisk.

their own words – like Shintō priest Tomokiyo Tanaka; Hiromi Isori and Keiko Saito, artisans carrying forward Ainu woodcarving and embroidery traditions; and karate master Kenjiro Ueda. You'll hear from the likes of sushi chef Naruki Takimoto, tea farmer Shinji Matsunobu and kabuki actor Hayato Nakamura.

For some, the love affair with Japan is as ephemeral as *sakura* (cherry blossom) – delicate, perfect and short-lived, a vacation fling destined to be a beautiful memory. For others, it's an obsession that lasts a lifetime.

I don't make it over to Harajuku that often anymore. These days my interests lie more in mending my pottery with *kintsugi* in the spirit of *mottainai*, or soaking in one of the thousands of onsen that dapple the countryside. Still, I remember the energy of those early days on Takeshita St, and the thrill that propelled me on the journey that I'm still on today. What sparked your love affair?

—Selena Takigawa Hoy, Tokyo-based Lonely Planet Destination Editor

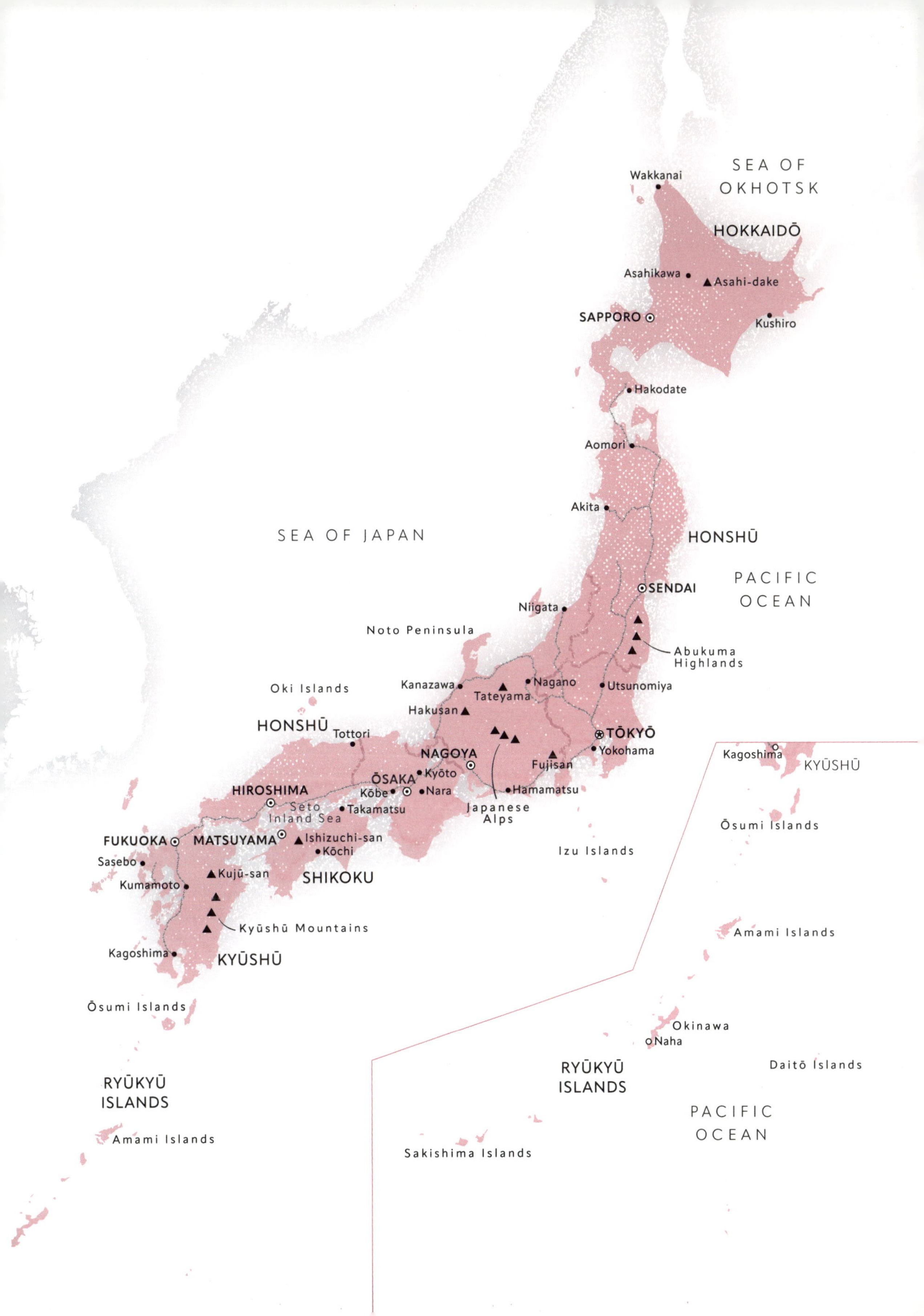

SEA OF OKHOTSK
Wakkanai
HOKKAIDŌ
Asahikawa
Asahi-dake
SAPPORO
Kushiro
Hakodate
Aomori
Akita
SEA OF JAPAN
HONSHŪ
SENDAI
PACIFIC OCEAN
Niigata
Noto Peninsula
Abukuma Highlands
Oki Islands
Kanazawa
Nagano
Utsunomiya
Tateyama
Hakusan
HONSHŪ
Tottori
TŌKYŌ
Yokohama
NAGOYA
Fujisan
ŌSAKA
Kyōto
Kōbe
Nara
Hamamatsu
HIROSHIMA
Seto Inland Sea
Takamatsu
Japanese Alps
FUKUOKA
MATSUYAMA
Ishizuchi-san
Kōchi
Izu Islands
Sasebo
Kujū-san
SHIKOKU
Kumamoto
Kyūshū Mountains
Kagoshima
KYŪSHŪ
Ōsumi Islands
RYŪKYŪ ISLANDS
Amami Islands
Kagoshima
KYŪSHŪ
Ōsumi Islands
Amami Islands
Okinawa
Naha
RYŪKYŪ ISLANDS
Daitō Islands
PACIFIC OCEAN
Sakishima Islands

Japanese History

The history of Japan has been shaped both by its isolation as an island nation and by its proximity to the Asian mainland. During periods of openness it has percolated the diverse ideas and cultures that have appeared on its shores; in times of retreat it has incubated its own distinctive way of doing things. Like most histories, Japan's is also one of conflict, tumult and soul-searching.

TOP Saga Prefecture's Yoshinogari Historical Park, reconstructed from the Yayoi Period.

BOTTOM A bronze bell or dotaku from the Yayoi Period, derived from Korean designs.

JŌMON PERIOD (14,000 BCE TO 300 BCE)

The ancestors of the Jōmon people crossed land bridges that connected Japan to Asia between 20,000 and 10,000 years ago, thanks to lower sea levels. Fishers, hunters and food-gatherers, the Jōmon (meaning 'cord-marked') are named for the pottery they created, which featured rope patterns pressed into the clay.

YAYOI PERIOD (300 BCE TO 250 CE)

Technologically advanced immigrants arrived, likely from the Korean Peninsula, introducing wet-rice farming and bronze toolmaking. This period was also named for its pottery, discovered in the Yayoi district of what's now Tokyo.

KOFUN PERIOD (250–538)

The creation of *kofun* – burial mounds in the shape of keyholes, which were codified according to status – indicate a society with increasing stratification. Thousands have been discovered, mostly in central and western Japan.

ASUKA PERIOD (538–710)
Named after the Asuka region of modern Nara Prefecture, this period saw a burgeoning empire – major artistic, social and political changes were established by the ruling Yamato clan. Buddhism (introduced from China via Korea) also took hold.

NARA PERIOD (710–794)
Japan's first permanent capital was established in Nara, in keeping with the Asuka-period practice of relocating the capital following an emperor's death. The new capital was modelled after Chang'an, capital of the Tang dynasty in China, with the Japanese patterning themselves after the Chinese and adopting the Chinese writing system. With a new written language, history was recorded and the first works of Japanese literature produced.

HEIAN PERIOD (794–1185)
By the end of the 8th century, Nara's Buddhist clergy had become so politically meddlesome that Emperor Kammu relocated the capital to Heian-kyō (present-day Kyoto). A period of peace and cultural refinement thrived under Nara's imperial court – until late in the period, when emperors began to devote more time to leisure and scholarly pursuits than to government. This created an opening for the warrior class, and power battles between the

Taira and Minamoto clans ensued. Widely considered to be the world's first novel, *The Tale of Genji* was written by lady-in-waiting Murasaki Shikibu.

KAMAKURA PERIOD (1185–1333)
Following victory in the Genpei War, the first shōgun Minamoto no Yoritomo imposed a new military regime in Kamakura, having been granted dominion by the now largely powerless emperor. The samurai warrior caste emerged, and feudalism became established in Japan. A *kamikaze* (divine wind) in the form of timely typhoons was credited for the repulsion of two attempted invasions by Mongol fleets.

MUROMACHI PERIOD (1333–1568)
With samurai support, Ashikaga Takauji deposed Emperor Go-Daigo, was proclaimed shōgun and established his government in Kyoto. The ensuing period of Ashikaga rule was called Muromachi (after the district of Kyoto in which it was based) until 1573, when its 15th shōgun, Ashikaga Yoshiaki, was driven out of Kyoto by Oda Nobunaga. Culture influenced by Zen Buddhism flourished during this period.

AZUCHI-MOMOYAMA PERIOD (1568–1603)
Named after Oda Nobunaga's Azuchi Castle and Toyotomi Hideyoshi's Momoyama Castle, this period featured near constant civil war until Hideyoshi unified Japan in 1591. After Hideyoshi's death in 1598, Tokugawa Ieyasu won the legendary Battle of Sekigahara in 1600 and established the Tokugawa shogunate in Edo, present-day Tokyo.

EDO PERIOD (1603–1868)
The Tokugawa shogunate closed Japan to the outside world and ushered in a significant period of peace and prosperity, under the rule of both the shogunate and some 300 regional *daimyō* (feudal lords). In 1639, all

LEFT The Japanese warlord Minamoto no Yoritomo.

CENTRE Emperor Meiji ruled Japan until 1912.

RIGHT A depiction of the deities Izanagi and Izanami in Japanese mythology.

foreigners were expelled under the policy of *sakoku*, beginning Japan's long period of isolation. In 1853, Japan was forcibly opened to Western trade by US Commodore Matthew C Perry, and the Edo period came to an end in 1868 with the Meiji Restoration.

MEIJI ERA (1868–1912)

The shogunate was abolished and Emperor Meiji reinstated as the supreme power. Japan, now open to the world, began a wholesale importation of Western ideas, leading to deep changes in social structure, internal politics, the economy, the military and foreign relations. Japan's growing confidence was demonstrated by the ease with which it beat China in the Sino-Japanese War (1894–5), then stunned Russia in the Russo-Japanese War (1904–5).

JAPAN'S CREATION STORY

Once upon a time, the male and female deities Izanagi and Izanami came down to a watery world from Takamagahara (the Plains of High Heaven) to create land. Droplets from Izanagi's 'spear' solidified into the land now known as Japan, and Izanami and Izanagi then populated it with gods. One of these was Japan's supreme deity, the Sun Goddess Amaterasu (Light of Heaven), whose great-great-grandson Jimmu became the first emperor of Japan, reputedly in 660 BCE.

This is the story of Japan's creation, as told by the young empire's first written accounts: *Kojiki* (Record of Ancient Matters; 712 CE) and *Nihonshoki* (Chronicles of Japan; 720 CE). These narratives form the foundation of Shintō religious beliefs and establish the divine lineage of the Japanese imperial family. They establish not only Japan, but the universe, the heavenly realm and the underworld, as well as an elaborate family tree of *kami* (gods).

ABOVE Emperor Hirohito on a tour of a bombed district of Tokyo during WWII.

TOP RIGHT Team Japan skateboarder Momiji Nishiya competes in the Tokyo 2020 Summer Olympic Games.

BOTTOM Launch Vehicle No 47 lifts off at the Tanegashima Space Center in 2023.

TAISHŌ ERA (1912–26)

On his death, Emperor Meiji was succeeded by his son Yoshihito, whose period of rule was the Taishō era. While WWI occupied the major powers, Japan took the opportunity to expand its economy via shipping and trade. Western-style democracy briefly took hold before giving way to militarisation.

SHŌWA ERA (1926–89)

Emperor Hirohito gained the throne in 1926. Rising nationalism was quickened by the worldwide economic depression from 1930 onwards. Japan invaded Manchuria in 1931, withdrew from the League of Nations in 1933, signed a tripartite agreement with Germany and Italy in 1940, and then launched itself into WWII by attacking Pearl Harbor in 1940. In 1945, after atomic bombs were dropped on Hiroshima and Nagasaki, Emperor Hirohito announced unconditional surrender. Postwar reconstruction saw economic growth in the decades following 1950, known as the 'Japanese Miracle'. Tokyo hosted the Summer Olympics in 1964, and Sapporo the 1972 Winter Olympics. A middle class emerged and from 1968, Japan officially became the world's second-largest economy after the USA.

HEISEI ERA (1989–2019)

In 1991, just two years after the Heisei Emperor ascended the throne, the

bubble burst and Japan's economy went into a tailspin. The 1990s were christened the 'Lost Decade', with more than 10 years of price deflation and stagnant GDP. On the positive side, the '90s saw anime and a number of Japanese media franchises gain worldwide popularity. Japan co-hosted the 2002 FIFA World Cup with Korea. The country's population peaked at 128 million in 2010, but has since been declining due to very low birth rates. In 2011, Japan was overtaken by China as the world's second-largest economy, though the major disaster of the year was the magnitude 9.1 Tōhoku Earthquake and tsunami that saw radioactive contamination from the Fukushima Daiichi Nuclear Power Plant. In 2019, Emperor Akihito abdicated; his eldest son, Naruhito, ascended the throne as the 126th Emperor of Japan.

REIWA ERA (2019–)

In 2019, Shinzō Abe became Japan's longest-serving prime minister, resigning due to health reasons the following year. He was assassinated while speaking at a public event in 2022. Due to the Covid-19 pandemic, the 2020 Tokyo Olympics were postponed until the summer of 2021. On a positive note, the economy was boosted by 37 million international visitor arrivals in 2024, while Japan became the fifth country to successfully land on the moon with the Smart Lander for Investigating Moon (SLIM) mission. In 2025, Sanae Takaichi won an LDP leadership election to become Japan's first female prime minister.

A MOVING CAPITAL

538

ASUKA PERIOD

The Asuka period saw Japan's capital relocated following the death of each emperor.

710

NARA

Nara became the first permanent capital of Japan in 710 CE.

794

KYOTO

Emperor Kammu relocated the capital to Heian-kyō (present-day Kyoto) in 794 CE.

1603

EDO PERIOD

The capital stayed in Kyoto, but the Tokugawa shogunate was based in Edo (Tokyo).

1868

TOKYO

The capital was moved from Kyoto to Edo in 1868, and the city renamed Tokyo.

Language

The language of Japan, spoken by more than 99% of the population, is Japanese (aka Nihongo), but just like English in the UK or the US, it comes in various guises.

The Japanese spoken on TV news shows and in the streets of Tokyo is regarded as standard Japanese, but regional accents and dialects are also used. A prime example is Osaka-ben. In the lively dialect of Japan's third-largest city, Osaka, *akan* replaces *dame* (meaning 'bad/don't'), *wakarahen* is used instead of *wakaranai* (I don't understand), and sentence endings take on a character all of their own, such as *atsui nen* instead of *atsui yo* for 'it's hot'.

Then there are Japan's other native languages: Ainu and Ryūkyū. With shared roots to Japanese, the Ryūkyūan language in Okinawa and parts of Kagoshima is spoken by an estimated 150,000 people, something that traces its roots to when the Ryūkyū Islands were a separate kingdom from Japan.

The Ainu language is more distinct. Spoken by the Indigenous Ainu, from Hokkaidō in Japan's far north, it has left a linguistic mark across the island: some 80% of place names here have an Ainu origin. Sapporo, for example, comes from the Ainu *sat poro pet*, meaning 'dry big river'. However, that doesn't mean the Ainu language is in a healthy place these days. While an estimated 14,000 people in Japan identify as Ainu and some 200,000 have Ainu ancestry, previous anti-Ainu policies (including a ban on Ainu in schools) mean there are now fewer than 10 people who speak Ainu fluently.

LEFT Calligraphy is a refined way to write the Japanese language.

READING JAPANESE

Anyone who gets the urge to learn how to read and write Japanese should be prepared for a long slog. Written Japanese is comprised of not one, but three sets of characters: *hiragana*, *katakana* and – the most difficult of the lot – *kanji*.

Hiragana and *katakana* are both sets of phonetic symbols, but with a differing look and varying uses. The more angular of the two, the 46 basic *katakana* characters are used for loaned words and foreign names, like ロンドン (*Rondon*) for London or テレビ (*terebi*) for television. In some cases, *katakana* words don't retain a connection to their meaning in their original language: take the word マンション(*manshon*), which doesn't refer to a mansion but rather to a condominium or apartment.

Hiragana also has 46 basic symbols, but they are more cursive in appearance and are used for verb

LEFT Ryūkyū dancers in Okinawa.

CENTRE Around 75,000 books are published in Japanese each year.

RIGHT Language etiquette is an extremely important element of Japanese society.

endings, grammatical particles and native Japanese words – especially in texts for children where the *kanji* might be too difficult.

Logographic *kanji* characters were introduced from China and represent nouns and the stems of most adjectives and verbs: things like 犬 (dog) and 好 (to like). There are a staggering 2136 *kanji* deemed essential for everyday use, plus many more that are used less frequently. To complicate matters, each *kanji* has more than one possible reading: *on-yomi* (literally 'sound reading') is based on the sound of the original Chinese, while *kun-yomi* (literally 'meaning reading') is the Japanese word that corresponds to the meaning of the *kanji* – so even a simple *kanji* like 水 (water) can be said as *sui* or *mizu*, depending on its use.

If *katakana*, *hiragana* and *kanji* are combined in a simple sentence, it might look like this: ジェーンは犬が好きです (Jane likes dogs). One other notable thing about this sample sentence is that it has a different word order to that of English: Japanese essentially uses subject-object-verb.

LOST IN TRANSLATION

No matter how much you study Japanese, some words will always be difficult to translate directly to English – even if they are simple expressions. *Yoroshiku* (and longer, more formal

variations) has many subtle uses, from 'nice to meet you' to 'give my regards to' or 'thank-you in advance.' The complication is that *yoroshiku* ought to translate to something like 'please be nice', yet that's not what it means

Japan's legion of onomatopoeia can also be tricky as they don't always have such a close connection to sounds as English onomatopoeia. *Doki doki* (nervous or love-struck) makes sense as it's the sound of one's heart beating quickly. But *niko niko* is to be smiley and *waku waku* is to be full of excitement or enthusiasm. If you drink a gallon of coffee and get so jittery that you can't sit still, then *sowa sowa* (fidgety) is the word for you.

LEVELS OF POLITENESS

Japanese is ranked as one of the hardest languages for English speakers to learn – something not helped by its varying levels of formality, typically based upon the situation and the person to whom one is talking. Take a very simple, everyday phrase like 'thank you'. Very casually, there's *dōmo*, or a little less casually *arigatō* – the things you'd say to friends and family. A more polite option is *arigatō gozaimasu*, which works well with strangers or staff at a restaurant. Basically, that's the all-round safe option, much like saying 'thank-you very much'. It could also be made more formal with *dōmo arigatō gozaimasu*.

There are also completely different versions available at each end of the politeness spectrum. For example, *osoreirimasu* or *osewa ni narimashita* in an important business setting, or a playful *sankyū* (the *katakana* for 'thank you').

Transport

From bullet train to rickshaw, plane to ferry – maybe even a water bison pulling a cart on the island of Taketomi – a trip to Japan can involve all sorts of transportation.

Japan's trains are perhaps its best-known mode of transport; after all, this is the country that gave the world the shinkansen (bullet train) in the 1960s, and is now developing even faster Maglev trains, which are expected to come into service around 2035 and can hit speeds of 505 km/h (414mph) – although in testing they have already broken the 600 km/h (373mph) barrier. That's almost double a shinkansen's top speed.

ABOVE The Shimanami Kaidō national cycle route links islands in the south of Japan.

RIGHT Even high-speed shinkansen have personalities.

In terms of everyday services, Japan has a well-earned reputation for super-efficient rail and subway networks, even if squeezing into a Tokyo commuter train during the morning rush hour can be a full-body workout. That level of efficiency is important in a country where most city dwellers get to work by public transport. That said, trains can be playful too, like the dinosaur-inspired Dino Liner in Fukui or JR West's cutesy Hello Kitty–themed bullet train.

In a nation comprised of more than 14,000 islands, not even trains can reach everywhere, but there is a wide network of domestic flights that connect 98 airports around the country, from Wakkanai in the far north to multiple islands in Okinawa. Then there are the ferry lines, which range from short hops around the art-filled islands of the Seto Inland Sea to the 24-hour, 1000km (620-mile) haul

south from Tokyo to the subtropical Ogasawara Islands.

In recent years Japan has promoted its cycling routes and there are great rides all over the country – including the island-hopping Shimanami Kaidō, which runs 70km (43 miles) from Onomichi to Imabari; the 200km (124-mile) Biwaichi which loops around Lake Biwa; and the scenic 102km (63-mile) Toyama Bay Cycling Route. That ought not be a surprise given that cycling is a major part of Japanese society. *Mamachari* (simple bikes with baskets) are as ubiquitous as vending machines – many people do the school run, buy groceries and other daily tasks on bicycles rather than by car.

MAJOR BULLET-TRAIN ROUTES

1 TŌHOKU SHINKANSEN
Tokyo to Shin-Aomori in the Tōhoku region, with stops at major stations like Sendai and Morioka.

2 TŌKAIDŌ SHINKANSEN
Tokyo to Nagoya, Kyoto and Shin-Osaka, where it becomes the San'yō Shinkansen.

3 SAN'YŌ SHINKANSEN
Shin-Osaka to Shin-Kōbe, Okayama, Hiroshima and Hakata (Fukuoka).

4 JŌETSU SHINKANSEN
Tokyo to Niigata, including a seasonal stop at the ski slopes of Gala Yuzawa.

5 HOKURIKU SHINKANSEN
Tokyo to Kanazawa, but also popular spots such as Karuizawa, Nagano and Toyama.

CULT
TRADI

URE

AND

TION

Indigenous peoples

LEFT Traditional Ainu huts in Akan-Mashū National Park.

RIGHT A demonstration of Ainu culture at Upopoy National Ainu Museum and Park.

THE AINU

While it's believed that humans arrived in Hokkaidō by crossing land bridges from north Asia some 25,000 years ago, a distinct culture evolved here around the 13th century CE. The people – who called themselves Ainu (meaning 'human') and their land *mosir* (meaning 'world') – were hunters, fishers and gatherers

The Japanese called Hokkaidō Ezo (or Yezo) and its people *emishi* (basically, barbarians), and it was considered a foreign land. Following the 1869 Meiji Restoration, however, the new government annexed Ezo, renamed it Hokkaidō – and colonisation began in earnest, ostensibly to halt and counter Russian expansion southward. This proved devastating for the Ainu: new regulations demanding assimilation prohibited the Ainu language and traditional ways of life. Discrimination was rife and many Ainu resorted to hiding their ancestry as deeply as possible.

With the general cultural upheaval of the 1960s, however, more and more Ainu began to speak out against entrenched discrimination and poverty, finding pride and common cause with other Indigenous peoples fighting for recognition and justice around the world. In 2008, following international pressure related to the upcoming G8

summit in Hokkaidō, and in response for calls by various UN bodies for Japan to recognise its Indigenous peoples, the Diet (parliament) passed a non-binding resolution that, for the first time, recognised the Ainu as an Indigenous people of Japan. But it wasn't until 2019 that the Diet legally recognised the Ainu.

After more than a century of forced assimilation and discrimination that saw Ainu culture and language almost disappear, there is now growing enthusiasm for an Ainu renaissance. Upopoy National Ainu Museum and Park, in Shiraoi, was opened in 2020. The northernmost of Japan's national museums, it is charged

AINU PLACE NAMES

Though few people can speak the Ainu language today, the old tongue has left an indelible mark on the map of Hokkaidō. The names of many mountains do not end with *-san* or *-yama* (as they do in Japanese), but with the Ainu word for mountain, *nupuri* – as in Niseko's Annupuri village and ski area. Iō-zan, meaning 'sulphur mountain' in Japanese, is known in Ainu as Atosa-nupuri (naked mountain). Similarly, *-nai* and *-pet* are the suffixes for river. The name of the northern city of Wakkanai literally means 'cold water river' in Ainu. The *-pet* becomes *-betsu* when pronounced in Japanese, and this has been incorporated into many Hokkaidō place names – such as Noboribetsu (meaning 'dark-coloured river'). *Shir* in Ainu means island, with Rishiri – the volcanic cone off the northern tip of Hokkaidō – translating to 'high island'. Intriguingly, many Japanese visitors also find place names in Hokkaidō to be exotic.

LEFT A woodcarver makes masks worn for traditional Okinawan Angama dances.

CENTRE Dancers perform at the Tanadui Festival on Okinawa's Taketomi island.

RIGHT A karate display at Shuri Castle in the historic Shuri district of Naha, the capital of Okinawa Prefecture.

with establishing an accurate and educational understanding of Ainu history and culture, and is a wonderful place to visit.

THE OKINAWANS

The Ryūkyū arc of islands stretches some 1200km (745 miles) southwest from Kyūshū to Taiwan, and is home to the people now known as Okinawans. While the issue of 'who originally came from where' in the various groups of islands is up for debate, after unification in the 14th century, the Ryūkyū Kingdom became a formal tributary state of China. In 1609, the islands were invaded by the Shimazu clan from southern Kyūshū and the Tokugawa shogunate laid claim to the Ryūkyū Islands, though they continued to be a tributary to the Chinese emperor. Due to this unusual three-way relationship, the islanders managed to maintain their Ryūkyūan culture and language. The Okinawa Islands were not considered part of Japan until being formally annexed (as Okinawa Prefecture) in 1879. Northern islands in the Ryūkyū archipelago became part of Kagoshima Prefecture.

Okinawans then suffered a similar fate to many Indigenous peoples around the globe. They lost control of their land and resources, and the Japanese government banned use of Ryūkyūan languages and pushed

assimilation. The islands suffered terrible devastation at the end of WWII, and were then occupied and controlled by the US before being returned to Japan in 1972. The ongoing presence of US military bases in Okinawa underlies what's still a strained relationship with the Japanese government.

Since 2008, multiple UN committees have said that Japan 'should expressly recognise the Ainu and Ryūkyūans/Okinawans as Indigenous peoples', but while Japan legally recognised the Ainu in 2019, the government maintains its position that there is no such thing as Indigenous Ryūkyūan peoples and languages. With Tokyo supporting the ongoing presence of Okinawa's US military bases, recognition of Okinawans as an Indigenous people is unlikely in the near future, as it would create demands for self-determination, control over natural resources and the return of land.

KARATE: OKINAWA'S DEFENSIVE EXPORT

To prevent internal rebellion in the 1500s, Ryūkyū islanders were banned from carrying weapons. In 1609, when the Shimazu clan from Satsuma (now Kagoshima) invaded, the weaponless locals could put up little resistance and were conquered easily. The Shimazu exploited the Ryūkyū Islands greedily and strictly enforced the 'no weapons' edict for the next 250 years. During this period, *te* (unarmed fighting methods) were developed in secrecy. Locals also gleaned techniques from Chinese traders and sailors, and later travelled to China to study martial arts. While the original characters for karate meant 'Chinese hand', when Okinawan karate was introduced to mainland Japan in the 1920s, the characters 空手 ('empty hand'), were used. Prior to WWII, karate gained increasing popularity in Japan; after the war, occupying troops took Okinawan karate back to the USA. Hollywood soon caught on, and spread karate around the globe via the silver screen.

Hiromi Isori & Keiko Saito

Born near Lake Kussharo in Hokkaidō, Hiromi Isori learned woodcarving from his Ainu parents. With his partner Keiko Saito, who practices Ainu embroidery, he runs Kussharo Factory, where their traditional crafts embody Ainu culture.

What kinds of works do you create, and how do they connect to Ainu values?
Hiromi: I grew up watching my parents make and sell folk crafts, so carving and creating things came naturally. Today, I mostly work with Ezo [the historical name of Hokkaidō] deer antlers and glass beads, into which I fuse Ainu patterns by firing them myself. It's a way of carrying forward what I learned as a child while also making what feels meaningful to me.
Keiko: After living with Hiromi, I began learning Ainu embroidery. Although I'm not Ainu, I approach patterns with respect, aiming never to make them feel fake while also adding my own originality. What started as making things for daily use has grown into work that I now share with others.

Ainu patterns are striking. What meanings do they hold?
Both: Patterns are talismanic – protective designs made with wishes for health and for safety, whether for oneself or others.

Nature is central to Ainu beliefs. How does that shape your work?
Hiromi: For us, it's instinctive. When harvesting wild vegetables or mushrooms, I thank the mountain *kamuy* (spirits) and leave some for the animals. That sense of coexistence flows naturally into my designs.
Keiko: I find inspiration in colours from nature or world events – like using flag colours in embroidery while wishing for peace.

What do Ainu teachings say about our relationship with the land? *Both:* We're taught that animals and plants choose people who will use them respectfully. All life is interconnected, so harming one place eventually harms us too.

What do you want readers to understand about Ainu culture?
Both: Our *kotan* (Ainu settlement) by Lake Kussharo is blessed with lakes, rivers, mountains and hot springs once used for making *attus* (bark cloth), woven from elm bark. This environment shaped our ancestors' way of life, and we carry that forward today. With the opening of the National Ainu Museum, more people can now encounter Ainu culture. But what matters most to us is regional character – the specific relationship between people and the land. Ideally, visitors would also come to Lake Kussharo, speak with us, and experience both this environment and an Ainu craft workshop first-hand.

Spirituality

LEFT A temple of the Shingon sect of Buddhism at Koyasan's Danjō Garan Sacred Temple Complex.

RIGHT The Shintō shrine of Tsugizakura-ōji on the Kumano Kodō pilgrimage route.

You are born Shintō and die Buddhist – or so the saying goes in Japan. In reality, things are a little more complicated. Both Shintō and Buddhism are deeply woven into Japan's cultural fabric, functioning in unison to form a combined set of spiritual practices. Nowadays some people even say 'born Shintō, married Christian, die Buddhist' on account of the contemporary popularity of white weddings.

The original saying has its roots in Shintō associations with birth, purification and renewal and with Buddhism's connection to death and the afterlife. When children are a month old, many parents take them to a shrine for an *omiyamairi* ceremony, where priests pray for their health and prosperity. Yet at the end of life, most funerals follow Buddhist traditions – with a wake, funeral ceremony and then cremation, plus special memorial days at fixed periods after death (including the seventh, 49th and 100th days, and the first, third, fifth and seventh years).

SHINTŌ

Of the two main religions, Shintō is the oldest in Japan, having been around in its earliest form since the 4th century BCE, at the start of the Yayoi period. Japan's main Indigenous religion, it revolves around the worship of spirits or deities (called *kami*) that reside in nature. Unlike many other

religions, there is no founder and no set scriptures, although the form of worship performed at Shintō shrines is highly ritualised.

As an example, take how visitors to shrines purify themselves and then pray. After entering the shrine's sacred ground, visitors stop at the *temizuya* (water font), where they use a ladle to scoop up water and perform ablutions: first by pouring water over their left hand, then right, and finally pouring a little more water into their left hand and using it to rinse their mouth – all done without ever letting the ladle touch the mouth and with none of the water being returned to the font. At the shrine's altar, praying is equally

TEMPLE OR SHRINE?

Shintō worship takes place at shrines, while Buddhism uses temples. Although these share stylistic similarities, there are easy ways to tell the difference between the two. First of all, temples and shrines have a suffix at the end of their name that will identify them. For temples, look out for *-ji* (as in Kinkaku-ji), *-tera/-dera* (Kiyomizu-dera) and *-in* (Ekō-in); for shrines expect to see *-jinja* (as per Hie-jinja), *-taisha* (Izumo-taisha), *-jingū* (Meiji-jingū) and less often *-gū*, *-myōjin*, *-sha* and *-yashiro*. You can also tell a Shintō shrine from a Buddhist temple by the architecture, most notably with the entrance to shrines being marked by *torii* gateways which look a little like a pi sign with a second horizontal crossbeam. When visiting a shrine, many people bow once before passing under a *torii* and then avoid walking directly through the centre, as that is the path reserved for the *kami*.

Nanrei Yokota

Chief abbot of the Engaku-ji branch of the Rinzai school, Zen Master Nanrei Yokota guides monks and lay practitioners through sitting Zen, rituals and teachings that connect centuries-old Zen wisdom with the challenges of modern life.

What forms of Buddhism are practiced in Japan?
Buddhism, founded by Shakyamuni Buddha in India in the 6th or 5th century BCE, was introduced to Japan in 538 CE. Over time, it evolved into several distinct schools, each offering a different path to enlightenment. Esoteric Buddhism focuses on ritual and mantra; Pure Land emphasises faith and chanting; Nichiren centres on devotion to the Lotus Sutra; and Zen, particularly the Rinzai school, emphasises *busshin* – the Buddha-nature inherent in all beings. Through *zazen* (sitting Zen), Zen practice aims to clear away mental clouds so this innate nature can shine forth.

How does Buddhism appear present in daily Japanese life?
A simple gesture – placing the palms together in *gasshō* – expresses reverence for unseen deities and Buddhas. Even Japanese people who call themselves 'non-religious' instinctively bow and join hands at temples or shrines. This reveals a deep cultural spirit: entrusting what lies beyond human control to a greater power and humbling oneself before it.

What role does Buddhism play in life's milestones?
Temples are central to funerals, where rituals not only guide the departed but also comfort the bereaved, providing an essential step toward moving forward in life. Coming of age and weddings likewise draw on blessings from Buddhas and deities. These ceremonies help people clearly recognise life's transitions and continue their journey with clarity.

How does Zen help the stresses of modern life?
Many people in Japan work without rest, whether in offices or at home. *Zazen* and mindfulness meditation deliberately turn awareness inward, revealing one's true state of mind – often forgotten in busy life. Whatever one's problems, awareness of the inner self is the essential first step to resolving them.

How can visitors experience Buddhism in Japan?
Many Zen temples open *zazen* sessions to the public. Etiquette varies, but the key is to approach each temple with respect, an open mind and a willingness to follow guidance. In doing so, visitors may glimpse the hidden meaning of Zen: that peace arises not from outside, but through one's inner self.

choreographed. Worshippers first throw a coin in the offering box, and then ring the bell once to get the attention of the *kami*. This is followed by two bows, two hand claps, a silent prayer with hands held together, and then a final bow before leaving the altar.

Many shrines have *kami* with specialities that attract worshippers who have specific prayers. For example, the famous Itsukushima-jinja in Miyajima – which is known for a giant *torii* (gate) that appears to be floating on water when the tide is in – has traditionally attracted prayers for safety at sea. At Suiten-gū in Tokyo, people come to pray for fertility and safe childbirth, while elsewhere other common specialities include prayers for good harvests, prosperity or good fortune in marriage.

While visiting a shrine, worshippers might also buy an *omamori* (amulet) to protect against misfortune or bring good luck. These vary by shrine, perhaps offering luck to students taking exams, safety when driving or more general things such as good health. Or they might spend a couple of hundred yen on an *omikuji* (fortune paper) – if it reveals bad luck, it is tied to a special rack or designated tree, so the bad fortune can't leave the shrine.

LEFT Hands are washed before entering a temple in Japan.

BUDDHISM

Compared to Shintō, Buddhism is a relative newcomer to Japan, having arrived from China and Korea in the 6th century and then spread quickly under imperial patronage. Today there are multiple schools (or sects) of Buddhism in Japan, with major sects including Nichiren, Shingon, Zen, Pure Land and Tendai.

Differentiation between these schools often comes down to the way in which believers seek enlightenment. An esoteric form of Buddhism founded by the monk Kūkai in the 9th century, Shingon focuses on mantras, holy chants and rituals – non-Buddhists could experience this with a stay at a temple in Kōya-san in Wakayama. Zen, on the other hand, places more importance on meditation, mindfulness and direct experiences, while Pure Land believes that faith in (and devotion to) the Amida Buddha can lead to rebirth in paradise.

When it comes to visiting a temple, in many respects it's similar to a shrine, as most worshippers follow the same purification ritual at the *temizuya*. But there is a difference in the way people pray. At a temple you might light a stick of incense (for a fee) and place it in the incense burner as an offering, and praying will then be done at the altar without clapping. You just put your hands together, bow, and silently say your prayer. As for the incense, there's a good chance you'll see others wafting the smoke over themselves – for good luck or to heal parts of themselves that are ailing.

OTHER RELIGIONS

Roughly 1% of the population of Japan is Christian. The faith was introduced by Portuguese Catholics in the 1540s, although after decades of increasing hostility towards Christians it was

LEFT A Christian cross in Shingō, Aomori Prefecture.

RIGHT Yamabushi monks walking over hot coals at the Takao-san fire-walking festival.

then banned (and made punishable by death) by the Tokugawa shogunate in 1614, during the Edo era. During that time, however, Christianity didn't disappear, but instead went underground in areas like Nagasaki, with 'hidden Christians' worshipping in secret – often concealing their rituals within Shintō and Buddhist practices, and sometimes carving crosses inside everyday objects.

Up in Aomori Prefecture, in the village of Shingō, there's a more unusual connection to Christianity: a grave claiming to be the resting place of Jesus. Amid the rise of nationalism during the 1930s, documents were discovered which supposedly showed that even Jesus was drawn to life in Japan. As the tale goes, Jesus first came to Japan in his 20s to study theology, then returned to Judea and was condemned to death. But here's the big twist: it's held that he did not die, and that it was Jesus's younger brother who perished on the cross, while Jesus managed to escape back to Japan – where he fell in love, married, raised several children and then died at the age of 106.

Beyond Buddhism, Shintō and Christianity you'll also find Shugendō, a syncretic religion combining elements of Shintō, Buddhism, Taoism and folk practices, but rooted in the idea that the mountains are sacred

JAPAN'S MOST SACRED SPOTS

1 DEWA SANZAN
Three sacred peaks where *yamabushi* ascetics commune with nature through activities such as waterfall meditation.

2 KŌYA-SAN
A mountainside town, full of temples, that's been the headquarters of Shingon Buddhism since the 9th century.

3 MEIJI-JINGŪ
Tokyo's most important shrine was built to enshrine the Emperor and Empress Meiji.

4 ISE-JINGŪ
Some 2000 years old, the country's most sacred shrine houses Amaterasu Ōmikami, the mythical ancestress of Japan's imperial family.

5 IZUMO-TAISHA
The annual Kamiari Matsuri here brings together gods from around the country.

ABOVE A torii gate at Fushimi Inari-Taisha near Kyoto.

areas where gods reside. A signature of Shugendō are *yamabushi* ascetics, typically dressed in white robes, who in sacred areas such as Dewa Sanzan commune with nature as part of a journey of spiritual rebirth – which includes meditating under chilly waterfalls, jumping over burning coals and taking long hikes through the mountains. That's something even non-*yamabushi* can experience nowadays in Dewa Sanzan by signing up for *yamabushi*-led programmes.

LOCAL PERSPECTIVE  SHINTŌ PRIEST

Tomokiyo Tanaka

Tomokiyo Tanaka is the senior priest at Iwashimizu Hachimangū, a 1000-year-old shrine located atop Otokoyama near Kyoto. Beyond his religious duties, he is engaged in interfaith peace-building and academic research on Shintō's spiritual philosophy.

What is Shintō? Shintō is the spiritual foundation of Japan. It has no founder or scripture. Instead, it honours the *yaoyorozu no kami* – the eight million deities believed to dwell in all things – through rituals and festivals that unite communities in gratitude and harmony. Rather than focusing on good and evil, Shintō values purity, sincerity and maintaining harmony between one's inner self and surroundings.

How is Shintō reflected in daily life? Shintō is like the air – quietly present in everyday life and at life's major milestones. Many important life events are celebrated at shrines, as a way of 'walking together with the gods' with family and loved ones. A baby's first shrine visit; the Shichi-Go-San ceremony for children aged three, five and seven; coming-of-age celebrations at age 20; and weddings – all are joyful rituals offering gratitude to the gods for life, growth and union. Throughout the year, Shintō customs continue in daily life. At New Year, people visit shrines to pray for safety and good fortune, display sacred *shimenawa* ropes at their doors, and participate in local festivals at shrines. These practices reflect a spirit of gratitude for all things and reverence for what cannot be seen, quietly connecting individuals, families and communities to the divine.

How does Shintō's reverence for nature shape Japanese culture? Mountains, rivers, trees, rocks, wind and sunlight – all contain divine spirits. Living in awe and gratitude toward these forces is the heart of Shintō, which underlies Japan's deep sensitivity to the changing seasons. From cherry blossoms in spring to harvest festivals in autumn, each moment celebrates coexistence with nature. In this land of frequent natural disasters, respect for nature's overwhelming power is deeply ingrained and expressed through rituals of prayer and thanksgiving – a reminder that nature's forces transcend human control.

What message can Shintō offer the modern world? The guiding principles of Shintō are harmony and gratitude. It reminds us that mountains, rivers and trees are sacred, and that coexistence – not domination – sustains life. In a divided, digital world, this spirit offers a quiet yet profound guide toward peace, connection and respect for all beings.

Samurai and ninja

ABOVE Hokusai's manga sketches of ninja were published in the 19th century.

TOP RIGHT Ashikaga Yoshiteru was the 13th shōgun of the Ashikaga shogunate.

RIGHT A Japanese samurai in the 1880s.

'Samurai' refers to high-ranking members of Japan's former hereditary warrior class. Also known as *bushi*, this class emerged during the 9th and 10th centuries, and many of the warrior clans within it claimed their descent from junior princes who had lost their imperial status. As the imperial court became mired in internal power struggles, the influence of the *bushi* rose; during the 12th century, they gained control over the court.

Japan's first shogunate was established after one warrior clan, the Genji, defeated the Heike in 1185. The head of the Genji was given the rank of sei'i tai-shōgun, and made de facto ruler of the country. After that, Japan was governed by a succession of military rulers (except for a brief interlude between 1333 and 1336, when an emperor managed to take back power), until the end of the Tokugawa shogunate in 1868. These rulers governed through a feudal network of vassals, but their power was frequently insecure; internecine conflict was a constant.

SAMURAI SWORDS

Back in the 11th and 12th centuries, high-ranking warriors fought on horseback using arrows. Their heavy swords, known as *tachi*, only served a backup role in battle. These warriors, however, were accompanied by low-status foot soldiers known as *ashigaru*, who did fight with blades. Many of these *ashigaru* formed the lowest rung within the warrior class. As they increased in number, playing an ever greater part in warfare, their sword evolved into what is now known as the samurai sword, the *uchi-gatana* (also referred to as *katana*, the Japanese word for sword).

By the second half of the 15th century, *uchi-gatana* had become the high-ranking samurai's primary weapon. Samurai armour also changed accordingly, since it was no longer arrows that it had to deflect but sword cuts and, later on, bullets. Firearms were introduced to Japan by the Portuguese in the 16th century, but only the *ashigaru* carried them.

Towards the end of the 15th century, the weakening of the Ashikaga – the second of Japan's shogunates – led to Japan splintering into numerous fiefdoms ruled by warring warlords known as *daimyō*. The battles of the subsequent century gave rise to the ideal image of what a samurai ought to be: loyal to his lord to the death. This era also saw the emergence of covert agents now called ninja.

WHAT IS A NINJA?

Ninja were not samurai. Although they sometimes engaged in killings and acts of arson, their chief role was information gathering. They spied out the terrain before a battle, or insinuated themselves among the opposing camp or within villages in enemy territory (conversational skills and a knowledge of local dialects came in handy) in order to gauge levels of morale and preparation.

Some ninja came from the lowest warrior class, that of the foot soldier. In some provinces they were recruited from the criminal classes (burglars were considered to excel at stealth); in others, they were the sons of peasants and landowners, appreciated for their detailed local knowledge. Ninja dressed as commoners, and often carried farm tools such as sickles that were specially adapted as weapons. Apart from being able to accomplish

such feats as swimming across moats unnoticed (using a reed as a snorkel) or scaling castle walls, they needed physical strength and stamina to find their way in the wilderness and to survive extremes of heat, humidity and cold.

SAMURAI IN PEACETIME

Peace finally descended upon Japan in the 17th century under the Tokugawa (or Edo) shogunate. Samurai were no longer needed for warfare, and a crisis of identity ensued. The shoguns of the Tokugawa dynasty dealt with this by turning the samurai into government bureaucrats, while drawing upon old-time battleground ethics in order to secure their allegiance. Fidelity, duty, self-sacrifice and honour were paradoxically enjoined upon them more than ever before.

After the arrival of Commodore Matthew C Perry and his US squadron at the mouth of Edo Bay in 1853,

ABOVE A portrait of the rulers of the Tokugawa shogunate.

TOP RIGHT The Sōma Nomaoi Festival, a 1000-year-old samurai horseback battle, held annually in Fukushima Prefecture.

BOTTOM Preparing for the samurai tradition of ritual suicide.

samurai already disaffected with a tired shogunate began to rally around the emperor in Kyoto – against both the increasing Western presence in Japan and the Tokugawa shogunate itself. Samurai hostility towards the presence of Westerners and their insensitivities to Japanese ways led to incidents of bloodshed, for which Western powers demanded the severest penalty. The shogunate obliged (as did the imperial Meiji government, which succeeded it in 1868), but both accorded condemned samurai the privilege of dying by ritual suicide – *seppuku*, or *hara-kiri* in common parlance – instead of being executed. These occasions were witnessed by Western dignitaries and reported in overseas press (with illustrations). Thus the idea of the 'happy dispatch' became indelibly connected with the Japanese in the Western imagination.

The imperial Meiji regime dismantled the samurai hierarchy. In 1876, former samurai were effectively banned from wearing swords, the symbol of their status. The Satsuma Rebellion of 1877 was their final, futile act of defiance against the tide of modernisation.

SAMURAI THROUGH THE AGES

Until the 15th century, samurai mainly fought on horseback. Large shoulder panels protected them against arrows.

Armour became lighter and less cumbersome once the sword (*uchi-gatana*) became the chief weapon of the samurai.

A samurai in his armour, photographed in the 19th century.

In peacetime, samurai had no need of armour; just a light helmet was worn when travelling.

Various ninja weapons held by the Iga-ryū Ninja Museum, including *shuriken*, so-called 'ninja stars'.

Ayano Uehara

Ayano Uehara, a senior director at Sōma City Hall, made history riding in the Sōma Nomaoi Festival – a 1000-year-old samurai horseback battle – after rules were amended to permit women. The festival preserves her hometown's culture and community.

Why is the annual Sōma Nomaoi Festival considered such a unique and important part of Japanese culture? The Sōma Nomaoi Festival is one of Japan's largest historic samurai events, where hundreds of mounted warriors don traditional armour, engage in mock battles and race to capture sacred flags. Beyond the spectacle, it preserves centuries-old samurai traditions, showcases the courage and skill of riders and brings the local community together, allowing visitors to experience a living connection to Japan's samurai heritage.

How does samurai culture continue to influence Japanese society today? Samurai culture is deeply woven into Japan's identity. Even beyond specific festivals, the values of courage, discipline and loyalty – core to *bushidō*, the samurai code of moral conduct – remain visible in daily life, in how communities honour history and in cultural practices that emphasise respect and responsibility.

Are there particular traditions or rituals that keep this heritage alive? Yes. Traditional skills – in martial arts, horse riding or ceremonial practices – are passed down by experts to younger generations. Craftspeople maintain and produce armour, banners and other cultural artefacts, ensuring that these symbols of samurai culture survive. These traditions are more than aesthetics – they embody centuries of history and moral principles.

How do individuals connect with this heritage today? People experience samurai culture both actively and symbolically. Watching demonstrations, participating in historical events or practising martial arts allows them to feel *bushidō* values first-hand. It's a way to engage with history, reflect on personal discipline and connect with Japan's past.

What challenges exist in preserving samurai culture? Ensuring participation across generations, including women and young people, is vital. Tradition must adapt to remain relevant, but the core principles – honour, courage, loyalty – should be preserved as a living influence on contemporary Japanese identity. In order to pass down 'samurai culture' to future generations, the key is to know one's own history and values, and to continue to take pride in them.

Ryokan

ABOVE A traditional ryokan with onsen near Kanazawa, Ishikawa Prefecture.

RIGHT Brewing tea at the Waki-Honjin inn in Nagano Prefecture.

Here's a bit of trivia: the oldest hotel in the world is a traditional Japanese inn, aka a ryokan. Established in 705 CE, the Nishiyama Onsen Keiunkan in Yamanashi Prefecture has been run by the same family for 52 generations.

The Keiunkan has gone through plenty of changes over the centuries, as has the concept of a Japanese inn. Back when the Keiunkan was in its infancy, inns began as *fuseya*, free rest houses that were run by Buddhist monks. During the Kamakura period in the 12th and 13th centuries, a kind of lodging called *kichin-yado* appeared, where guests paid only for the firewood used to cook their own food.

When the road network began to develop in the 17th century, following the onset of the Edo period, more Japanese began travelling and the inns now called ryokan started to take on a more familiar shape – with lodgings called *hatago* for the common traveller, and more luxurious honjin for travelling feudal lords (as well as *waki-honjin* for their entourage).

Today, the archetypal traditional ryokan is a welcoming retreat with tatami-mat guestrooms that feature futon, *shōji* (screen doors) and minimal decor, and where the experience typically involves shedding your daily clothes for a *yukata* (a light cotton kimono), soaking in hot-spring baths and enjoying multi-course dinners centred on seasonal local produce. You'll notice little moments of Japanese hospitality too, such as the way futon are prepared when guests are at dinner or how slippers always seem to be perfectly aligned and waiting for you whenever you leave the tatami.

But that doesn't mean all ryokan are the same. Some have outdoor communal baths surrounded by nature; others offer the option of in-room hot-spring bathing; and some are known as much for their cuisine as anything else. Many are in heritage buildings that creak underfoot, but there are also plenty of newer ryokan that merge traditional aesthetics with contemporary luxury. Then there are *minshuku*, a kind of family-run B&B with more modest traditional rooms and simple meals. There's something for (almost) every budget.

One more bit of trivia: Nishiyama Onsen Keiunkan might be old, but it isn't the oldest business in Japan. That honour goes to a construction company called Kongō Gumi, established in 578 CE.

HOW TO WEAR A YUKATA

1. Ryokan either supply *yukata* in rooms or have a selection in the lobby; keep underwear on when wearing them.

2. Slip arms through the sleeves, tuck the right side of the *yukata* around the left hip, then bring the left side over the right hip.

3. Ensure the bottom of the *yukata* is evenly aligned on both sides.

4. Wrap the long sash around the waist (women) or hip (men) two or three times.

5. Tie the sash into a bow, positioned in front or behind.

Kohei and Manami Yamada

At Hanamurasaki, sixth-generation owner Kohei Yamada and his wife Manami reimagine the ryokan as a cultural salon. After studying art in California, Kohei returned to Yamanaka Onsen, Ishikawa, to blend tradition and innovation with hospitality.

What role does a ryokan play in Japanese culture?
A ryokan is more than a place to stay – it's a cultural hub. Through hot springs, nature, food, art and craft, guests experience the spirit of a place. Each ryokan tells the story of its region and its people.

Hanamurasaki has been in your family for six generations. How are you able to balance tradition with change?
For us, inheriting and creating are inseparable. Even the ryokan masters, awarded the title of Living National Treasures and deemed cultural assets, were once challengers. Tradition is not about guarding the past, but daring to create something new that endures. That's why we've renovated with local artists and craftspeople, while preserving traditional features such as tatami flooring, *shōji* screens and tranquil displays in *tokonoma* alcoves – reimagined in a modern way.

Food is central to the ryokan experience. How do you approach it?
Kaiseki, a Japanese multicourse meal, is like capturing the seasons on a plate. Each dish highlights seasonal ingredients and reflects the local character. We meet our producers, learn their stories, and serve what should truly be eaten here and now. Local sake and wines from the region, Yamanaka lacquerware and Kutani porcelain add depth – the food and crafts complement each other. It's also about the spirit of *ichigo ichie* – treasuring each encounter as once-in-a-lifetime.

How do art and craft fit into the experience?
For us, *terroir* is not only food and drink, but also art, craft and antiques. The works of contemporary artists who live in Hokuriku and draw inspiration from its landscapes and heritage are part of the daily environment, not static displays. Hospitality is about sharing local beauty and skills while supporting artists to continue their craft.

What is your hope for the future of ryokan?
In a time of change, ryokan can connect travellers and communities. They offer something hotels cannot – the chance to step into Japan's culture, tradition and spirit. For international guests seeking authenticity, ryokan are more relevant than ever.

Yuru-kyara

LEFT Nasu Tourism's mascot Kyubii, inspired by the legend of the nine-tailed fox said to reside in the Sesshoseki Stone near Mt Nasu.

RIGHT Shopping for Chiikawa souvenirs in Kiddy Land, Tokyo.

Fluffy, cutesy, big-eyed characters pop up everywhere in Japan, from credit cards to cosmetics to official government documents. Familiar manga-derived creatures such as Pokémon or megastar characters like Hello Kitty are commercial creations, but others – known as yuru-kyara – are appealing mascots specifically designed to represent a region, a company brand or a local government. Their purpose is to nurture emotional attachment among residents and users.

Japan has a long tradition of personifying animals and commodities, which stems from ancient folklore and Shintō beliefs. This was further solidified during the Edo period, when stories of ghosts and spirits featured frequently in books and in *ukiyo-e* woodcut prints. This history is said to have laid the foundation for Japan's nuanced *kawaii* culture (p200), which encompasses a wide range of cuteness.

The yuru-kyara phenomenon began in the early 2000s, when local authorities started deploying mascots to boost tourism and grow a sense of community and pride among residents. Kumamoto Prefecture's PR character Kumamon plays an active role in various contexts promoting the region. Merchandise featuring Kumamon's illustration generates annual sales of approximately 170 billion yen. This successful model inspired many other

local governments, and there are now over 1500 yuru-kyara representing towns and regions across Japan.

The yuru-kyara trend peaked around 2020 but the mascots are still popular: in 2025, Gotōchi Character Carnival saw 48,000 people gather in Gunma Prefecture to meet 120 mascots. Yuru-kyara also have a loyal fan base – many characters have more social media followers than the mayors of the regions they represent. Fans flock to buy merchandise from stores like Kiddy Land and Tokyo Station's Character Street, as well as from regional 'antenna shops'. And many indulge in yuru-kyara experiences at theme parks such as Sanrio Puroland and Chiikawa Park.

THE EVOLUTION OF YURU-KYARA

The charm of popular characters relies not just on their appearance but also on the way their story and personality are curated. Kumamon's round face and red cheeks are the epitome of formulated cuteness, but other characters have more colourful, often edgy personalities. Inspired by the fusion of cells and water, Myaku-Myaku (official mascot of the 2025 Osaka World Expo) deviates from the standard of cuteness, but has become a major hit despite initial criticism. Former yuru-kyara illustrator Nagano has taken this trend to the next level. Her cartoons depicting the everyday struggles of hamster-like character Chiikawa deeply resonate with fans and have grown the most influential character account on X (with over 4.4 million followers). Chiikawa's success showcases the Japanese cultural affinity with characters that have well-developed backgrounds and emotional depth.

Geisha

TOP Maiko (apprentice geigi) clad in colourful kimono at Nabejaya in Furumachi, Niigata City.

RIGHT A geisha walking in Kyoto's Gion district.

Geisha, formally known as *geigi* or *geiko*, are professional entertainers who preserve the traditions of various schools of traditional Japanese dance and music. They usually perform their art in the seclusion of private dining rooms for patrons, and afterwards join their company, pouring sake and making conversation. Presenting an idealised version of femininity, they are the epitome of discretion, grace and attentiveness.

Geisha first appeared as a distinct class around the 1730s, but courtesans were entertaining patrons with dance and music from at least the 11th century. By the 16th century, Japanese military rulers began creating official brothel quarters in Kyoto in order to control the presence of the city's prostitutes and to extract tax from them. In Edo (now Tokyo), the first official brothel quarter – named the Yoshiwara – was established by the Tokugawa Shogunate in 1617. After it burnt down in 1657, it was rebuilt to the north of city and named Shin-Yoshiwara (the 'New Yoshiwara').

Initially, the official brothel quarters of Edo, Kyoto, Osaka and Nagasaki were home to talented, highly cultured courtesans of the highest status (known as *tayū*) who sang, danced and played musical instruments. These women, however, became too expensive even for the

GEISHA TODAY

Geisha were formerly indentured to geisha houses, often from childhood, and were weighed down by enormous debts that they were obligated to repay through work they could not turn down. Indentured servitude in the sex trade formally ended in Japan with the passing of the Anti-Prostitution Act in 1956. Today, becoming a geisha is just another career choice – but geisha are becoming increasingly rare.

richest of their patrons, and this class of courtesan had disappeared by the middle of the 18th century. Thereafter, musical entertainment in the brothel quarters was provided by geisha, who usually performed in the teahouses where patrons ate and were entertained before going on to one of the brothels to meet their chosen courtesan. In Edo's Shin-Yoshiwara, the distinction between geisha and courtesans (even the low-class ones) was strictly enforced; geisha were prohibited from selling sex.

In Edo, however, and in other cities and towns, there were unofficial pleasure quarters where such proscriptions did not apply. Edo's popular Fukagawa district was well known for its stylish geisha,

who were summoned to entertain at restaurants and teahouses. But there were many more women for whom art was merely a pretext – and they were known as *korobi-geisha* (stumbling geisha), because they danced badly and had tripped up morally.

FROM MAIKO TO GEISHA

Cities such as Tokyo and Kanazawa still have geisha, and Kyoto has five official districts, known as *hana-machi*, where geisha work. Gion, the most famous, is divided into two *hana-machi*.

The first step to becoming a modern Kyoto geisha involves joining a geisha house and learning what the day-to-day geisha life entails. After being accepted by a geisha house, the aspirant will lodge there, undertaking everyday chores. She will learn the geisha's special dialect and their elaborate etiquette, and begin her training in dance and music.

Only when the mistress of the geisha house and the dance and music instructors agree that an aspirant has potential is she allowed to move on to the next stage – that of becoming a *maiko* (apprentice geisha). She formally enters a bond of sistership with a senior geisha, who will act as her mentor, and begins to make appearances at evening engagements; if this goes well, she will officially become a *maiko*. It is the *maiko* who wear long-sleeved,

LEFT A scene from Kyoto's Fukagawa district during the Edo period.

RIGHT A maiko or apprentice geisha in Kyoto's Gion district.

colourful kimonos, as well as dangly hair ornaments and *pokkuri* (clogs).

Maiko continue with their intensive training in dance and in music, including singing and the mastery of instruments such as the three-stringed *shamisen*, along with a variety of traditional Japanese flutes and drums. After five or six years, the decision will have to be made whether a *maiko* has attained the high level of expertise required of a full-fledged geisha. If she hasn't, she will have to leave the world of the geisha.

Once a *maiko* becomes a geisha, she dresses as a mature young woman. She wears her hair in the *shimada* style, with fewer ornaments. Her kimonos become more subtle in colour and style, with shorter sleeves. She will also decide whether to specialise in dance or music. Musician geisha appear alongside dancers, but in many geisha communities they perform dressed in a subdued fashion, without intricately styled hair or elaborate makeup.

Geisha and *maiko* usually only make appearances for private engagements at select restaurants and teahouses. However, in four out of the five Kyoto *hana-machi*, they put on annual theatrical performances, such as the Gion Kōbu quarter's Miyako Odori and Ponto-chō's Kamogawa Odori in the spring, and the Gion Higashi's Gion Odori in late autumn.

ABOVE Geisha and maiko perform at Gion Higashi's Gion Odori in autumn.

Beniko Hatsuyanagi

In Niigata's historic Furumachi district, Beniko Hatsuyanagi is an esteemed geigi (as geisha are known locally) and head of the Geigi Association. Born in the heart of Furumachi, she helps preserve the arts, traditions and hospitality of the profession.

What does it mean to be a geisha?
In Niigata, it's pronounced *geigi*, but the meaning is the same: 'people of the arts'. Being a *geigi* means dedicating yourself to traditional performing arts such as singing, *shamisen*, dance, tea ceremony and flute, alongside mastering the art of conversation. Our guests and conversations vary, so staying curious about the world is essential to connect meaningfully.

How does one become a geisha?
In Niigata, women typically start between 18 and 22 years old and work as salaried employees. They apply online, live independently, have paid holidays and can marry if they choose. This is different from Kyoto, where girls can start as young as 15, often live in shared geisha houses called *okiya*, and earn fees per engagement rather than a salary.

Has the number of geisha changed over time?
Geisha culture reached its peak approximately from the 1890s to the 1930s, with tens of thousands working across Japan. After WWII, the number of working geisha declined sharply due to social change, economic hardship and the growth of more modern entertainment. Today, only a few geisha districts remain active.

Are geisha performances always the same?
Our dances, costumes and music change to reflect the seasons – plum blossoms in spring, fans in summer, autumn leaves in fall and snowy landscapes in winter. This seasonal expression helps guests experience the spirit of Niigata through our art.

How does someone arrange to see a *geigi* performance in Niigata?
Guests can book a traditional restaurant in Furumachi and request *geigi* entertainment. The performances include dance, music and even playful drinking games, in a relaxed and welcoming atmosphere. *Geigi* are not only entertainers but also guardians of Niigata's cultural heritage, preserving traditional folk songs and classical pieces that might otherwise have been lost over time.

Celebrations

LEFT The Shuni-e or Omizutori ceremony of repentence at Nara's Tōdai-ji features fire and water.

RIGHT The Nebuta Festival is a summer highlight of Aomori.

Midsummer in Japan sees giant floats paraded around Aomori for the annual Nebuta Matsuri, while thousands of dancers take to the streets of Tokushima in Shikoku for the 450-year-old Awa Odori and fireworks light up the night sky over Tokyo's Sumida River. That's just the tip of the summer celebrations that unfold across the country. In fact, at any time of year, there will be a major celebration of some sort happening – whether that's a rite of passage, a Shintō harvest ritual, a centuries-old festival that started to celebrate a new castle, a get-together of anime lovers – or all manner of other events. Simply put, Japan loves a celebration.

THE HISTORIC

It probably won't come as a surprise that Kyoto – which served as Japan's capital for close to 1000 years – is home to some of Japan's most historic celebrations. Featuring multiple events throughout July (including two

processions of giant decorated floats), the Gion Matsuri has been held since 869 CE, when it began as a way to appease the gods in the hope they'd protect the city from a plague. Even older, the Aoi Matsuri's procession of people in Heian-era dress (staged in May) is said to date to the 6th century, when it was also designed to please the gods – in this case, to ask for a good harvest after several years of poor crops.

But it's not just Kyoto that has ancient festivals. In Nara, the capital before Kyoto (from 710 to 784), the Shuni-e or Omizutori has been held at the temple of Tōdai-ji since the year 752. The two-week event in March has multiple components and is a combination of repentance and purification, but is best known for monks carrying large, burning bundles that send sparks flying through night sky.

THE MODERN CLASSICS

Not all major events and celebrations have historic roots. With Fuji Rock and Summer Sonic, Japan has two contemporary summertime music festivals that draw big Japanese and international performers. In Sapporo, meanwhile, the annual Snow Festival is a relative newcomer, having started in as a minor event in 1950 in which local schoolchildren created ice sculptures. It now

MAJOR HOLIDAY PERIODS

NEW YEAR

OSHŌGATSU
Japan's New Year holiday is a big family get-together, with special foods, gifts of money to children and TV specials.

APR-MAY

GOLDEN WEEK
A cluster of four national holidays between 29 April and 5 May.

MID-AUG

O-BON
The summer holiday in mid-August, where many return to their home towns and remember their ancestors.

SEP

SILVER WEEK
A small grouping of national holidays in September, where some take extra days off to create a long break.

NOV

BUNKA NO HI
'Culture Day' is celebrated with special events and free entry to museums and galleries.

TOP Sapporo's Snow Festival, viewed from the Observation deck of its TV Tower in 2024.

BOTTOM Participating in the World Cosplay Summit in Nagoya.

attracts more than two million visitors annually, with teams from around the world crafting giant, intricately designed snow and ice sculptures.

Japan has also gradually begun using events as way to promote diversity. Osaka, for example – the first city in Japan to launch a website aimed at LGBTIQ+ travellers – is home to the Rainbow Festa in October, with a parade and live music. Likewise, Tokyo's LGBTIQ+ community and allies come together for a host of parades and events during Tokyo Pride in June.

The country's legion of *otaku* (the word given to people obsessed with such things as manga and anime) have carved out annual celebrations of their own, too. For folk who like dressing up as characters from video games, anime and books, the world's largest get-together of cosplayers happens at the World Cosplay Summit in Nagoya; gamers get the hugely popular Tokyo Game Show. Twice a year, Comiket in Tokyo is a manga extravaganza, where independent manga artists and other creatives come together to showcase what they've been working on.

THE QUIRKY

Japan also stages celebrations that at first glance appear unusual – a prime example being the Kanamara Matsuri in Kawasaki, aka the 'Steel Phallus Festival'. Taking place on the first Sunday of April, this event centres around a procession of large, portable shrines shaped like penises, with stalls along the route selling snacks in similar forms and even *daikon* (radishes) carved into distinctive phallic shapes. Nowadays it's light-hearted fun for most festivalgoers, but its original purpose was a mix of prayer for safe childbirth and invocations from the area's sex workers for protection against STDs. Today, profits from the event go to HIV research.

Elsewhere in Japan, there are plenty of *hadaka* (naked) festivals, typically featuring men clad just in loincloths. These include the 500-year-old Saidai-ji Eyō festival in Okayama, where the climax features thousands of near-naked men scrambling around the grounds of Saidai-ji temple in darkness, in the hope of claiming one of two lucky *shingi* (sacred sticks).

TOKYO'S BIGGEST EVENTS

SUMIDAGAWA HANABI TAIKAI
Tokyo's premier fireworks display plays out above the Sumida River on the last Saturday of July.

ASAKUSA SAMBA CARNIVAL
Asakusa parties to samba beats at this colourful September event.

KŌENJI AWA ODORI
Thousands of dancers take to the streets of Kōenji in late August for Tokyo's largest dance festival.

KANDA MATSURI
Kanda Myōjin shrine is the focal point of this major procession of portable shrines in May.

SANNŌ MATSURI
Another shrine festival, Hie-jinja's celebrations in June feature processions and performances of traditional music and dance.

Other notable additions to Japan's list of esoteric events include crying festivals, like the *nakizumō* (meaning 'crying-baby contest'), held at various places around the country – one major such event takes place at Tokyo's Senso-ji temple in April. These *nakizumō* see contactless bouts between pairs of one-year-old infants, each being held by a sumo wrestler, where the winning baby is the one who cries first; if both start bawling at the same time, then victory goes to whoever cries loudest. While that might sound odd, it's not done out of cruelty but on the basis of an old saying that translates to something like, 'Crying babies grow (healthily)'.

LEFT Children are taken to shrines on specific occasions.

RIGHT Carp flags fly during Kodomo-no-hi (Children's Day) in May.

RITES OF PASSAGE

Some Japanese celebrations are more about marking moments in time. One that takes place across the country on 15 November (or the nearest weekend) is Shichi-go-san (Seven-Five-Three), where girls aged three and seven and boys aged three and five get dressed up in kimono or *hakama* (a type of pleated, skirt-like trousers) to visit their local shrine and receive blessings. On one of those years, many families will also pay for commemorative photo shoots of their children in traditional outfits – it's one of those photos of childhood that almost everyone will rediscover at some point once grown up.

When children have reached adulthood, there is Seijin-no-hi (Coming of Age Day) on the second Monday of January. This is still celebrated at the age of 20 in some parts of Japan, despite the age of adulthood (for things such as voting

and marriage) having been reduced to 18 in 2022. That's partly out of tradition, but also because the legal drinking age in Japan is still 20, and Seijin-no-hi is known for its drinking parties – not a year passes without some coverage of Seijin-no-hi events that have drunkenly gone off the rails. Other than drinking, it's a time to dress up in a traditional kimono or a smart suit and attend congratulatory events at the local municipal hall.

Besides Shichi-go-san and Seijin-no-hi, there are many other youth-focused celebrations. On Kodomo-no-hi (Children's Day) on 5 May, many families and local municipalities hang windsock-like carp banners called *koinobori* outside, something rooted in an old tale of a carp becoming a dragon and representing how children can be strong and courageous. Kodomo-no-hi once focused on boys only, and some families also display miniature samurai helmets and armour within the home.

Then there's Hina Matsuri on 3 March, which gets translated as Doll Festival or Girl's Day. This is when families pray for the health and wellbeing of young girls, although the event is best known for displays of ornamental *hina* dolls; clad in traditional court dress from the Heian era, these represent an emperor, empress, attendants and musicians, and are all set on a step-altar.

ABOVE Displays of ornamental dolls are created for Hina Matsuri (Girl's Day) in March.

LIFE-
COMM

STYLE AND UNITY

Wabi-sabi

ABOVE Mino ware pottery from the late 16th century exemplifies simplicity and imperfection.

TOP RIGHT A woodblock print of Sen no Rikyū preparing tea.

BOTTOM A Buddhist temple built in honour of Toyotomi Hideyoshi and his wife Nene.

Virtually every explanation of wabi-sabi will include phrases like 'rustic simplicity', 'understated elegance' and 'appreciation of beauty that is imperfect, impermanent or incomplete' – alongside words such as humble, subdued, flawed, natural and unpretentious. If an object – irregularly shaped tea bowls or a gnarled, weathered tree – has any of the above characteristics, it can be said to be wabi-sabi.

The term originated in the 16th century, when Murata Jukō introduced the *wabi-cha* style of tea ceremony, which emphasised simplicity and imperfection over technically perfect, polished beauty. Jukō and later tea practitioners such as Sen no Rikyū challenged the rules of beauty by championing common Japanese pottery over imported Chinese ceramics, challenging people to find beauty and significance in humble everyday items.

Wabi-sabi's appeal has waxed and waned. *Wabi-cha* reached its apotheosis with Rikyū, but had become thoroughly unfashionable by the second quarter of the

TEA, POLITICS AND WABI-SABI

The person most associated with wabi-sabi ideals is the tea master Sen no Rikyū. He is credited with many significant developments in tea practice, from the *nijiriguchi* (crawl-through) tea-room entrance to the use of handmade Raku ware and of natural materials such as thatch and plaster to build teahouses.

Tea and politics were inseparable during the late 16th century. Under what was known as the *onchanoyu goseidō* (rule by tea), a tea-ceremony licence was officially required for samurai houses to qualify as a 'proper' samurai family. As the personal tea master to *daimyō* (feudal lord) Oda Nobunaga and his successor Toyotomi Hideyoshi, Sen no Rikyū wielded great influence and power. However, Hideyoshi preferred a more showy, extravagant style of tea, and as Rikyū's increasingly popular wabi-sabi ideals threatened to undermine his authority, he eventually ordered Rikyū to commit ritual suicide (*seppuku*).

17th century, supplanted by *kirei-sabi (*elegant, refined rusticity) as championed by tea master Kobori Enshū. The late 1960s and early '70s saw a resurgence of interest in wabi-sabi aesthetics. One contributing factor was the early-20th-century Mingei Movement, which emphasised the beauty of ordinary, utilitarian handmade objects. Another factor was the export of Japanese ideas such as Zen, in tandem with the 1964 Tokyo Olympics and the 1970 Osaka Expo. Terms like 'wabi-sabi' were used as a convenient shorthand for describing traditional Japanese culture, which in turn rekindled domestic interest in these ideas.

Wabi-sabi remains popular and relevant today. One reason, says creative consultant Joanna Kawecki, is because 'the term offers an alternative to perfectionism and consumerism.' In a time that's increasingly shaped by AI, wabi-sabi is a reminder to remain grounded and appreciative of the real, imperfect world and, as Kawecki asserts, to 'recognise the beauty in humble simplicity.'

Onsen

ABOVE Some onsen offer hot-sand baths.

TOP Leave your shoes at the entrance of an onsen and put on a pair of traditional sandals.

RIGHT The hot springs at Otani Sansō ryokan in Nagato Yumoto Onsen.

All onsen are hot springs, but not all hot-spring sources count as onsen. To legally qualify as one, the Japanese Hot Springs Act of 1948 stipulates that the waters must be at least 25°C (77°F) at source and contain specified amounts of minerals such as sulphur, iron or magnesium.

Japan's tradition of hot-spring bathing dates back at least 1300 years, as glowingly described in essays by Heian-era writers like Sei Shōnagon. Many onsen were considered sacred, and had shrines or temples dedicated to them; Edo-era poet Matsuo Bashō wrote about worshipping at Yuzen (Onsen) Shrine in Nasuyumoto Onsen in his masterwork *Oku no Hosomichi* (The Narrow Road to the Deep North). And just as Britain's Victorians sent patients to recuperate along the coast, so too have the Japanese used onsen as balneotherapy. Early on, only aristocrats had the means to travel and indulge in *tōji* – long-stay hot-spring therapy, which they would enjoy for weeks or even months. (Genuine convalescences aside, the *Nihonshoki* – the second-oldest chronicle of classical Japanese history – notes that Prince Arima faked an illness and went bathing to avoid political problems at court.)

The practice of *tōji* spread to various other classes of society from the early 17th century onwards, when domestic travel became safer. People were

permitted to travel only for specific reasons, such as religious pilgrimages and hot-spring cures, so these were appropriated as useful pretexts for sightseeing. The proliferation of illustrated guidebooks detailing hot-spring sites only fuelled this boom. Even in the 20th century, *tōji* remained an option for the wealthy. Writers like Osamu Dazai and Yasunari Kawabata famously spent months recovering and writing at hot-spring inns, and onsen towns feature in the novels of both.

However, improved healthcare accelerated the overall shift at onsen from therapy to tourism. Onsen towns responded by adding new facilities and services to entertain bathers: theatre troupe Takarazuka Chorus were engaged to perform at Takarazuka Shin Onsen in 1914. Enormous hotels sprung up in the postwar years and onwards, catering to large groups of salarymen travelling together. Today, onsen remain one of Japan's most beloved natural resources. The reasons for visiting them may have changed over time, but their fundamental effect remains the same – there's nothing so restorative as a hot bath.

TATTOO CULTURE AND ONSEN

In Japan, tattoos have long been associated with the *yakuza* (Japanese mafia), and so subject to a social reflex of fear. Many hot springs historically barred tattooed guests, despite tattoos elsewhere carrying cultural significance or cachet among fashionistas. But attitudes are shifting. In 2016, Japan's Tourism Agency encouraged flexibility and websites such as 'Tattoo-Friendly Onsen' list welcoming facilities. While the stigma does linger a little, society is moving toward greater acceptance.

1 KINOSAKI ONSEN
Traditional townscapes, lush surroundings and seven tattoo-friendly public hot-spring baths.

2 BEPPU
At Japan's highest concentration of hot springs, visitors can 'hell-steam' meals using geothermal heat.

3 IBUSUKI ONSEN
'Baths' in volcanically heated sand at this seaside town offer a twist on the usual hot-spring offerings.

4 TAKARAGAWA ONSEN
This mountain-surrounded outdoor bath is one of Japan's few remaining mixed-gender baths.

5 DŌGO ONSEN
Said to be Japan's oldest hot spring, dating back some 3000 years.

LOCAL PERSPECTIVE  ONSEN OWNER

Kazuhiro Otani

Born in Nagato Yumoto, Kazuhiro Otani is the fifth-generation owner of Otani Sansō ryokan, custodian of Ontō bathhouse and proprietor of luxury ryokan Bettei Otozure. He works with local schools to pass Japan's bathing culture to future generations.

What do you find most appealing about hot springs?
For me, their greatest appeal lies in what I call their 'place capital' – how nature, history, culture, stories and human activity condense into a single spot. At Ontō public bathhouse, water has bubbled naturally for over 600 years, welcoming everyone from feudal lords to local children. A hot spring strips us back to our natural selves, restoring a sense of peace. In that sense, onsen are a modern-day utopia.

Across Japan, hot springs often have 'discovery legends'. Why are these stories important?
Most legends attribute a spring's discovery to animals, monks or divine revelations from Shintō gods or Buddhist deities. Their purpose was to prevent monopolisation: by rooting springs in shared myths, they became public goods for the whole community. These stories form what I call 'narrative capital' – preserving hot springs as public spaces right at the heart of Japanese society.

Bathing etiquette can feel strict to newcomers. How do you explain it?
Rather than restrictions, I see them as expressions of care. *Yudō* – the 'Way of the Bath' – teaches three principles: appreciation of the everyday, compassion toward others, discipline in pausing to reflect and face oneself. Washing first and keeping towels out of the tub ensure harmony. Even modest gestures, like holding a small towel, reflect *hajirai*, a sense of modest reserve. Embracing *yudō* allows visitors to enjoy both the bath and the calm state of mind it fosters.

Beyond bathing itself, what is it that makes onsen towns memorable?
What stays with visitors is the unique atmosphere – food, architecture and the traditions of local people. At Ontō, children grow up measuring themselves against the 1m-deep (3ft) bath, a memory passed down for generations. Nagato Yumoto also embodies Shintō and Buddhist syncretism, rooted in the founding legends. In gratitude to the Zen monks of the local temple Tainei-ji, the Shintō deities Sumiyoshi Daimyōjin blessed the village with the Ontō spring. This blend of faith, ritual and practice fosters tolerance, mindfulness and communal care, making a soak in the onsen not just a bath but a cultural journey through centuries of Japanese life.

Mottainai

ABOVE Sorting through the recycling in Kamikatsu in Shikoku, a zero-waste town.

Translated roughly as 'what a waste' or 'don't waste that', mottainai is a common Japanese word that might be deployed when a meal is left unfinished or a perfectly usable item is about to be thrown away. In recent years, it's also become a buzzword for sustainability – a single word that embodies the four Rs: Reduce, Reuse, Recycle and Respect.

Although Japan still has room for improvement when it comes to sustainability – ranking 19th in the UN's 2025 Sustainable Development Goals report – mottainai manifests itself in varied ways, new and old. One approach to reuse that's often highlighted is the Edo-era art of *kintsugi*, with which broken ceramics are repaired with *urushi* lacquer that's been mixed with powdered gold, silver or platinum, in the process creating new works of art that celebrate an item's imperfection.

Far newer is Japan's strict system of waste separation: in many municipalities residents must sort household rubbish into multiple categories, helping to reduce landfill and, arguably, making people more aware of what they're using and discarding. In terms of recycling, there are laws in place to mandate the correct processing of things like old household appliances, and relatively high recycling rates for items such as PET bottles.

As for the fourth R, mottainai-infused respect might relate to a simple appreciation of everyday items and how they came to be owned, or a gratitude to the people who made them. That in turn can inspire valuing and taking care of even the simplest items – meaning people are less likely to waste them.

Like other Japanese buzzwords, the mottainai concept has begun to go global, something that was helped by the late Kenyan activist Wangari Maathai giving a speech to the UN in praise of mottainai initiatives after visiting Japan in 2005. Kenya has since launched a Mottainai Green tree-replanting project, while other initiatives with a mottainai label have popped up in Vietnam, Indonesia and the US. In 2025, the result of the United Nations Environment Programme's annual Youth Day was the Mottainai Youth Declaration to promote zero-waste societies and better environmental governance.

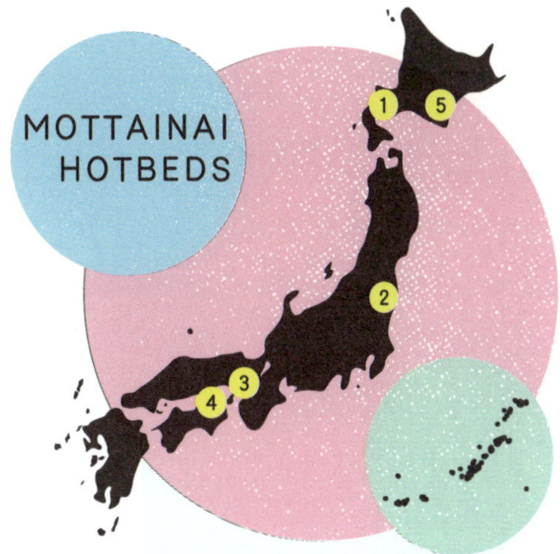

1 NISEKO
This top winter-sports destination has also been designated as an Eco-Model City by the Japanese government.

2 MICHINOKU COASTAL TRAIL
This 1000km (621-mile) trail was established to help protect the coastline and rebuild communities affected by the 2011 tsunami.

3 TAMBA SASAYAMA
One of many old castle towns restoring and reimagining historic streetscapes and buildings.

4 KAMIKATSU
Since the early 2000s, Kamikatsu town has been the pioneer of Japan's zero-waste movement.

5 HIDAKA-SANMYAKU-ERIMO-TOKACHI
Designated Japan's 35th (and largest) national park in 2024.

Longevity

LEFT Tsutomu Takamine and his water buffalo Kai-kun ferry passengers to Yubu Island's botanic garden.

RIGHT Nutritious nattō (fermented soy beans) are a key component of Japan's traditional washoku cuisine.

With an average life expectancy of 87, nobody around the world lives longer than Japanese women; and with an average age of 81, the men don't do badly either. One factor often cited to explain this longevity is Japan's low obesity figures, which in turn promote lower rates of heart disease and common forms of cancer. Where the USA has an obesity rate above 40% – judged by a body mass index (BMI) greater than 30 – fewer than 5% of Japanese fall into the same category. Nutrition plays a key role in this, with traditional *washoku* (Japanese cuisine) low in calories, sugars and processed fats, but also high in such things as fish, fresh vegetables, rice and probiotic-rich foods like *nattō* (fermented soy beans).

While modern-day Japan certainly doesn't live on *washoku* alone, an understanding of food choices and nutrition is ingrained from an early age. All public elementary and junior high schools are required by law to provide healthy school meals, and schools have a full-time food and nutrition teacher who is also responsible for overseeing school-meal programmes.

Active lifestyles are another factor. Japan is a place where people in urban areas tend to forego driving cars and instead cycle, walk and use the efficient public transport systems to get around; and where, thanks to the

principles of *ikigai* (p76), people tend to remain busy in the community long after retirement age.

Preventative healthcare plays a role too. Companies are required to provide all employees with an annual health check-up, which typically includes a range of thorough screenings. If you aren't employed, no problem: anyone aged 40 to 74 can get a free or subsidised check, if they are enrolled in the national health insurance system. Speaking of that, national health insurance covers at least 70% of the cost of a doctor's visit or medical treatment, so while healthcare isn't free for all, the barriers for it are low.

THE LAND OF CENTENARIANS?

In 2025, Japan hit a new landmark for ageing, when the number of people aged 100 or older reached 100,000 for the first time. Coupled with a declining birth rate, that level of ageing brings some issues. Some 30% of the population is already aged 65 and over, and that's expected to hit 40% by 2050, further raising social welfare costs and shrinking the workforce. There could be a surge in social isolation, too, with more senior citizens being predicted to live in single-person households.

Exactly how old some Japanese are, however, is a matter of contention. Firstly, many birth records were lost during WWII, so the age of people born before then can at times be sketchy. Then there's the issue of false social security claims: in 2010, a government audit found that 82% of centenarians claiming benefits were actually deceased.

LOCAL PERSPECTIVE  RYŪKYŪ CUISINE EXPERT

Kazumi Kayo

Born in Okinawa, Kazumi Kayo founded Yonner Food in Naha in 2007 to preserve and share Ryūkyū culinary wisdom. A qualified nutritionist, she teaches Okinawan home-cooking, court cuisine and Blue Zone-inspired dishes, sharing the island's food culture.

What makes Okinawan food culture unique?
Okinawa's food culture has developed through centuries of exchange with other countries. During the Ryūkyū Kingdom era, influences came from China, Thailand, Indonesia and Japan; after WWII, [North] American food culture was introduced. While undergoing many changes, Okinawans accepted these influences flexibly and created a cuisine of their own.

Which foods do you think Okinawans are most proud of?
Perhaps *gōya* (bitter melon). *Gōya champuru* stir-fry [a summertimes stir-fry usually with tofu and other vegetables alongside *gōya*] has spread across Japan but could only have been born in hot Okinawa. Another is pork. Out of gratitude for life, Okinawans eat every part of the pig except its oink – bones for broth, offal for the finest dishes of hospitality, belly meat for many recipes. Pork is truly indispensable in the cuisine of Ryūkyū.

How do you think Okinawan food expresses Okinawa's unique culture?
Okinawan cuisine retains the island dialect, and I try to write dish names using it. For example, *jiimāmi-dofu* means 'peanut tofu': *jiimāmi* combines *jii* (earth) and *māmi* (bean), literally 'bean that grows in the ground.' Today, fewer and fewer people speak the dialect, but losing it means losing identity itself.

What role do you think food plays in Okinawan health and long life?
Okinawan food follows the idea of *ishoku-dōgen* – 'food is medicine'. It is rooted in the belief that eating wisely prevents illness before it happens. In summer, water-rich gourds cool the body. If vital organs become weak, pork offal or blood are eaten to restore strength. To counter oxidation from strong sunlight, people eat purple vegetables such as *beni imo* (sweet potatoes). Many dishes arose from such everyday wisdom, and I believe this is what gave rise to longevity. Following the simple, rational eating practices of our ancestors is key to long, healthy lives. This is why I work to preserve and pass down this food culture.

Ikigai

LEFT A weaver at Koho Nishiki-ori Studio in Kyoto works with his loom, preserving traditional techniques.

RIGHT Retired Japanese seek ikigai by way of second careers, working in bookstores such as this Tokyo shop.

The Japanese term ikigai has no direct English translation, but it's a concept that has resonated around the world. In *The Little Book of Ikigai*, scientist Ken Mogi describes ikigai as the 'pleasures and meaning of life' and 'the reason for getting up in the morning.' While these might sound like a New Age catchphrases, Japanese ikigai has its origins in the Heian period. Derived from the words *iki* (life) and *gai* (value), ikigai essentially encapsulates a sense of purpose and joy in living.

The importance of purpose is well known to contemporary medical researchers, and is often associated with longevity. Mogi's book describes a seven-year study conducted by Tōhoku University's School of Medicine where 50,000 people between the ages of 40–79 were given a questionnaire; one question asked respondents if they had ikigai. Mortality rates among those who answered 'yes' was significantly lower than those who said 'no'.

While the concept seems elemental, the phenomena of ikigai is anything but. *Ikigai: The Japanese Secret to a Long and Happy Life* by Spanish authors Héctor Garcia and Francesc Miralles sold five million copies worldwide and was translated into 70 languages. And the concept of ikigai isn't only a part of life in Japan: Hong Kong can also lay claim to some of the planet's longest life-expectancy rates.

'The elderly want to be respected, have flexibility and want to learn more things', says chairman of the Hong Kong Society of the Aged Dr Kim Mak Kin-wah. 'They can also do things they could not afford to do when they were paying their mortgage, and have aspirations that are completely different – as long as they are willing to learn new things.'

Japanese people often take up second careers post-retirement, becoming booksellers, coffee baristas or artisans. Many are attracted to pursuits that empower them to engage in meaningful interactions and contribute to wider society. This is deemed more important than how much they are paid. Purpose, of course, needn't be job-related – it can be as fundamental as projecting and experiencing love. Gerontologists often point to the phenomena of two spouses, one caring for the other. When one dies, the other often joins them not long after.

HOW TO MANIFEST IKIGAI

COMMUNITY
Being part of a community is integral to ikigai – whether it's through involvement in a special interest, a subculture or a neighbourhood project.

CONTRIBUTING TO SOCIETY
Engaging in activities that are useful and make a positive impact on society are key to increasing ikigai.

LOVE
In all its manifold forms – caring for, nurturing and loving each other – love is the backbone of ikigai.

PASSION
A sense of enthusiasm applied to all aspects of life is crucial to achieving ikigai.

TALENT
Ikigai is achieved by flourishing in a field that you are good at, or applying dedication to mastering it.

Car culture

LEFT The beautiful lines of a Japan-made Toyota 2000GT sports car from the 1960s.

RIGHT Car modifiers regularly congregate at the iconic motorway rest stop of Daikoku between Tokyo and Yokohama.

The popular image of Japan's car cultures is of modified cars, bathed in the neon lights of skyscrapers and with tyres smoking as they gracefully slide sideways around bends. Drifters – never mind that they have been largely outlawed – have long been popularised in movies and such manga as *Initial D*, but there's a lot more to Japan's car scene than these flamboyant drivers.

The car industry took off in the 1960s with the introduction of vehicles from the ever-practical Toyota Corolla to elegant sports cars such as the Nissan Fairlady Z and the Toyota 2000GT. Japan is still famous for its modern engineering marvels – the Nissan Skyline GT-R, Honda NSX and Toyota's Lexus LFA each represent world-first advances in technology. The Toyota Automobile Museum in Aichi Prefecture and Ishikawa's Motorcar Museum of Japan trace the country's stellar history of car manufacturing.

With such potent performance under their feet, some Japanese pitted their cars against each other. From the late

1980s until 1999, the Mid Night Club raced (illegally) along the highway from Tokyo to Yokohama in high-end sports cars, reaching speeds in excess of 300km/h (190mph). At the same time in Osaka, the local street racers were known as *kanjōzoku* and exclusively drove Honda Civics and Integras. Up in the mountains, 'touge' racing saw illicit head-to-heads between drivers drifting around the twisting roads.

Influential though Japan's street-racing scenes have been beyond the country's borders, there are less adrenaline-fuelled subcultures to explore. Decorating vehicles is as popular as modifying their performance. Trucks festooned with colourful lights, vivid paintjobs and extra bodywork signify vehicle owners' dedication to *dekotora* culture, which evolved in the 1970s. The *itasha* culture is about adding graphics depicting scenes and characters from manga, anime and video games to your car.

Other Japanese car cultures prize the vehicle itself. Whatever type of car you can imagine, from luxury sedans to vintage Volvos, there will be Japanese fans that celebrate it and gather for outings. With densely populated cities, tax incentives for compact cars created the kei car, which could be no more than 1.48m (5ft) wide and powered by an engine more at home in a motorbike. The earliest examples date from the 1950s, but they're still made today.

JAPAN'S CAR SUBCULTURES

KEI CARS

Miniaturised vehicles to fit in Japan's narrow urban streets and compact spaces.

DORIFUTO

The art of drifting cars, sometimes employed to race up twisting hillside roads.

KANJŌZOKU

Illicit street racing in highly modified cars, originally on the Kanjō loop of Osaka.

DEKOTORA

Trucks elaborately decorated with lights, extra pipes, artwork and a lot of chrome.

ITASHA

Regular cars with cute graphics or paintjobs, sometimes featuring anime characters.

LOCAL PERSPECTIVE  KEI CARS EXPERT

Fumihiko Kondo

Based at Daihatsu's Humobility World in Osaka, museum director Fumihiko Kondo explains how Japan's kei cars – small in size but big in ingenuity – became cultural icons shaped by postwar necessity, narrow streets and a talent for doing more with less.

How did kei cars first emerge in Japan? Kei cars – *kei* meaning 'light' – originated in 1949, when the Japanese government introduced a new vehicle classification to stimulate mobility and industry at a time when materials were scarce. Kei cars are the smallest category of four-wheeled vehicles that are allowed to travel on Japan's expressways. The kei class set strict limits on size and engine size, so people could afford to own and operate cars during the country's postwar recovery. Early models were tiny – 150cc engines and under 3m [10ft] long – but as standards expanded and technology advanced, kei cars grew into practical everyday vehicles. They were literally shaped by Japan's landscape, engineered to navigate narrow streets, tight corners and dense neighbourhoods.

Why have they become such a distinctive part of Japanese culture? Japan's rapid urbanisation fostered an instinct for maximising function in compact spaces. Kei cars embody this: small yet roomy, economical to run, easy to park. They fit seamlessly into daily life. Their diversity also mirrors Japanese creativity: from tall, box-shaped family cars like the Move to tiny pickup trucks such as the Midget – and even mini sports cars.

What design traits make kei cars ideal for urban Japan? A compact footprint, tall cabin space, great fuel economy and an impressively tight turning radius all suit dense city living. Kei cars concentrate sophisticated engineering into small frames, constantly improving safety, quietness and comfort while remaining within strict size and engine limits.

How do kei cars shape social life and mobility? Kei cars are a cornerstone of daily life in Japan, with 54.5 per 100 households [as of 2023]. They are a first car, a daily companion or a vital lifeline in areas with limited public transport. In rural communities, it's common for households to have one car per person. Kei vans and trucks handle logistics, from parcel deliveries to family-run shops, while welfare-adapted models support wheelchair users and the elderly.

What lies ahead for kei cars? Advances in electric-vehicle technology are bringing kei-sized EVs to the market. In addition, with the spread of autonomous driving and car sharing, cities may shift from a model of 'ownership' to one of 'use'. Yet their essence remains the same: small, capable and woven into Japanese life.

250

Running

LEFT Japan has abundant running trails and traffic-free paths.

RIGHT Relay runners hand over the sash during a Hakone Ekiden long-distance relay race.

From forest trails to city loops, Japan offers a variety of running trails. While jogging as a fitness pursuit only became popular in the postwar era, Japan has a long tradition of endurance running that is rooted in *ekiden*, famous long-distance relay races inspired by the country's Edo-period courier system. Messengers would carry official communications between post towns, or official rest stops, along major routes such as the Tōkaidō, and passed a *tasuki* (sash) in lieu of a baton. In 1917, the first *ekiden* was a marathon-style relay from Kyoto to Tokyo; today, the Hakone Ekiden is a national annual event staged on 2 and 3 January, starting near the Imperial Palace in Tokyo and finishing in the mountains of Hakone.

Japan's cities have excellent running infrastructure, and urbanites make good use of the well-maintained, night-lit paths. Seasonal changes add extra charm, from *sakura* (cherry blossoms) in spring to vibrant autumn leaves. Popular routes include Tokyo's Imperial Palace Loop (a

classic 5K run), the trails through forested Yoyogi Park and, a little over an hour south of central Tokyo, the coastal trail at Shōnan Beach in Kanagawa. In Kyoto, the run along the Kamo River combines nature and city life. Running groups also flourish across Japan (particularly in major cities), staging community runs or focusing on disciplines such as *marason kyōshitsu* (marathon training). Trail running is also popular, especially in areas like Takao near Tokyo, the forests around Hakone, and in the Japanese Alps.

Japanese runners observe a distinct etiquette, keeping to the left side of the pavement, avoiding blocking pedestrian traffic and maintaining a quiet, respectful demeanour in public spaces. On trails, it's expected that runners stay on designated paths, minimise noise and yield to hikers or locals enjoying nature. Runners out at night wear bright or reflective clothing.

JAPAN ON THE RUN

Japan has a vibrant marathon scene, characterised by enthusiastic crowds, clockwork-like organisation and races staged in all seasons. Held in early spring, the Tokyo Marathon is one of the world's largest urban races, taking runners past iconic landmarks like the Imperial Palace and Tokyo Tower, and through atmospheric Asakusa district. The city's traditional Hakone Ekiden showcases teamwork and endurance, with teams of runners covering long distances across the city and into the countryside.

There's also a race around Japan's iconic peak: the late-winter Mt Fuji Marathon offers runners a scenic yet challenging route, combining forested trails, volcanic landscapes and views of lakes and mountains. Further south, the early winter Nara Marathon offers a picturesque route through ancient temples, historic streets and deer-filled parks. October's Sapporo Marathon up in Hokkaidō is famous for mountain views along the route.

Susumu Hara

Head coach of Aoyama Gakuin University's track and field team, Susumu Hara has led the team to become the most successful in the history of the Hakone Ekiden, Japan's most prestigious long-distance relay. He has authored several books on running.

Could you explain what *ekiden* it is and why it's so popular in Japan today?

Ekiden is a long-distance relay race where runners pass a sash, or *tasuki*, from one teammate to the next. The most famous, the Hakone Ekiden, is a round-trip race covering more than 200km [124 miles] between Tokyo and Hakone – a true test of endurance and teamwork. The first *ekiden* was held in 1917, inspired by Japan's old courier system. What makes it special is how it fuses individual endurance with collective strength. A marathon is a personal challenge, but in *ekiden*, every runner's effort directly affects the team. The drama of 'entrusting your spirit to the next runner' moves people deeply.

Why does long-distance running resonate so strongly with the Japanese?

As seen in Japanese martial arts and craftsmanship, steady effort to master a single pursuit and the ability to endure hardship are considered virtues. Long-distance running training embodies this philosophy – strength cannot be built overnight. It requires daily accumulation, struggle and perseverance even when results are not immediately visible. This also overlaps with Japan's work ethic. Diligent, sincere effort and the sense of responsibility to see a task through are exactly the qualities long-distance runners develop.

The Hakone Ekiden is watched nationwide every New Year. Why is it so important?

Beyond sport, it inspires people. Watching students give their all reminds viewers of the power of perseverance and hope, creating a shared emotion that unites generations.

What lesson does running teach about life?

Running mirrors life: there are steep climbs and gentle descents, but if you keep moving, the goal comes into view. Every effort we make today becomes a *tasuki*, carrying our spirit to the future – to the next generation, and to a better society.

Skiing and snowsports

TOP Looking out at volcanic Yōtei-zan from Niseko resort.

BOTTOM A cable car glides over snow and ice at Zaō Onsen ski resort, Yamagata Prefecture.

Every winter, millions flock to Japan's *yukiguni* (snow country) for its feather-light powder and steaming onsen (hot springs) – not to mention affordable lift passes and a culture that balances thrills with tranquillity.

Modern skiing reached Japan in 1911, when Austrian Theodor von Lerch introduced alpine skiing to Niigata. Two decades later, Hannes Schneider – the 'father of modern skiing' – helped turn it into both sport and business. By the mid-20th century, ski resorts blanketed Honshū and Hokkaidō, welcoming experienced and first-time skiers alongside backcountry adventurers. Snowboarding carved into the scene in the 1980s and '90s, transforming from a rebellious subculture into a mainstream pursuit. The 1998 Nagano Winter Olympics cemented Japan's global reputation, showcasing its powder, hospitality and mountain culture to the world.

What makes Japan's snow so extraordinary? Icy winds sweeping across the Sea of Japan pick up moisture, then collide with Honshū and Hokkaidō's mountains, dumping some 10m (33ft) of dry, light snow each season – perfect for powder-hounds. Many resorts also sit beside natural hot springs, creating that quintessential après-ski experience of soaking in a steaming *rotemburo* (outside bath) amid drifts of snow.

But the future of Japan's *yukiguni* is shifting. Major destinations like Niseko and Hakuba are thriving, but smaller resorts face shorter seasons and financial strain. Climate change is forcing adaptation and a pivot toward year-round tourism. Organisations like Protect Our Winters Japan promote sustainability, clean energy and climate action to help safeguard Japan's legendary powder.

In Nozawa Onsen Village, a century-old ski club has shaped generations, teaching kids about nature through skiing. Born and raised in Nozawa Onsen (and currently its mayor), former pro skier Yuta Ueno is looking ahead: 'The last 100 years were built on skiing. For the next 100, we have to think differently.' While snowfall remains steady here, warmer temperatures are changing the landscape. Ueno plans to channel Nozawa's snow-blessed prosperity into its future – shaping the village into a year-round well-being destination. 'If one day we lose the snow,' he says, 'people will still come to soak in the onsen, eat good food and feel welcome.'

1 NISEKO
(Hokkaidō) World-famous powder, extensive runs, vibrant nightlife and luxe, international flair.

2 APPI KŌGEN
(Iwate) Popular for its deep powder, modern facilities and spacious slopes suitable for all abilities.

3 ZAŌ ONSEN
(Yamagata) This resort offers a unique winter landscape with its iconic *juhyō* ('snow monsters' – ice-glazed trees).

4 HAKUBA VALLEY
(Nagano) Olympic host with diverse backcountry terrain, deep snow and beginner-to-expert runs across multiple resorts.

5 NOZAWA ONSEN
(Nagano) Historic hot springs, consistent powder and an authentic Japanese skiing experience.

Martial arts

LEFT Training with bo staffs in a park in Naha City, Okinawa.

RIGHT The record-breaking 2016 karate demonstration on Naha's Kokusai St.

For centuries, *budō* (Japanese martial arts) have shaped Japan's culture, philosophy and sense of self. Over the years – and especially after the 1868 Meiji Restoration signalled the end of the samurai class – martial arts transitioned from battlefield necessities to refined disciplines emphasising education, ethics and personal and spiritual development. In the late 19th and 20th centuries, schools and universities adopted karate, sumo, judo and kendo, integrating them into physical education programmes and modernising training methods. This ensured that Japan's traditional martial arts not only survived, but also adapted and eventually gained international recognition, attracting practitioners across the globe.

KARATE

Arguably Japan's most famous martial art, karate originated in the Ryūkyū Kingdom (modern-day Okinawa) in the 15th century. It was influenced by Chinese martial arts and emphasises striking techniques – punches, kicks and open-hand strikes – while cultivating mental focus, discipline and respect. The sport spread to mainland Japan in the 1920s and quickly expanded overseas.

Legendary Okinawa *sensei* (teacher) Choko Kiyuna has spent his life

championing and preserving the spirit of karate. Raised in a family steeped in the art – his father and brother trained under the renowned Chōtoku Kyan, a key figure in shaping Okinawa's Shōrin-ryū karate style – Kiyuna's roots run deep. Now in his late 80s, he continues to train students at his Risshikan Main Dōjō. 'In the past, karate was practiced behind closed doors. It was a private, personal practice,' Kiyuna recalls. 'After WWII, with the presence of American troops, Okinawans began to take pride in karate and to share it as part of our culture.'

As an advisor to Okinawa Dentō Karatedō Shinkōkai (which promotes and preserves karate), Kiyuna helped establish Okinawa Karate Day, a celebration that attracts thousands of practitioners to Naha's Kokusai St for spectacular group demonstrations. In 2016, the event made history with a Guinness world record: 3973 *karateka* (karate practitioners) performing a *kata* (choreographed sequence of movements) in unison – a powerful testament to the enduring legacy of Okinawa's most famous cultural export.

HOW TO SUMO

STEP ONE
Wrestlers step into the *dohyō*, clapping hands and stamping feet to purify the sacred ring.

STEP TWO
They face off, crouching low and with fists touching the ground, waiting for the referee's signal to start the clash.

STEP THREE
At *tachi-ai* (initial charge), wrestlers collide with explosive force, aiming for a dominant grip or push.

STEP FOUR
Techniques include shoves, thrusts, trips and throws, each designed to unbalance and overpower the opponent.

STEP FIVE
The bout ends when a wrestler touches ground or exits the ring; the opponent is declared the winner.

SUMO

Japan's national sport, sumo has roots stretching back over 1500 years. Originally a Shintō ritual to entertain the gods, it has become a highly ritualised professional sport. Sumo wrestlers – *rikishi*, meaning 'men of strength' – compete in *dohyō* (circular rings), relying on strength, balance and technique to force opponents out of the *dohyō* or to the ground. *Rikishi* lead highly disciplined lives, waking before dawn for gruelling hours of training and following a carefully scheduled daily routine of chores, practise and rest. This regimen is fuelled by a high-calorie diet centred on *chanko-nabe*, a stew of meat, fish vegetables and rice that's eaten in massive portions to maintain their size.

Major sumo *honbasho* (tournaments) take place six times a year, with the most famous held in Tokyo's Ryōgoku Kokugikan in January, May and September. Other tournaments are staged in Osaka, Nagoya and Fukuoka throughout the year. Tickets are sold online in advance or at the arena, with options ranging from ringside seats to more affordable upper-level seating, and they sell out quickly. The tournaments start with lower-ranked wrestlers, while top bouts typically run in the afternoon and evening. Aficionados also visit sumo stables to watch training sessions.

TOP A sumo tournament in Tokyo.

BOTTOM RIGHT A kendo-style demonstration with wooden swords.

BOTTOM LEFT Japanese archery was used by samurai.

OTHER DISCIPLINES

Now a worldwide Olympic sport, judo was developed by Jigorō Kanō in 1882, and evolved from older jujutsu schools. It's an accessible sport for people of all sizes, as it focuses on using an opponent's force against them rather than brute strength. Techniques include throws, pins and joint-locks.

The 'way of the sword', kendo emerged from *kenjutsu* (samurai swordsmanship) and is a living connection to Japan's samurai heritage. Today, though, the swords are bamboo *shinai*, and practitioners wear *bogū* (protective armour). Timing, precision and cultivation of the warrior spirit are key. While kendo is competitive, with full-contact sparring, aikido is non-competitive, focusing on harmonising with an opponent's energy redirecting attacks, and neutralising conflict without causing injury.

Ninjutsu – the traditional art of the ninja – emphasises stealth and evasion. While often romanticised in popular culture, modern schools teach historical techniques alongside survival skills which are still practiced today in areas such as mountainous Togakushi, the birthplace of Togakure-ryū (the 'School of the Hidden Door', one of the oldest traditions within ninjutsu).

Kyūdo, Japanese archery, is a meditative practice based on mental presence, form and breathing. These techniques were adapted into *yabusame* (mounted archery performed at a gallop) as a training technique for warriors and a Shintō ritual to pray for protection. *Yabusame* demonstrations are featured in festivals such as November's Meiji Jingu Autumn Festival in Tokyo and at the Shintō shrine of Tsurugaoka Hachimangū in Kamakura.

LOCAL PERSPECTIVE  KARATE MASTER

Kenjiro 'Kenny' Ueda

Kenjiro Ueda is a 7th-dan master of Shōrin-ryū and Shitō-ryū karate and a kobudō (traditional martial arts) practitioner. As CEO of Ageshio Japan, he offers specialist karate travel experiences that immerse visitors in Okinawan martial arts.

What are the origins of karate?
Karate was born during the Ryūkyū Kingdom era, when Okinawa was an independent kingdom engaged in cultural exchange with China. It began as *tie* (手, 'hand') and evolved under influences from Chinese martial arts. In parallel, Ryūkyū *kobudō* developed, using everyday tools such as staffs and sickles as weapons when carrying arms was forbidden. Together, these traditions shaped what we now know as Okinawan karate. By the 20th century, karate had spread from Okinawa to mainland Japan and beyond, becoming both a martial art and a cultural legacy practiced by over 100 million people worldwide.

Do all Okinawan dōjōs teach the same style?
Okinawa has around 400 dōjōs rooted in three main lineages – Shuri-te, Naha-te and Tomari-te – each named after the village where it developed. Shuri-te emphasizes speed and linear movement, Naha-te focuses on breathing and conditioning, and Tomari-te values practical, fluid techniques. Together they represent the diversity and depth of Okinawan martial culture.

How does karate reflect Okinawan culture?
Karate is not just combat – it is a philosophy of life. Training cultivates courtesy, patience and self-discipline, qualities deeply tied to Okinawan values. As karate pioneer Gichin Funakoshi taught: 'There is no first attack in karate.' He also advised: 'First control yourself before attempting to control others.'

What sites does Ageshio introduce in Okinawa?
Across Okinawa, many sites embody the spirit of karate – from grandmasters' dōjōs to monuments and statues of past masters, and historic shrines. Visitors can find inscriptions with the teachings and philosophies of these masters – timeless reminders that the true essence of karate lies not in conflict, but in harmony.

人生

Surfing

LEFT Surfing Fujisawa's Shonan Beach, in the shadow of Mt Fuji.

RIGHT Pro surfer Amuro Tsuzuki of Japan training at Tsurigasaki Beach in Chiba.

As an island country, it shouldn't come as a surprise that Japan has a surfing culture with deep roots – far earlier than many realise. It's said that Japanese wave-riding dates back to the Edo period, as an 1821 haiku by Dokurakuan Kanri describes children in Yamagata Prefecture skimming waves on *itago*, small wooden belly boards made from boat-floor planks.

Modern surfing arrived in two waves. After WWII, US soldiers based at Yokosuka naval base brought fibreglass longboards to Kanagawa's Shōnan Coast and to the coastline of Chiba Prefecture. This inspired Japan's first generation of surfers, who began shaping boards and riding waves. In 1965, the Nippon Surfing Association (NSA) was established, overseeing competitions, athlete development and international representation. The second wave, in the late 1970s to early '80s, coincided with the buoyant national economy of Japan's 'Bubble Era' phase. Miyazaki became a popular honeymoon destination; the Japanese holidaymakers who flocked to beach resorts such as Aoshima were exposed to surfing, and riding waves was thus integrated into the country's mainstream leisure culture.

In recent years, the local surf scene has gained international acclaim: in 2018, Japan hosted the ISA World Surfing Games in Tahara, where

Japan secured a historic team gold medal. The country also reached an Olympic milestone at the Tokyo Summer Games (held in 2021), when Tsurigasaki Beach in Chiba hosted the first ever Olympic surfing competition.

Japan has a diverse range of surf breaks along its extensive coastline, which tend to have the best waves during the typhoon season (August to November). Off the mainland, Okinawa offers a long swell-window between late summer to early spring. Up north in Hokkaidō, hardy adventurers can go from riding deep powder snow to surfing winter barrels. Surrounded by sea and shaped by its varied coastline, Japan's surfing culture continues to grow and evolve.

1 SOUTHERN CHIBA

Consistent beach breaks near Tokyo, popular with beginners and intermediate surfers seeking easy access.

2 SHŌNAN COAST

Mellow waves and a lively surf culture; a quick, go-to escape for first-timers and city-dwellers.

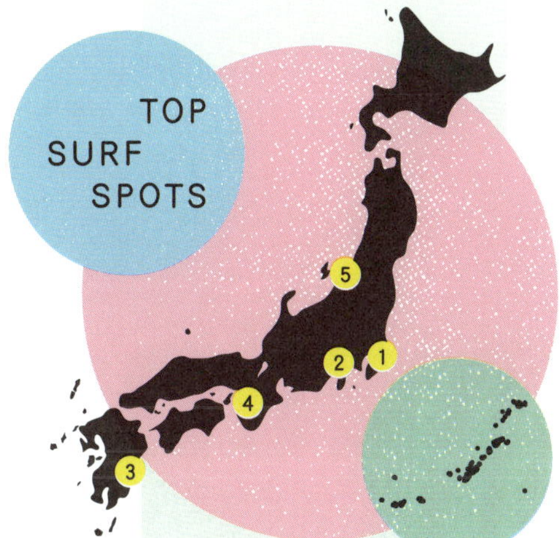

3 MIYAZAKI AND SOUTHERN KYŪSHŪ

Tropical, sunny coastline with world-class point breaks that attract surfers chasing fun waves.

4 WAKAYAMA

Uncrowded beaches with reliable swells. Isonoura is a well-known surf spot in the Kansai region that draws in local surfers.

5 NIIGATA

Remote waves along the Sea of Japan. The swell here is more seasonal and can be rough; conditions vary greatly.

Shinrin-yoku

LEFT It's possible to find quiet, green spaces even in Tokyo, such as Hibiya-kōen.

RIGHT Contemplating nature at Pinaisāra-no-taki on Iriomote Island.

Shinrin-yoku is a catchy Japanese term, coined in 1982 to promote the health benefits of going for a relaxing walk in the woods. The civil servant who came up with it had a vested interest (he ran the Japanese Forestry Agency at the time), but he believed that woodlands have a positive role to play in helping people overwhelmed by modern life to de-stress, to recharge their physical and mental energies and to rediscover pleasure in life.

Shinrin-yoku translates as 'deep-forest bathing', and the concept of bathing is a positive and pleasurable one to the Japanese, since it's associated not with the task of washing but with the enjoyment of plunging, immersing and soaking oneself in warm, all-embracing water. Shinrin-yoku also suggests the idea of total immersion – but in this case, in the natural world, specifically among trees.

The idea is that shinrin-yoku should involve an enjoyable rather than a gruelling amount of physical exercise, usually in the form of walking; the aim is not to punish the body

by engaging in a strenuous physical workout – it's to repair it. Freeing oneself from stress is an important part of this. Shinrin-yoku involves being kind to yourself, and taking your time. There's no point trying to escape from daily worries and anxieties by attempting more than you can cope with.

By opening up the senses – sight, smell, sound and even touch (albeit while avoiding doing damage to plants and steering clear of poisonous ones), the mind is released from the shackles of self-absorption. Concentrating on the here and now allows both body and spirit to become alive to the immediate environment, and to reconnect with the natural world. And shinrin-yoku can be enjoyed any time of the year, whether bathing in the greenery of a summer forest canopy, where sparkling light flickers through the leaves and branches; or filling the lungs with bracing, cleansing air and listening to the sound of crackling hoarfrost beneath the feet in a winter forest. It is all about healing oneself through nurturing a respect and love for nature.

FOREST-BATHING ESSENTIALS

PICK A PLACE

A riverside picnic spot along Aomori Prefecture's Oirase-gawa provides a place to rest in nature.

DON'T RUSH

But gentle activities such as horse riding or cycling can also be a means of enjoying woodland.

FIND YOUR FOCUS

Be mindful of your breathing. Be still and inhale deeply and exhale slowly. Your mind may wander. This is good.

ENGAGE YOUR SENSES

Painting and sketching can be a way of connecting with the natural world.

GO ALONE OR WITH A FRIEND

A guide is not necessary but if you take companions, ensure you're on the same wavelength.

Hara hachi bu

LEFT Encounter a million ways to enjoy tofu in Japan.

RIGHT Harvesting locally grown vegetables is very hara hachi bu.

In Japan's far south, on tropical Okinawa Island, people well into their 80s and 90s (and even centenarians) enjoy healthy, thriving lives. Some say their secret is hara hachi bu – which translates as 'stomach eight parts out of ten' and refers to eating until roughly 80% full. This Confucian principle champions moderation over indulgence, encouraging pausing before feeling completely stuffed. The result is a gentle, almost effortless form of calorie reduction linked to steadier energy, healthier weight management and happier digestion. Eating slowly helps too, easing pressure on the gut and warding off bloating and discomfort. With its focus on balance, awareness and restraint, hara hachi bu is often credited as one pillar of Okinawans' remarkable longevity alongside local superfoods and *moai*, strong community ties.

Paired with the Okinawan belief in *kusui mun* (food as medicine), locals have long shaped their wellbeing through mindful eating. 'The most important internal organs are our digestive organs,' says Yukie Miyaguni, a traditional Chinese medicine practitioner and chef of traditional Okinawan cuisine. 'No matter how high-quality or nutrient-dense your food is, if your stomach and intestines aren't in good condition, digestion becomes a burden.' She likens the digestive

system to a blender: ingredients tossed in whole or packed to the brim won't blend smoothly, and the machine may overheat. Likewise, overeating strains the gut; leaving a little 'space' helps everything run smoothly and leaves you comfortably satisfied shortly after.

Putting hara hachi bu into practice is refreshingly simple: it's just slowing the pace of a meal, chewing thoroughly and taking pauses to let the stomach signal its needs. Using smaller plates, keeping portions modest and stopping just before feeling full is also important, as are tuning into genuine hunger cues rather than habits or distractions, and savouring flavours and textures without scrolling or watching TV.

EAT LIKE AN OKINAWAN

The centuries-old Okinawan diet centres on sweet potatoes, vegetables, tofu, seaweed and pork. After WWII, however, North American foods gained popularity, edging out traditional dishes. As a hospital nutritionist, Yukie Miyaguni saw the health impact up close: near US bases, residents favoured fries and coffee and showed higher rates of obesity and lifestyle diseases, while rural elders who stuck to local foods and practised *kusui mun* enjoyed better health. Their intuitive choices highlighted the connection between health and diet.

Based an hour from Naha, Okinawa's central hub, Miyaguni hosts medicinal cooking classes. After an introduction to the traditional Okinawan diet, participants' skin, tongue and energy levels are assessed. Miyaguni also recommends tailored foods and teaches students how to make dishes they can recreate at home, so maintaining healthy eating habits long after they visit.

Hiking

LEFT Yamabushi climb sacred Ōmine-san in Tenkawa, Nara, in 1928.

RIGHT Trekking up to the summit of Miyanoura-dake on Yakushima.

Japan is a hikers' paradise. Over 70% of the country is blanketed in mountains – from the iconic peaks of Honshū's Japan Alps to the volcanic landscapes of Kyūshū and Hokkaidō – and the uplands are laced with a network of trails, which weave through onsen towns, pass sacred shrines and deliver breathtaking vistas that have inspired poets, pilgrims and mountaineers for centuries.

Hiking in Japan is deeply tied to spirituality and tradition. Long before it became a leisure pursuit, *yamabushi* monks practised ascetic mountain training, trekking remote ridges in search of enlightenment. In the late 19th century, Western explorers mapped Japan's mountains. The British missionary and mountaineer Walter Weston, who documented his climbs across Nagano, Toyama and Gifu Prefectures, helped popularise the term 'Japanese Alps'. His vivid accounts introduced these dramatic landscapes – craggy peaks, deep valleys, alpine meadows – to hikers in Japan and around the world. Today, hiking is a national pastime embraced by people of all ages, including active octogenarians who still scale their local peaks for health and for the sheer joy of it. Many stay in Japan's popular *yamagoya*, rustic mountain lodges that offer hearty meals, futon-style sleeping mats and a cosy refuge after a long day

on the trails. They also provide connection with other walkers: evenings are communal, with hikers sharing stories over dinner before turning in early for a sunrise start.

Japanese hiking culture emphasises respect for others (uphill hikers always have the right of way) and for mountain traditions. Trails are meant to be shared calmly and courteously, and carrying out trash is essential – as is treading lightly and speaking softly, especially near shrines or temples. Respect for nature is equally key: Japan's mountains are rich with wildlife, with trails taking hikers into the territory of macaques, deer or shaggy *kamoshika* (the goat-antelope serow). Upland forests are also home to alpine species such as copper pheasants, woodpeckers and the rare *raichō* (rock ptarmigan), a snow-white bird revered for its resilience in harsh alpine winters. Bears roam, too: the *tsukinowa-guma* (black bear) in Honshū and Shikoku; and the larger, more aggressive *higuma* (brown bear) in Hokkaidō.

HIKING ROUTES

1 KAMIKŌCHI TO YARIGATAKE
An adventurous multiday hike in Honshū's Northern Alps features rugged peaks and alpine meadows.

2 DAISETSUZAN NATIONAL PARK
Vast wilderness, volcanic landscapes and rare wildlife await in Hokkaidō.

3 SHIKOKU 88 PILGRIMAGE TRAIL
This popular pilgrimage route connects temples and passes through rural villages and forested hills.

4 KUMANO KODŌ PILGRIMAGE TRAIL
Ancient paths meander through cedar forests on this UNESCO World Heritage–listed trail on Honshū's Kii Peninsula.

5 NAKASENDŌ TRAIL
A cultural trek through Nagano and Gifu in Honshū, taking in serene forests, historic inns and Edo-era towns.

MOUNTAIN TRAILS

No Japanese mountain is more iconic nor more frequently summited than 3776m (12,288ft) Mt Fuji. Over 200,000 hikers ascend Japan's highest peak annually, mostly during the official hiking season (from early July to early September), when trails are clear of snow and *yamagoya* open their doors. Many start their at night to watch sunrise from the summit. But given its challenging, rocky terrain, many heed the saying 'A wise man climbs Fuji once; a fool climbs it twice', and make hiking up Fuji a once-in-a-lifetime experience.

Beyond Fuji, the Japan Alps offer spectacular trekking. The Northern Alps feature the rugged peaks of the Hotaka range and Tateyama; the Central Alps are home to Kisokoma; and the Southern Alps host Kitadake. Multiday routes – like Kamikōchi to Yarigatake – reward hikers with alpine meadows, glassy rivers and panoramic ridgelines, while shorter routes in the Alps (often doable in a day) provide access to the same grandeur with less exertion. Drawn by a love of hiking and snowboarding, trekking guide Kohei Nishida traded Tokyo's bustle for the Alps' crisp mountain air and founded Shinano Discovery, guiding hikers along some of Japan's most scenic and lesser-known trails. 'Hiking in Japan offers incredible variety,' he says. 'In the Japan Alps, you trek from *yamagoya* to *yamagoya* with sweeping alpine views. Elsewhere, there are ancient pilgrimage routes and gentle *satoyama* (countryside) walks through forests. On the Pacific side, evergreen woods dominate, while the Sea of Japan side gets heavy snow and has deciduous forests. You can experience different scenery even in the same season.'

Many Japanese hiking routes also offer an enticing mix of culture and nature: the Amatomi Trail, linking Nagano Station with the summit of Madarao, passes through charming villages and Kurohime's beech forest, and incorporates the historic Togakushi Kodō pilgrimage path. Nishida recalls one memorable moment while maintaining Kurohime's trails: 'After a long day, I looked up to see a bear sitting in a mulberry tree, happily eating. Our eyes met, but it just kept munching,' he laughs. 'You need to be especially careful around bears, but that was quite a cute moment.'

English-language trail information can be limited, especially on less-visited mountains; on popular routes, signage often notes distances, difficulty levels and emergency contacts. Given Japan's famously fickle weather, with sudden rain and fast-changing mountain conditions, Japanese hikers are attuned to checking forecasts, wearing weather-appropriate clothing, carrying proper gear (including bear bells) and using GPS navigation when hiking without a guide. Preparation is key to enjoying Japan's trails safely.

TOP LEFT Grilling fresh char in a mountain lodge at the end of a day's hiking.

TOP RIGHT A sacred shika deer at Kasuga Taisha shrine.

CENTRE Approaching the Zuishinmon Gate on the Togakushi-jinja approach walk, Nagano.

BOTTOM The Kumano Kodō trail begins behind Takijiri-ōji, once held to be the entranceway to the abode of the gods.

Baseball

TOP LEFT Matsutarō Shōriki, media mogul and founder of Japan's iconic Yomiuri Giants baseball team.

TOP RIGHT A baseball game between Japan and South Korea at the Tokyo Dome.

BOTTOM Teruaki Sato of the Hanshin Tigers hits a two-run double.

Baseball is far more than a game in Japan: it's the country's most beloved team pastime, filling school fields and stadiums alike with a passion unmatched by any other team sport. With dramatic home runs, choreographed cheering sections and legendary athletes, Japanese baseball (*yakyū*) is thrilling and theatrical.

Baseball was brought to Japan in the 1870s by American educator Horace Wilson, but it was 1934 that truly changed the game. Owner of *Yomiuri Shimbun* newspaper Matsutarō Shōriki invited American Major League Baseball (MLB) stars Babe Ruth, Lou Gehrig and Jimmie Foxx to Tokyo for exhibition matches against the All-Nippon team, made up of Japan's top amateur talent. The tour packed stadiums with ecstatic fans, and Shoriki's squad became the iconic Yomiuri Giants. Just two years later, Japan's first professional league was formed, evolving into today's Nippon Professional Baseball (NPB) league, with its Central and Pacific divisions.

Now regarded as the world's strongest league outside MLB, NPB is a national institution – and Japan's baseball scene has made its mark globally. Japanese teams have won the Little League World Series 11 times, making it the third-most successful country in the tournament's history; and home-grown stars such as Hideo Nomo, Ichiro Suzuki and Shohei Ohtani have carried Japanese precision and flair to MLB. Around seven million Japanese – roughly 5% of the population – now play baseball, and every spring and summer, the annual Kōshien (the National High School Baseball Championship of Japan) grips the nation. For young players, reaching Kōshien can be life-changing as many professional stars first make their names there.

Over time, Japanese baseball has developed a style all its own. Games pulse with energy thanks to organised cheering, colourful banners and team-specific songs belted out in unison. The rivalry between the country's most popular teams – the Yomiuri Giants and Hanshin Tigers – is one of Japan's great sporting traditions. At the cavernous Tokyo Dome, fans deliver rousing choruses of *Tōkon Komete* (meaning 'with fighting spirit'); in Kansai, passionate Hanshin Tigers supporters are famed for their booming chants of *Rokkō Oroshi* (referencing the powerful wind that sweeps down from the Rokkō range).

EVOLUTION OF JAPANESE BASEBALL

1872 Baseball arrives in Japan (via American educator Horace Wilson), sparking early school and community interest.

1934 Babe Ruth, Lou Gehrig and Jimmie Foxx tour Tokyo and play against the All-Nippon team (later the Yomiuri Giants).

1950s Japan's baseball culture solidifies: Nippon Professional Baseball is established with Central and Pacific Leagues.

1960s Japanese players excel in Little League and international tournaments, marking Japan's global presence.

2000s Japanese stars like Ichiro Suzuki shine in MLB, inspiring new generations; domestic leagues thrive.

Meditation

LEFT Priest Keno Miura meditating at Dairyū-ji.

RIGHT Dairyū-ji is a temple tucked into the mountains of Gifu.

The Japanese version of Mahayana Buddhism (which arrived from China around the 7th century), Zen has significantly shaped Japanese culture, from aesthetic sensibilities and daily practices to the arts. One particularly widespread Zen practice is meditation, a form of experiential wisdom that has become popular not just among Buddhists (where it's a core exercise in the study of self), but also among secular enthusiasts.

Dairyū-ji is a Sōtō-sect Zen temple in Akita, established over 800 years ago, where *zazen* (seated meditation) is a fundamental aspect of training. Head priest Keno Miura explains that 'Because Buddha meditated under the Bodhi tree and attained enlightenment, meditation is a central part of Sōtō school activity, but *zazen* is not just done with the goal of attaining enlightenment. Sitting itself is the gateway to peace, and while meditation is central, it is only one part of a daily lifestyle practice that even includes how one eats and prepares food. Enlightenment might sound inaccessible, but by meditating, one notices small things in our daily life, and the process of becoming aware is an expression of enlightenment.'

In Sōtō Buddhism, practitioners face a wall when meditating, although this differs between the sects; at Dairyū-ji, they face views of the resplendent Zen

garden. *Zazen* focuses on posture, in order to breathe naturally and gently. 'We say *chōshin* (align the posture), *chōsoku* (regulate the breath) and *chōshin* again (adjust the mind)', says Keno Miura. 'When the first two are balanced, the mind follows.' He also asserts that even two minutes of quiet can reset the mind. 'Having the experience of *zazen* is like a tool, and you can apply it to everyday life. When you are doing *zazen*, things like age, gender, job, social status and whether you have money or not – none of that matters. While you are sitting, you're not comparing yourself with anyone. You sit calmly, letting your mind and body refresh.'

MEDITATION AND MINDFULNESS

Mindfulness is an aspect of meditation that has its roots in Buddhism, being a core component of the practices that make up the Noble Eightfold Path (the route to enlightenment).

Like meditation, mindfulness is also popular with secular enthusiasts; Gretchen Miura of Dairyū-ji teaches a form of meditation that focuses on mindfulness. 'Mindfulness simply means being aware of what is happening right now, without judgement', she explains. 'Daily life contains many chances to practise mindfulness, and meditation grows out of that awareness. It means staying with the pain and difficulties without running from them. Modern society encourages us to avoid discomfort, even though that is part of being human. Meditation is about allowing yourself to fully exist in your own life.'

FOOD AND DRINK

Noodles

ABOVE LEFT Devour noodles on a night out anywhere in Japan.

There's no doubt, Japan knocks back oodles of noodles and must be the only country in the world where museums dedicated to noodles are must-visit attractions. The hype is well and truly justified – Japan's noodles know no equal in quality, subtlety, presentation and sheer style, and everyone has their favourite iteration (many also have an *anaba*, their 'hidden gem' of a noodle shop). In terms of noodle types, the big three are ramen, soba and udon.

RAMEN (ラーメン)

These days renowned around the planet as a Japanese phenom, ramen is thought to have arrived in Yokohama with Chinese immigrants in the early 20th century and was originally known as *shina-soba* (Chinese noodles). It was quickly adopted and adapted to Japanese tastes, going on to become a classic comfort food. If a small town in Japan has only one restaurant, odds are it's a ramen shop.

Basic ramen is a big bowl of crinkly wheat-based noodles in broth, served with toppings such as *chāshū* (sliced roast pork), *moyashi* (bean sprouts), *menma* (fermented bamboo shoots) and an egg. The broth can be made from pork, chicken bones or dried seafood and is often a top-secret combination of some or all of the above, falling somewhere on the

spectrum between *kotteri* (thick and fatty) and *assari* (thin and light). It's typically seasoned with *shio* (salt), *shōyu* (soy sauce) or a hearty miso – though at less orthodox places, anything goes. In Hokkaidō, the city of Sapporo specializes in *miso-ramen*, while up the road in Asahikawa, it's *shōyu-ramen* and down south in Hakodate, the locals laud their *shio-ramen*.

Ramen is cheap eats in Japan. Avoiding labour costs, some places may require patrons to order and pay from a vending machine or a screen. Many ramen shops will also have *yakimeshi* (fried rice) and *gyōza* (pan-fried dumplings) on their menu.

ABOVE RIGHT A Japanese chef prepares soba noodles by hand.

Ramen is also often served as a cold noodle salad, often with mushrooms and ginger.

For an absorbing window into Japan's ramen world, Juzō Itami's classic 1985 movie *Tampopo* comes highly recommended; an oldie but a goodie, it follows the efforts of a female noodle-shop owner striving for ramen perfection.

SOBA (そば)

The popularity of soba (buckwheat noodles) arose not due to their delicate aroma or distinctive, subtle, elegant-but-earthy taste, but with buckwheat's ability to deter starvation. Packed with nutrients, it flourishes in thin mountain

soils where nothing else will and, with its rapid 75-day passage from seed to grain, it made an excellent backup whenever the rice crop failed.

Soba is traditionally sliced by hand to make *teuchi-soba*, but as the dough easily breaks when stretched after kneading, it is often either sliced by machine or, in the case of *teuchi*, *tsunagi* (a binding agent) is added, usually wheat flour. A ratio of 20% wheat flour to 80% soba is said to produce the finest results, though some purists swear by the dark, 100% *soba jūwari*. Soba noodles are a light brownish-grey in colour and the width resembles spaghetti.

Soba is eaten hot, cold or stir-fried. Hot soba comes in a bowl of broth, while cold soba is presented on a *zaru* (bamboo-grid tray) to be dunked in a separate cold *tsuyu* (dipping sauce). Added to the sauce are ingredients such as *sarashi-negi* (sliced spring onion), grated *daikon* (radish), *katsuo-bushi* (bonito flakes), *yuzu* (fragrant Japanese citron), *uzura-tamago* (quail egg) and, of course, wasabi.

Yaki-soba is a stir-fried noodle dish of soba with thinly sliced pork and vegetables (such as cabbage, carrots and onions), all tossed in a savoury, tangy sauce and topped off with pickled ginger, *aonori* (green dried seaweed) and bonito flakes.

While there are many cheap and cheerful soba shops, there are also a number of more upmarket restaurants – and while the weather may be a factor in choosing whether to eat hot or cold soba, the choice is just as likely to come down to personal preference.

TOP LEFT Noodles are served at Udon Sakaeda restaurant in Kagawa.

CENTRE Ramen is a quick and easy meal for busy people.

TOP RIGHT Vending machines across Japan dispense noodles.

STANDOUT NOODLE DISHES

ZARU-SOBA
Cold soba, laid out on a bamboo-grid tray and dipped in a sauce that's served in a separate bowl.

CHASHU-MISO-RAMEN
A hearty *miso-ramen* topped off with thick slices of roast pork and other condiments.

YAKI-UDON
Stir-fried udon noodles with thin-sliced pork, vegetables and a tangy sauce

SANUKI-UDON
Thick, chewy udon noodles in a tasty broth; speciality of Kagawa Prefecture.

HIYAMUGI
A popular style of udon noodles that are particularly favoured by children – they're often coloured pink or green.

UDON (うどん)

White-wheat udon noodles come in a various shapes and thicknesses, and there are many regional varieties. As with soba, udon is eaten hot in a broth, cold with a dipping sauce or stir-fried as *yaki-udon*.

On the island of Shikoku, Kagawa Prefecture is so enamoured with its local speciality *Sanuki-udon* that it has nicknamed itself '*udon-ken*' (meaning 'udon prefecture'), and though it is the smallest of Japan's 47 prefectures, it boasts some 800 udon shops. Known throughout Japan, the thick, dense and chewy *Sanuki-udon* is said to have arrived from China about the same time as Buddhism (in the mid-6th century).

Also of the udon family, *sōmen* is a thin, round noodle similar in thickness to angel-hair pasta; it's particularly popular in summer, eaten cold with a soy-based dipping sauce and *umeboshi* (pickled plum). *Kishimen*, a speciality in Aichi Prefecture, is a thin, flat noodle served in a seasoned soup; *hiyamugi* are thin, round udon noodles that are often coloured green and pink, making them popular with children.

Seafood

LEFT A fishing boat departs from Rausu port on Hokkaidō.

RIGHT Sashimi is artfully arranged at a kaiseki restaurant.

Surrounded by the sea, with cold currents sweeping down from the frigid north and warm currents from the subtropical south, Japan is blessed with an incredible variety of seafood. Its nutrient-rich waters deliver an enormous bounty of seafood delights to the country's chefs.

SEASONAL SEAFOOD DELIGHTS

Japan prides itself on having four distinct seasons, and along with changes in scenery and temperatures come differing types of seafood – all nutritious, reasonably priced and delicious. Summer is the season for *saba* (mackerel), *unagi* (eel), *ika* (squid) and *uni* (sea urchin). Autumn is famous for *kaki* (oysters), *sanma* (Pacific saury) and *ayu* (freshwater sweetfish); winter for *hotate-gai* (scallops), *kani* (crab), *buri* (yellowtail amberjack) and *tako* (octopus). *Kisu* (whiting), *kanpachi* (amberjack) and *katsuo* (bonito) are popular in spring.

SEAFOOD DESTINATIONS

Areas of Japan are known for their *meibutsu* (local speciality), many being seafood related; Japanese domestic travellers often visit a destination with the specific goal of trying the local *meibutsu*.Hiroshima is known for its *kaki* (oysters), while Kōchi is renowned for *katsuo-no-tataki* (seared bonito). Aomori is famous for its *hotate-gai*

(scallops) and Hokkaidō for its *kani* (crab), *sake* (salmon) and *kombu* (kelp). Many head to Rishiri Island, off the northern tip of Hokkaidō, to try its legendary *uni* (sea urchins), while at the western tip of Honshū, the city of Shimonoseki is known for its *fugu* (pufferfish), poisonous if not prepared in the correct manner by a qualified chef.

One of Osaka's great street foods is *takoyaki* (octopus balls), while Nagoya is known for its *ebi-furai* (fried breadcrumbed prawns). Hakodate on Hokkaidō is a place to eat *kaisendon* (raw seafood on rice) for breakfast at the morning fish market.

IN DAILY MEALS

The importance of seafood in the daily life and diet of the Japanese is on display in the seafood section at any local supermarket. There's usually a mind-blowing array of prepared sushi and sashimi, along with grilled, fried and chilled fish and shellfish. *Yaki-zakana* (grilled fish) is a common way of consuming seafood at home, often eaten for breakfast and dinner alongside rice, miso soup and other accompaniments.

POPULAR FISH

MAGURO (TUNA)
Top quality *maguro* can generate unbelievable news-making prices at morning fish markets.

SABA (MACKEREL)
Grilled *saba* is an affordable fish dish in Japanese households, eaten at breakfast or dinner.

SAKE (SALMON)
Taken from the sea and rivers of Hokkaidō, *sake* (or *shake*) is a traditional food of the Ainu.

TAI (SEA BREAM)
Eaten on happy occasions such as weddings; the name is based on a pun – *omede-tai* means 'congratulations'.

FUGU (PUFFERFISH)
Japanese law strictly regulates who can prepare this potentially poisonous culinary thrill.

Sushi

ABIVE Sample super-fresh sushi at Tsukiji Outer Market in Tokyo.

RIGHT Chef Naruki Takimoto (see over the page) prepares sushi in his eponymous restaurant.

Essentially, sushi is raw fish and rice seasoned with vinegar. The most common style is *nigiri-zushi* (hand-formed sushi), made by deft-fingered chefs who quickly press slivers of raw fish onto bite-sized mounds of rice. The fish isn't always raw and is sometimes lightly seared or grilled. *Tamago-yaki* (slightly sweetened rolled omelette) is also served on rice in the *nigiri-zushi* style, and *inari-zushi* sees the rice stuffed inside pockets of deep-fried sweetened tofu.

Maki-zushi is rolled sushi which, in Japan, is generally fairy simple, involving fish or vegetables rolled into rice that is wrapped in *nori* (dried seaweed). *Maki-zushi* hasn't evolved along the same lines as it has in the US, and you're unlikely to come across anything like elaborate California or Philadelphia rolls.

Unless otherwise instructed by the chef, who may have pre-seasoned some pieces, patrons dip each piece lightly in *shōyu* (soy sauce), which is poured from a decanter into a small dish provided for that purpose. *Nigiri-zushi* is usually

made with wasabi, though patrons can order without wasabi by saying *'Wasabi-nuki de onegai shimasu'*.

Sushi is one of the few foods in Japan that it is perfectly acceptable to eat with your hands, even at high-end places. Slices of *gari* (pickled ginger) are served to refresh the palate.

Sushi-ya (sushi restaurants) come in all shapes and sizes. High-end places can be frighteningly expensive, especially if patrons order the *omakase* (chef's choice) course, which is usually the pick of seasonal delicacies. At a mid-level place, diners can order à la carte or from a selection of set menus that usually include ten to twelve pieces. Sushi can also be had very cheaply at *kaiten-zushi*, where plates of sushi are sent around the restaurant on a conveyor belt and patrons can just grab whatever looks good.

The *kaiten-zushi* model was forced to evolve further in 2023 when a bout of what was labelled 'sushi terrorism' hit the country. The perpetrators caused havoc in hygiene-obsessed Japan by touching and even tainting food on conveyor belts and then leaving plates to circle the restaurant. *Kaiten-zushi* chains now go to extreme lengths to ensure that their sushi makes the journey from kitchen to table in perfect condition. These days, patrons can order from tablets and the sushi is whizzed out to the patron's specific booth in an 'express lane'.

HOW TO EAT SUSHI

1 WITH YOUR HANDS
It's perfectly acceptable to eat sushi with your hands (even at high-end places!).

2 ORDER À LA CARTE
Just point to the fish in the refrigerated glass case on the counter.

3 ORDER A SET
A most economical way to eat sushi; sets usually consist of 10 to 12 pieces.

4 AT KAITEN-ZUSHI
Ready-made sushi sent around a restaurant on a conveyor belt: grab what you fancy.

5 LIGHTLY DIP
Dip each piece lightly in *shōyu* (soy sauce), poured into a bowl from a small decanter.

Naruki Takimoto

Chef Naruki Takimoto trained for 10 years at prestigious sushi restaurants in Tokyo before opening Naruki in 2022. In his hometown of Himi, a fishing port on Toyama Bay, he serves sushi that showcases some of Japan's finest, freshest seafood.

What does sushi represent in Japanese culture?
Sushi embodies centuries of Japanese tradition, using ingredients at the heart of Japan's diet – rice, fish, soy sauce and vinegar. Simple in appearance, it distils the Japanese spirit into a single bite. Sushi is accessible to everyone, from casual conveyor-belt restaurants to refined *omakase* [refined multi-course dining] counters, and is enjoyed on both special occasions and ordinary days.

What is required to become a sushi chef?
High-end sushi requires around 10 years of training. I spent seven years at Kyubey in Tokyo, a renowned sushi house founded in 1935. From my first year, I prepared fish – removing heads, gutting, handling hundreds of shrimp daily – and washed more than 50kg [110lb] of rice each day. It took six years before I could work at the counter. Culinary school can teach basics in a year or two, but mastery comes only from years of hands-on experience.

How do you balance tradition with innovation in your sushi?
I focus on authentic Edomae sushi, highlighting the natural flavours of the seafood rather than adding extra ingredients. Enhancements come only from the same ingredient, like shrimp heads or grilled shells for a sauce.

What are a sushi chef's most important tools?
Good knives are essential. I buy mine from Nenohi near Tsukiji Market, custom-made by skilled craftsmen. Sharpness, balance and feel are critical. These bespoke hammered knives can take up to two years to complete and last a lifetime with careful use.

How do you engage with customers while preparing sushi?
Hospitality is at the heart of Japanese culture. We recognise the life in everything – from the fish to the flowers – and give thanks. That extends to customers: I constantly ask, 'How can I make them happy?' While preparing dishes, I respond quickly to questions without breaking focus, aiming to make diners feel relaxed and comfortable.

What do you recommend drinking with sushi?
A clean, dry sake refreshes the palate and harmonises with the delicate balance of rice and fish, naturally complementing the sushi.

Rice

TOP The coastal rice terraces of Fukui Prefecture.

RIGHT Ricefield artwork made by the Japanese Agricultural Cooperative in Asahikawa, Hokkaidō.

The Japanese don't just consume *okome* (rice) all day, every day – they venerate it. What's more, it's Japanese-produced *Oryza sativa japonica* or nothing. To protect domestic rice farmers, there are strict caps on the import of foreign rice, and imports are carefully controlled.

Short-grained, translucent *japonica* differs from its relatives *indica* and *javanica* in possessing amylopectin, the element that gives it its wonderful texture and slightly glutinous quality. The Japanese adore it. Yet their passion for it comes not merely from its taste – in the past, a meal was simply incomplete without the inclusion of *okome*. Though its consumption rate has lowered in recent decades, rice is the building block on which a Japanese meal is based, the core helix at the heart of the Japanese culinary DNA. In its uncooked form it is *okome*, the '*o*' denoting respect, '*kome*' meaning rice. Cooked Japanese-style, it is called *gohan* – the '*go-*' prefix is the highest indicator of respect, denoting rice or meal (some may use the more informal *meshi*, meaning something akin to 'grub'). When it's included in fusion cuisine and Western-style fast-food favourite *yōshoku*, it is termed *raisu*. Such is its importance that when a Japanese person asks another if they've eaten, they say '*Gohan o tabemashita ka*?' (Have you eaten rice?).

RICE IN THE NORTH

Hokkaidō is known for its produce, and now grows more rice than any other prefecture. But before cold-resistant varieties were developed in the early 20th century, rice was hardly grown here at all. Missing rice – their staple before heading north – perturbed Meiji-era immigrant farmers were encouraged to produce potatoes, which grow well in cold climates, thereby establishing a 'potato culture'. American advisors also suggested wheat and dairy cattle, which did well at similar latitudes in the US; today, potatoes, bread, milk and cheese feature more in Hokkaidō food culture than in the rest of Japan.

These days, with cold-tolerant, early-maturing *japonica* varieties, rice is grown even in Hokkaidō's chilly north. The area around central Asahikawa is known for its high-quality rice, including varieties that contribute to the fame of local sake (such as that made in Otokoyama).

Regional varieties of rice proliferate. Top varieties in the Japanese rice world are *koshihikari* and *sasanishiki*, found throughout the archipelago but especially renowned in Niigata, Fukui and Akita Prefectures.

PREPARATION AND CULTIVATION

Traditionally rice was steamed in a large cauldron, set over an earthenware hearth fuelled with *maki* (wood). This steaming process even has its own verb – *taku* – which is used exclusively to describe rice preparation. Today, style has succumbed to convenience, and nearly every restaurant and private home relies on the electric *suihanki* (rice cooker). The rice grains are rinsed thoroughly in

ABOVE Rice is left as an offering at memorials for the deceased in Japan.

RIGHT Mochi rice cakes are shaped around a soft filling.

cold water to remove excess starch, swished by hand in a circular scooping motion until the mix loses its cloudy appearance. The rice is then placed in the *suihanki*. *Hakumai* (white rice) has an equal amount of water added, while *genmai* (brown rice) has 50% more. After cooking for 20 to 30 hands-free minutes, the rice is almost ready for serving – but it's usual to let it sit (or *murasu* in Japanese, which originally means 'steam') for 10 minutes, after which it's deemed to be ready.

Automation has also come to dominate the cultivation process, with the rural *min'yō* (folk songs) and hours of backbreaking toil replaced by the clank and clatter of rice planters in spring and harvesters in autumn. Rice fields have changed shape too. Thanks to significant investment, tiny terraced paddies in geographical nooks and crannies up narrow side-valleys have been largely replaced with sizeable rectangular paddies that can be serviced by mechanical planters and harvesters. Planting and harvesting rice by hand – by the crooked bent-over *o-bāsan* (grandmothers), who worked in the fields for decades – is today restricted to deeply rural rice-producing areas.

RICE AND RITUAL

The omnipresence of rice in Japanese life has also led it to carry spiritual connotations. Even in ultramodern Tokyo, a child will often be taught to scoop a small amount of white rice from the *suihanki* to offer to the spirits of deceased ancestors in the family's *butsudan* (home altar), before heading to school carrying a lunchbox filled with assorted bite-sized goodies – and, of course, some cooked rice.

Zen monks have long recognised the importance of food and the act of eating as part of their religious practice. When the great Zen master Dōgen wrote his *Tenzo Kyōkun* (Instructions for the Zen Cook) in 1237, he was especially reverent about the simple act of washing and cooking rice: 'Keep your eyes open. Do not allow even one grain of rice to be lost. Wash the rice thoroughly, put it in the pot, light the fire and cook it'.

At Japanese funerals, the custom is also to leave out a bowl of rice with chopsticks stuck upright, hence the strict taboo against leaving one's chopsticks in rice during everyday meals.

TYPES OF RICE

HAKUMAI

Daily white rice (often called sushi rice outside Japan), universally used in every dish.

GENMAI

Unpolished, unrefined, brown rice rarely spotted outside organic restaurants, as it lacks the glow of simple *hakumai*.

BLENDED RICE

Includes *shichi-buzuki* (70% white, 30% brown), *go-buzuki* (50-50) and *san-buzuki* (30% white, 70% brown).

MOCHI-GOME

Glutinous version of regular rice, used for sticky *mochi* rice cakes served around New Year.

NANATSUBOSHI

This high-quality, cold-resistant variety is grown extensively in Hokkaidō.

Foraging

LEFT A basket of foraged mountain vegetables at Dewaya restaurant (see over the page).

RIGHT Ainu women use a mortar to prepare food in the 1920s.

Foraging is a very popular pastime in Japan – a country where anyone armed with a basic knowledge of local flora could get lost in the mountains for days and not suffer from a lack of food. A surprising amount of the lush natural vegetation that covers the islands is not only edible, but absolutely delicious.

Sansai (mountain vegetables) have been an integral part of the Japanese diet for centuries, as the mountains provided one of the few food sources that could be relied on during hard times. Poor rice harvests, famine and burdensome taxes often forced peasants to turn to the mountains for sustenance. And as part of their religious practices, *yamabushi* (mountain ascetics) were restricted to a diet of *sansai* while on pilgrimages.

Strictly speaking, only edible plants that grow wild in the mountains are considered *sansai*, but in a broader sense, those that grow along riverbanks, rice paddies and forest verges are also *sansai*. Some of these vegetables are now cultivated commercially, but Japanese still go on outings in spring and early summer to pick them in the uplands.

Many types have nutritional and medicinal value. A bowl of *sansai-soba* usually includes the likes of *warabi* (bracken), *zenmai* (fiddlehead fern), *yamabuki* (butterbur) and *nemagari-take* (bamboo-grass shoots).

There are some notable seasonal joys. Spring is the time for fresh *takenoko* (bamboo shoots), as well as *sansai* such as *fukinoto* (unopened butterbur bud), often added to miso soup. In autumn, the main prizes are *matsutake* (prized mushrooms) and sweet *kaki* (persimmons).

It's worth noting that *sansai-tori* (mountain-vegetable foragers) are not the only creatures out there with an interest in the tasty wild offerings that are up for grabs. Many bear attacks in Japan happen not to hikers, but rather to foragers who are out there searching for the same delicacies as the bears; bear-awareness is a wild-food collectors' essential here.

AINU CUISINE

Hokkaidō's Indigenous people, the Ainu, draw their ancestry back to the island's earliest settlers, and a distinct Ainu culture emerged some 700 years ago. They were hunters, fishers and gatherers, settling along salmon runs and coastal plains. After the formal annexation of Hokkaidō in 1869, the Meiji government tried to assimilate the Ainu, banning traditional practices such as hunting – but following legal recognition of the Ainu as an Indigenous people of Japan in 2019, a renaissance is underway. This includes a recovery of traditional Ainu cuisine, which made use of ingredients such as wild-caught salmon and deer, seaweed, foraged shoots and roots, millet, bear fat and fish oil. A growing number of Hokkaidō restaurants now serve Ainu dishes such as *ruibe* (half-frozen salmon sashimi), *pocche* (fermented-potato dumplings) and *ohaw* (a soup of salmon or venison and wild vegetables).

LOCAL PERSPECTIVE  CHEF AND FORAGER

Haruki Sato

Haruki Sato is the fourth-generation chef-owner of Dewaya in Yamagata, a restaurant famed for its seasonal mountain cuisine. In 2023, he opened a chef's-counter restaurant on-site to share the cultural and ecological value of wild mountain vegetables.

What do *sansai* mean to Japanese food culture?
Gathering wild mountain vegetables is not simply about eating – it is a cultural practice that reconnects us with nature. Today, supermarkets provide any ingredient year-round, and many children no longer know that mushrooms are an autumn food. Experiencing the mountains first-hand awakens a sense of *shikisaikan* – an awareness of the seasons that is deeply rooted in Japanese life. Eating with the rhythm of the seasons reminds us that food is part of a larger natural cycle.

You describe *sansai* as linked to ecology as well as cuisine. How so?
A mountain once touched by human hands needs care; if abandoned, it quickly grows wild. By venturing into the mountains to gather *sansai* and mushrooms, people help maintain the ecosystem. The act of harvesting teaches respect for nature: you take only what you need and leave the rest to thrive. In this way, *sansai* cuisine is both the continuation of food culture and a form of environmental stewardship.

What role do the seasons play in your cooking?
In Japanese cuisine, the seasons are everything. Spring's shoots, summer's coolness, autumn's harvest, winter's stillness – by reflecting them in food, meals naturally connect with the rhythms of life. At Dewaya, we avoid over-decoration and let the ingredients shine. I often feel that it is not we who are expressing the seasons, but rather the mountains themselves teaching us how to present them. This awareness shapes not only the dishes but also the way we prepare and serve them.

How have elders in your community influenced you?
Their influence is profound. Older generations live by *mottainai* – never wasting anything. Their creativity in using every part of what the mountain provides is astonishing, and their practical wisdom informs how we cook, preserve and present ingredients.
This knowledge is at risk of disappearing, so I see it as my duty to listen carefully, preserve their words, and pass them on. Their teachings remind me that respecting the land, the seasons and every ingredient is at the heart of Japanese cuisine.

Konbini

LEFT A konbini near Kawaguchi Train Station and Mt Fuji.

RIGHT Ready-made bentō boxes for convenience at a konbini.

When Japanese university students first move out of home, one thing they always check is the distance between potential new living quarters and a konbini (convenience store). And this extends well beyond students: there are legions of time-poor workers, far from loved ones or just single, who depend on the existence of their local konbini, many of which are open 24 hours a day, 365 days a year.

Top-selling konbini products all form part of *nakashoku*, 'home meal replacements' that bridge the gap between home cooking and eating out – plus alcoholic drink concoctions, hot and cold tea and coffee, single-serve bread snacks, dependable *onigiri* (rice balls) and ready-to-eat bentō meals, alongside side dishes that can round out a quick dinner.

Konbini also stand in for plenty of other tasks a parent might perform, from dispensing cash at ATMs to facilities for customers to pay bills, book concert and plane tickets, send packages and print official government documents from smart photocopiers. Their toilets can also be a godsend for anyone caught short. In essence, they serve as extensions of Japanese homes, which are often shoebox-sized with tiny kitchenettes that don't have enough space to store one large weekly shop – konbini aren't replacing supermarkets, simply complementing them.

COMMUNITY LIFE-SAVERS

To many residents of Japan's smaller suburbs, the mere presence of one ever-bright store projects an aura of safety to the neighbourhood. In depopulated rural towns, konbini offer an escape from isolation and provide vital food and supplies.

Convenience stores can also be a lifeline during natural disasters, when the government uses these ubiquitores stores as bases from which to distribute emergency supplies. Many konbini turn themselves into emergency support centres, opening their doors for people to use their taps, toilets and electricity. After earthquakes, some konbini have activated mobile stores to deliver supplies to hard-to-reach areas, while convenience-store chain Lawson sent drones to bring food to the large elderly population in radiation-affected zones around Fukushima after disaster struck. Following the 2024 Noto Peninsula earthquake, FamilyMart delivered *onigiri* and bread to evacuation shelters, 7-Eleven sent bottled water and Lawson distributed hand-warmers and energy bars to emergency crews.

Beyond just being convenient, konbini specifically target the needs of Japan's elderly, who increasingly live alone. Konbini workers are trained in assisting older adults who wander in confused or with an emergency, and in contacting community support centres (local agencies that help the elderly).

In daily life, konbini also promote lesser-known Japanese ingredients and can be joyous ambassadors of culinary adventure. When a konbini chain launches a drink or sushi dish using Ōita-grown *kabosu* (Japanese lime) to an audience of millions, it not only creates business for local farmers, but also accustoms the tastebuds of people across Japan to a new flavour.

Wagashi

LEFT Wagashi crafted by Yasuhiro Hikiami (see over the page).

TOP RIGHT Yasuhiro Hikiami uses wagashi crafting scissors to create fine details, such as petals.

BOTTOM Wagashi for sale at Hikiami Kogetsudo in Toyama (see over the page).

Sweets in Japan are usually considered an accompaniment to tea, as they offset the bitterness of matcha. They're known as wagashi (和菓子) – as opposed to *yōgashi* (洋菓子), Western-style cakes, biscuits and baked goods. The character 和 is read *wa*, meaning Japanese, and it's also used in other contexts such as *washoku* for Japanese-style meals.

The basic ingredients of wagashi are rice and *anko*, a sweetened paste of red azuki beans. Flavour (usually subtle) and design (often exquisite) are influenced by the seasons. In spring wagashi may be shaped like cherry blossoms or wrapped in cherry leaves; in autumn they might be golden-coloured, like fall leaves, or flavoured with chestnut.

Okashi-ya (sweet shops) usually have open shopfronts with wares laid out in wooden trays to entice passers-by. Gorgeous displays of delicate and beautifully presented wagashi are also sold in *depachika*, set in the basement floors of department stores; these Aladdin's caves of gustatory delights have been go-to spots for gifts and special-occasion treats since the 1930s. Showcasing Japan's most splendorous food creations, *depachika* sweets sections can look like jewellery shops, their cases full of gleaming jelly orbs, *mochi* shaped like flowers and candies embedded with cherry blossoms.

Classic wagashi include *daifuku* (a soft *mochi* enveloping a dense centre

of *anko*); and *warabi-mochi* (bracken-starch jellies dusted in *kinako*, a sweet toasted soybean flour). Others to look out for include *sakura-mochi*, a rice cake with bean paste and pickled cherry-blossom leaf; and fish-shaped *taiyaki*, little cakes filled with *anko* paste or other sweet fillings. Introduced by 16th-century Portuguese traders, *castella* is a dense, rich sponge cake that's a specialty of Nagasaki.

Kyoto wagashi, known as *Kyō-gashi*, are a staple of the city's culinary heritage, famous for their delicate, seasonal motifs. Often filled with *anko*, the cinnamon-flavoured *yatsuhashi* comes either baked (hard) or uncooked (soft), and is traditionally shaped like a *koto* (Japanese harp). *Jo-namagashi* are often shaped like seasonal flowers.

WAGASHI ESSENTIALS

AZUKI

The azuki (written with the characters for 'little bean') is used extensively to prepare wagashi.

KYŌ-GASHI

Kyoto's confectionary: the city has a long tradition rooted in tea ceremonies and wagashi-making.

ANKO

Sweet jam or paste made from azuki and other beans.

KASHIWA-MOCHI

Formed from glutinous rice with a sweet filling, wrapped in an aromatic oak leaf.

MOCHI

Cakes made of glutinous *mochi-gome* rice that's pounded then steamed.

Yasuhiro Hikiami

Yasuhiro Hikiami is a wagashi chef and the fourth-generation owner of Hikiami Kogetsudo, a traditional wagashi shop in Toyama. His work elevates confectionery into edible art, with each sweet reflecting time, place and the beauty of impermanence.

What are wagashi?
Wagashi are traditional Japanese sweets made from rice flour, beans, sugar and natural gelling agents like *kuzu* (a starch from plant roots) and agar (a jelly from seaweed). They're often shaped into delicate designs and are typically enjoyed with green tea. In the tea ceremony, they express the spirit of hospitality and the changing seasons.

How do wagashi designs vary?
A sense of the seasons – *shiki* – is central to wagashi. Through design and ingredients, a sweet can stir memories or emotion. Cherry blossoms, for instance, may recall school graduations or starting a new job – transitions that happen in spring. In this way, a single sweet can unlock a flood of feelings.

What role do the senses play in how wagashi are experienced?
Wagashi engages all five senses: sight, touch, taste and smell, while their poetic names evoke sound. These names often come from classical poetry, seasonal phrases or place-names. Ideally, wagashi acts as a 'switch', awakening memories through sensory experience – a uniquely Japanese art form.

What part of Japanese culture does wagashi help people understand?
Wagashi embodies *omotenashi*, or heartfelt hospitality. It connects many aspects of Japanese culture – ceramics, calligraphy, gardens, architecture and the tea ceremony.

Any favourite motifs you often return to?
One is three chrysanthemums, symbolising longevity. I designed it for a ritual offering at Meiji Shrine, which honours Emperor Meiji and Empress Shōken. As the flower of the imperial family [the chrysanthemum features on Japan's imperial crest], it felt especially fitting. Another is a leaping sea bream, an auspicious symbol of vitality and celebration. It was taught to me by my mentor, Masaru Sasaki, and I continue to make it as a tribute to him and what he passed on to me.

Wagyū

LEFT Wagyū is grilled at Korean-style barbecue places called yakiniku.

RIGHT A farmer brushes a Tajima Wagyū beef cow at his farm in Sayō, Hyōgo Prefecture.

Japan's wagyū beef has developed a cult status both in Japan and abroad thanks to its rich *shimofuri* (fat marbling), which makes for very melty, tender, tasty meat. The characters for wagyū (和牛) simply mean 'Japanese cattle', but the modern meaning refers to four breeds known as *kairyō-wagyū* (improved wagyū), which are recognised as distinct breeds and came into being as a result of crossbreeding with mainly European cattle following their introduction in the 1870s.

Before the opening of Japan in the mid-19th century, traditional Japanese culture held the cow as a sacred animal and eating meat was banned. There were Japanese native cattle, but rather than being raised for meat or producing milk, they were used mainly as draft animals to plough fields. The story goes that in 1856 US Consul General Townsend Harris ordered a cow be brought to the consulate, which was slaughtered, roasted and consumed – much to the shock of locals. This killing of the cow is said to

be one of the inauguration acts of modern Japan, whereby old conventions were cast aside and Western ideas quickly accepted. Things really took off in 1872 when Emperor Meiji announced that he enjoyed eating beef and a law was passed that broke the two great rules for Buddhist monks, allowing them to get married and eat beef.

All of a sudden, eating meat was promoted as a sign of civilisation, modernity and a way to build up the military. Foreign cattle were imported and crossbreeding was encouraged, particularly early in the 20th century. These days, 97% of all wagyū raised in Japan is of the Japanese Black breed of 'improved wagyū' – though to confuse matters, there are over 320 brands of wagyū, mostly named after the region in which they are raised. Particularly well known are Kōbe, Matsuzaka and Ōmi beef.

Unsurprisingly, such pedigree meat doesn't come cheap, but as wagyū is very rich, a small portion is generally quite enough. In terms of preparation, wagyū is often seared at high temperature on a *teppan* (steel hotplate), then diced and served with rice and miso soup. Diners also grill strips of wagyū over coals at Korean-style barbecue places called *yakiniku*; eat it in hotpot-style dishes such as *sukiyaki* or *shabu-shabu*; or order it at steakhouses paired with wine.

GAME MEAT

Japan has a long history of using euphemisms to skirt politely around topics that make people uncomfortable or that flout accepted rules. To circumvent prohibitions against eating four-legged creatures, *inoshishi* (wild boar) became known as *yama-kujira* (mountain whale), as it was fine to eat fish from the sea. *Inoshishi* is now a popular game meat, though in most cases, the 'wild' boars are actually farmed. Similarly, horsemeat is known as *sakura-niku* (cherry meat) and is considered a tender, healthy delicacy, particularly as *basashi* (horsemeat sashimi). Its pink colouring is said to resemble cherry blossoms, and it's a local speciality in Nagano and Kumamoto Prefectures.

With deer being viewed as divine messengers of the gods in the Shintō religion, *shika-niku* (venison) is often referred to euphemistically as *momiji-niku* (maple meat), as it is thought to be particularly tasty in autumn. Wild deer has long been on the menu for the Indigenous Ainu people of Hokkaidō

Kaiseki-ryōri

TOP Dumplings are served on a skewer with mugwort tofu at a kaiseki restaurant.

RIGHT Matcha tea and sweet delicacies are part of the cha-kaiseki ritual.

Often labelled Japanese haute cuisine, there are actually two kinds of Japanese meal styles called kaiseki-ryōri. Said to date back to the 16th century, the oldest is known as *cha-kaiseki* (茶懐石), and is a simple yet elegant meal that the host of a *chaji* (formal tea gathering) serves to guests before the ceremonial tea.

Over the last few centuries, however, a modern kaiseki has also evolved, and it's one of the world's most refined cuisines. This is a meal consisting of a large number of exquisitely presented small dishes, usually served on a separate tray to each member of a gathering. Consisting of a large number of exquisitely presented small dishes, kaiseki-ryōri (会席料理) is usually served to each member of a gathering on a separate tray, and it's the kaiseki style that many visitors to Japan have heard about and are most likely to have the opportunity in which to partake.

Modern kaiseki-ryōri is Japanese cuisine at its finest. Ingredients, preparation, setting and presentation come together to create an aesthetically sophisticated dining experience. Key to kaiseki-ryōri is seasonal freshness – the ingredients should be at the height of their flavour, with only subtle seasoning used to enhance them. Equally, the table settings and garnishes are chosen to complement the ingredients and to evoke seasonality.

CHA-KAISEKI

The goal of *cha-kaiseki* (tea kaiseki) creators is to produce a stylised yet simple banquet that sets diners up perfectly for the all-important tea ceremony that follows. Designed to complement rather than overpower the tea, it is rooted in Zen principles and emphasises seasonal, fresh ingredients, typically following an *ichijū-sansai* (one soup, three dishes) structure, with the focus on hospitality and aesthetics. Its rituals reflect Zen spiritual heritage, and just as there are prescribed ways of handling the utensils and receiving the tea during a simple tea ceremony (where matcha tea and confections are served), every movement in *cha-kaiseki* follows precise etiquette.

Cha-kaiseki is considered the forerunner of modern kaiseki dining – more austere, but embodying the essence of *omotenashi*, the Japanese spirit of wholehearted hospitality; every detail reflects the host's thoughtfulness and desire to bring joy to the guest.

For the most authentic kaiseki-ryōri experience, patrons dine at a *ryōtei*, a sophisticated and elegant traditional restaurant that is about as pricey as dining can get in Japan, often with private rooms and elegant garden views.

Many high-end ryokan serve a kaiseki-ryōri dinner that is included in the price of an overnight stay (and is one of the reasons that ryokan charge a per-person rate rather than a room rate to guests). The meal is prepared and laid out for guests with meticulous, artistic style in a private room or dining room. The number of small plates can be quite mind-boggling, and foreign guests tend to crack the same old joke – 'I'm glad I'm not the dish-washer here!'

Bentō

LEFT A basic bentō with white rice and a pickled plum to represent Japan's flag.

CENTRE A more sophisticated style of bentō, served on shinkansen trains.

RIGHT High-speed sustenance.

These days, bentō is a word recognised around the planet – but it has humble beginnings, dating back to the 8th century when travellers carried *hoshii* (steamed rice that had been dried under the sun). *Hoshii* was long-lasting, compact, lightweight and could be eaten with either hot or cold water, making it the perfect one-the-go food.

During the Edo period, farmers filled wooden containers with rice and *umeboshi* (pickled plum), taking them out to the fields as a lunchbox. Fishers headed out to sea with *funa-bentō*, a tub-shaped wooden container of rice; the tub could be used for floatation if disaster struck. During cherry blossom season, aristocrats and feudal lords took elaborately decorated *jūbako* (tiered food containers) to *hanami* (blossom-viewing parties), while theatre-goers bought *makuno-uchi bentō* ('between the acts' bentō) during intermissions at kabuki and noh performances.

Japan got its first railways in the 1870s, at the start of the Meiji era. While trains revolutionised transportation, they

didn't initially move at bullet-train-like speeds – resulting in the emergence of *ekiben* (p 000), bentō to be consumed during a train trip. This started a romanticised *ekiben* culture, in which people enjoyed local delicacies while gazing out of train windows at the passing scenery.

Eating a bentō while watching bouts at a sumo tournament became a quintessential part of the experience; housewives also prepared *aisai-bentō* (bentō 'made with love') for their husbands to take to work for lunch (some still do), and in the 1990s, parents slaved over creating *kyara-ben* (character-themed bentō, depicting popular anime characters) for their children.

At its most elegant, bentō comes in a black lacquerware box with compartments to keep warm and chilled dishes apart. Handled with great care, they are often wrapped in a *furoshiki*, a square of traditional cloth which is knotted at the top to carry the box; a valuable box and *furoshiki* can be a great source of pride to its owner. At the cheapest end of the scale, simple bentō from a *konbini* come in basic plastic containers. But while a bentō may be as fine as a top restaurant meal, the simplest is a *Hinomaru-bentō*, designed to resemble the Hinomaru (Japanese flag): white rice with an *umeboshi* (pickled plum) in the middle, representing the red sun on a white background.

BENTŌ TODAY

While bentō may have initially evolved as 'portable meals' eaten outside of home, the modern bentō has taken on a whole new twist. Nowadays, workers, students, singles or those short on time are buying bentō to take home. Tasty bentō can be bought at specialist stores, supermarkets and *konbini* in most neighbourhoods and towns at reasonable prices, rivalling the effort and cost of buying groceries and cooking a meal.

One of a number of bentō chains, Hokka-Hokka-Tei (Hot Hot Shop) has over 2000 locations throughout Japan (mostly located near train stations) where customers can purchase an astounding range of takeaway bentō to eat on the move or bring back home. There are no tables and chairs at which to eat, but there are seasonal specials, a rewards-points system, cashless payments and delivery for those who don't want to leave home (or their work desk). It's not the romantic image of a bentō, but it's certainly practical.

Shōjin-ryōri

LEFT Shōjin-ryōri cuisine at Jokiin temple in Kōya-san.

RIGHT The Buddhist temples of Kōya-san.

Although shōjin-ryōri (vegetarian temple cuisine) had existed in some form since the 6th century, it became widespread following the popularisation of Zen Buddhism in Japan a century later, which strongly demanded a spiritual practice even at the meal table: Zen monks consider cooking and eating as both a meditation and an opportunity for learning.

While shōjin-ryōri is served at the 50 or so temple lodging-houses that offer accommodation to visitors at Kōya-san in Kansai, it has also recently emerged in some of Tokyo's most acclaimed restaurants. Though shōjin-ryōri has has its roots in simplicity, the centuries-old perfecting of the craft appeals to chefs who are keen to embrace not just the myriad techniques but also the spiritual focus and mindfulness. The Zen master Dōgen, who pioneered this approach, believed shōjin-ryōri could align mind, body and soul – similar to the practice of a tea ceremony.

This is best represented by explaining *sanshin*, the 'three minds' of Japanese Zen Buddhism: *daishin* (the big mind), *rōshin* (the parental mind) and *kishin* (the precious mind). Shōjin-ryōri chefs need to possess all of these as they prepare ingredients, sometimes using methods that require hours of painstaking repetition. *Daishin* maintains motivation and calm, *rōshin* cares for and respects the ingredients

and the diners and *kishin* involves working with gratitude and pleasure.

The 'rule of five' is also an important part of shōjin-ryōri cuisine, stemming from *wuxing* (the five phases of Chinese philosophy). Underpinning cyclical balance, the rule of five applies to *goshoku* (five colours; white, red, black, yellow and green). It also must be incorporated into *gomi* (five flavours; sweet, sour, salty, bitter, umami). Finally, it should also be part of the *gohō* (five techniques; fried, simmered, raw, steamed, grilled).

Before eating, monks chant the five Zen reflections: be grateful, aware of imperfections, strive to improve them, eat for good health, fulfil obligations.

YUBA

Yuba (soy-milk skin) is a staple of shōjin-ryōri and a speciality of Kyoto. Highly nutritious despite its simplicity, yuba is a high-quality plant-based protein, packed with calcium, potassium, magnesium, vitamin B and fibre.

A dried form of *yuba* is added to soups; served fresh it's a marvellous accompaniment to sake and is eaten with grated wasabi and *sujōyu* (soy-sauce vinegar). *Dekitate-yuba*, the just-made stuff, is the best. Its creation is a time- and labour-intensive process in which *tōnyū* (soy milk) is allowed to curdle over a low heat, with the skin then plucked from the surface using either chopsticks or equipment especially designed for the process.

Yuba also features heavily in *butsu-ji*, Buddhist funerary cuisine served to relatives and mourners on the night preceding the funeral at the *otsuya* (wake). Meat and fish are strictly forbidden preceding a funeral.

Izakaya

LEFT Drinks ready to pour in an izakaya.

RIGHT The streets of Shinjuku in Tokyo host a range of izakaya.

The Japanese equivalent of a pub, izakaya (literally meaning 'drinking house') are found all over Japan. While formerly viewed as a little rough around the edges, and easily spotted by *aka-chōchin* (red paper lanterns) hanging outside, they now range in style from those with a quiet, neighbourhood-bar atmosphere to others sporting a rowdy, raucous pub vibe or aiming for a modern restaurant-style minimalism.

Izakaya are a one-stop shop, involving food and drinks all in one: a variety of plates to be shared are ordered for the table a few dishes at a time, along with rounds of beer, sake, *shōchū* (a strong distilled spirit), whisky, mixed drinks or even wine. Non-alcoholic options are also available. Just drinking is generally frowned upon, and Japanese patrons always order at least a few plates of food. While some smaller izakaya are yet to evolve from having their menu scrawled in chalk on a blackboard, those that are frequented by foreign tourists often have a picture menu or, more recently, a tablet with images of the dishes and the menu in

a variety of languages. There's often a buzzer at the table to call waiting staff, but if there's a tablet, patrons are expected to sort out ordering food and drinks by themselves.

There are traditional, family-run izakaya, often with rustic interiors, that serve sashimi and grilled fish to pair with sake, while more modern and stylish izakaya can have very creative menus. At the other end of the scale, there are large, inexpensive chains, popular with students, that often serve Western pub-style dishes such as chips and pizza slices. Chains targeting students and a younger clientele may also have *tabe-hōdai* (eat as much as you like) and/or *nomi-hōdai* (drink as much as you like) deals; these always have a time limit, often of 1½ hours.

Izakaya usually levy a small *otōshi* (cover charge), which includes a small plate to snack on while drinks are brought from the bar and the kitchen prepares the food order. Larger chain izakaya are generally smoke-free, but some small, older spots may allow smoking in a designated area.

CLASSIC IZAKAYA DISHES

AGEDASHI-DŌFU
揚げだし豆腐

Deep-fried tofu in a *dashi* (fish) broth, usually garnished with grated *daikon* (radish) and ginger.

EDAMAME
枝豆

Salted and boiled fresh soy beans, which are picked while they're still young.

GYŌZA
餃子

Famous pan-fried dumplings, typically filled with pork mince, cabbage and vegetables.

HIYAYAKKO
冷奴

A cold block of tofu with soy sauce and spring onions; silky smooth and creamy.

KARAAGE
唐揚げ

Fried chicken with a crispy exterior and juicy interior, and an enduringly popular izakaya snack.

Markets

ABOVE The exterior of Tsukiji Outer Market.

RIGHT TOP The public can buy snacks and ingredients at Tsukiji Outer Market.

BOTTOM Access to Tsukiji's fish auctions is restricted to trade buyers.

Every city and sizeable town in Japan has some form of market, be that fish markets in coastal regions, quaint morning markets in mountainous rural towns or large, busy metropolitan wholesale markets. While the locals turn up looking for ingredients for their daily meals, they also offer an intriguing window into the local food culture, which differs vastly countrywide.

Sapporo Jōgai Ichiba (Sapporo Curb Market) features some 80 shops and restaurants lined up along several blocks outside the Central Wholesale Market. It specialises in Hokkaidō seafood and local produce, with both locals and tourists coming to try the freshest sushi or *kaisendon* (seafood over rice) or for breakfast in one of the many restaurants that open from early.

Contrastingly, historic Hida-Takayama, in the mountains of Gifu Prefecture in central Japan, is known for its two morning markets selling locally produced fruit and veg, pickles, miso and other homemade goods.

At the western end of Honshū, the city of Shimonoseki has long held the reputation as being the *fugu* (pufferfish) centre of Japan; its Karato Ichiba specialises in *fugu*, and Japanese visitors turn up here to try this potentially deadly delicacy – as sashimi, fried, in a hotpot or in a clear soup.

Makishi Kosetsu Ichiba is the central produce, meat, fish and general market

of Okinawa's capital, Naha. It's like a different culinary world down here, with all kinds of Okinawan foodstuffs from pig's face, feet and stomach to colourful fish and shellfish, alongside farm-fresh tropical fruits and unique vegetables like *gōya* (bitter melon) and *hechima* (sponge gourd).

Nomi-no-ichi (flea markets) are widespread throughout Japan, often held in temple and shrine grounds on fixed dates (such as the first Sunday of each month). Like flea markets everywhere, anything and everything is for sale, and many a foreign visitor has picked up their favourite souvenir of Japan at a local *nomi-no-ichi*. It's best to arrive early.

Tokyo City Flea Market, at Oi Racecourse parking lot, features over 600 vendors and is open most weekends. Tokyo's twice-monthly Oedo Antique Market is legendary, while in Kyoto, the shrine Kitano Tenmangū and temple Tō-ji have their own secondhand markets for kimono, ceramics and various artisanal objects, along with food stalls.

1 HAKODATE ASA-ICHI, HOKKAIDŌ

Daily public market spanning four city blocks, with seafood and produce.

2 TOYOSU FISH MARKET, TOKYO

The largest seafood market in the world; renowned for its morning tuna auctions.

3 NISHIKI MARKET, KYOTO

Known as 'Kyoto's kitchen' and a lively retail market selling fresh seafood, produce and cookware.

4 KUROMON-ICHIBA, OSAKA

Long, covered shopping arcade filled with stalls, shops and restaurants.

5 KŌCHI SUNDAY MARKET, SHIKOKU

Japan's biggest open-air market, running for over 300 years.

Beer

LEFT There are approximately 500 craft breweries in Japan.

CENTRE A flight of craft beer to taste at Yanaka Beer Hall.

RIGHT The distinctive exterior of Sapporo Beer Museum.

The Japanese love *biiru* (beer) and drinking it is an essential part of contemporary culture, with summer beer gardens and *izakaya* (pubs; p142) countrywide serving it up in bottles (*bin-biiru*), or as *nama-biiru* (draft beer) in frosted, handled *jokki* (glasses).

Although it's thought that Dutch traders introduced beer to Japan in the 17th century, it was virtually unknown before the arrival of the US navy in 1854. With the opening of Japan to foreign trade, imported beers became available, mostly in foreign-settlement areas. The Japanese upper classes took to the new brew, and in an astute move Norwegian-American William Copeland opened Yokohama's Spring Valley Brewery in 1869; it later became Kirin, one of Japan's largest breweries.

Following the Meiji Restoration, Japanese travelled around the world to learn new skills and bring them home. In 1876, German-trained Seibei Nakagawa became the first brewer for Kaitakushi (Pioneer) Beer, set up by the Hokkaidō Development Commission as part of the economic development of Japan's new northern land. Beer was deemed a necessity in the frigid north as, in those days, cold-resistant varieties of rice hadn't been developed, meaning there was no rice to make the sake that burgeoning numbers of new immigrants required. Privatised in 1886, Kaitakushi Beer became the Sapporo

Beer Company, these days known right around the globe.

The big four breweries of Kirin, Asahi, Sapporo and Suntory (along with Okinawa's Orion) still dominate, with 90% of the Japanese beer market, but the mainstream brews they produce are pretty similar – nearly all are pale lagers using light malts and with moderate hop content. To the delight of true ale lovers, however, the production of *ji-biiru* (local beer) is on the rise. Craft ale has been constantly evolving and new, independent craft breweries keep popping up around the country.

And the Japanese beer scene isn't lacking in innovation. Hokkaidō's Abashiri Beer introduced the world to *bilk*, a concoction of 70% beer and 30% local milk (it didn't survive, due to poor sales). Abashiri also produces some of the most colourful beers on the planet, from the startlingly blue Ryūhō (drift-ice) Draft to the alarmingly green Shiretoko Draft, which echoes the verdant hues of the local national park.

JAPAN'S BEER FESTIVALS

1 SAPPORO
The Sapporo Ōdōri Beer Garden is Japan's largest, in full swing from mid-July to mid-August.

2 TOKYO
Held in Saitama, near Tokyo, the Keyaki-hiroba Beer Festival in mid-May features craft beer.

3 NAGOYA
Nagoya's BBW (Belgian Beer Weekend) in late April/early May features speciality imported beers, food and live music.

4 OSAKA
Staged in Tennō-ji Park, Ten-shiba Frühlingsfest is a Japanese 'Oktoberfest' (in late April/early May).

5 FUKUOKA
The Beers of Japan Festival at Fukuoka Castle showcases craft ales.

Sake

LEFT Sake barrels are stacked at the Ise Jingu Shintō shrine.

CENTRE Rice is washed at Ishizuchi Shuzo sake brewery before fermentation.

RIGHT The finished product at Kozue restaurant on the 40th floor of Tokyo's Park Hyatt Hotel.

The so-called 'drink of Japan', sake has existed for as long as the country's history has been recorded – and odds are a lot longer. From their *Omiya-mairi* (the first visit to a Shintō shrine at one month old) to the *O-soshiki* Buddhist funeral rites, sake accompanies every stage of Japanese life. It plays an important part in many Shintō rituals (including wedding ceremonies), and Shintō shrines often display huge sake barrels in front of their halls (most renowned is the huge, colourful wall at Tokyo's Meiji Jingu). These barrels are called *kazari-daru* (decoration barrels), and they're empty of liquid yet full of spiritual importance. At festivals and Shintō rites, people visit a shrine and will be given sake to drink in order to feel closer to the spiritual world.

Known since the postwar period as *Nihonshu* (Japan sake) to distinguish it from Western-style alcoholic drinks, sake is often termed 'rice wine' outside of Japan, but this is a misnomer: it's made through a fermentation process using grain, somewhat akin to beer-making. Key to the sake-making process are good *okome* (rice), good *mizu* (water) and the magical *Aspergillus oryzae*. The latter is the dark greenish-yellow, fine-powder *kōji*, a fermenting agent that is added to steamed white rice, converting sugar to alcohol. This process takes between

one and two months from start to finish, and the sake is ready to drink as soon as it drips from the barrel. It has an alcohol content of somewhere between 15% and 17%. Sake, unlike wine, does not have vintage years – its quality depends solely upon the conditions under which it is made and, foremost, the skill of the sake-maker. Nor is there the broad regional variation that affects wine – it is the maker rather than the location which determines a sake's calibre.

TYPES OF SAKE

All sake is graded into one of two main categories: the everyday Futsū-shu; and premium, special-designation Tokutei meishō-shu, which is divided into several types according to the degree to which the rice used to make it has been 'polished' to remove the outer

SAKE'S SPIRITUAL SIDE

Sake's place in religious life comes from its associations with rice – the food of the gods – and its symbolic purity, and it is consumed (often in large quantities) at every major rite-of-passage event in a Japanese person's life.

In the Shintō wedding ritual, the bride and groom seal the marriage via the *sansankudo* ritual, exchanging sake cups and drinking sake; this invokes the gods to intervene to help the couple and, through the sharing of sake, come closer together and create a bond of friendship. Sake is offered to the family *butsudan* (the altar that houses the spirits of one's departed ancestors), and at family graves during the midsummer O-Bon festival commemorating ancestors, when the spirits are thought to return to this world. It is proffered to the roadside Buddha statues that dot the countryside, and is a feature – both ritually symbolic and earthily practical – at every *matsuri* (festival).

ABOVE Sake cups are exchanged at Shintō wedding ceremonies.

RIGHT Sake ready to serve at an izakaya.

grain, and whether distilled alcohol has been added. Main Tokutei meishō-shu types include top-of-the-heap Daiginjō, always a brewer's flagship sake and made with rice milled so that 50% or less of the original size of the grains remains; it's an intensely crafted, complex sake, and is very expensive. Ginjō is another high-priced, complex sake, made with rice polished so that 60% of the original grain remains; it's also fermented at lower than average temperatures, using special yeast. Junmai is pure sake, made simply of rice, water and *kōji* without the addition of sugar, starch or additional alcohol; no more than 70% of the rice grain remains after milling. Honjōzō is similar to Junmai, but with a small amount of alcohol purposefully added to enhance its fragrance.

The first two are generally reserved for special occasions; the latter pair are for regular drinking. *Nama-zake* refers to sake that has not been pasteurised and can fall into any of the classifications mentioned above; it needs to be drunk quickly once the bottle has been opened. *Nigori-zake* is a cloudy, unfiltered sake in which some of the lees (yeast deposits) have been allowed to remain. It is not a particularly delicate brew, yet it is a popular warming drink in late winter or early spring. Its alcohol content is generally lower than other types of sake.

SAKE EXPERTS

A professional *kikisake-shi* (sake sommelier) will judge a sake using a small white *ochoko* cup which has an appraisal mark (two concentric circles) imprinted in the bottom, for judging colour and clarity. The best colour is *aozae*, a slight yellow with a tinge of blue. If sake has a brown shading, it most likely has too many sub-flavourings, while a completely colourless sake will have a flat, two-dimensional flavour. As with a wine sommelier, a *kikisake-shi* uses an arsenal of specialist phrases to describe sake's qualities. Some of the simpler terms are *amai* (sweet), *karai* (dry), *koku ga aru* (a phrase implying an earthy depth), *kuchiatari* (a sake's initial impression or effect) and its opposite *kire* (the tail), and *okubukai* (suggesting deep complexity).

HOW TO DRINK SAKE

1 ETIQUETTE

It's polite to fill everyone else's glass; don't fill your own glass (usually a younger person pours for an older person).

2 TEMPERATURE

Sake is generally drunk *hiya* (cold), when it is called *reishu*; otherwise it's *atsukan* (hot) or *nurukan* (warm).

3 SERVING

Hot or cold, sake will usually be served in a *tokkuri* (ceramic sake pot), with a small *ochoko* cup for drinking.

4 DRY OR SWEET

Sake's sweetness/dryness is based on a *Nihonshu-do* numerical scale, ranging from +20 (extremely dry) to -15 (ultra-sweet).

5 FOR CONNOISSEURS

The finest sake is always drunk cold. Hot options are reserved for when getting warm takes precedence.

LOCAL PERSPECTIVE  SAKE EXPERT

Marie Chiba

Marie Chiba is an influential voices in the new sake movement. She studied at the National Research Institute of Brewing and owns sake bars Eureka! in Tokyo and Marie in Bangkok. She has authored a sake-themed manga and a book on sake food pairings.

Sake is often called Japan's national drink. Could you explain its cultural role? Sake is more than a beverage – it's part of Japan's spiritual and social fabric. It's offered at shrines to thank the gods for the rice harvest, shared at weddings and New Year celebrations, and poured for others at gatherings to show respect and strengthen bonds. Unlike wine, which can ferment naturally, rice requires careful preparation and *kōji* mould to become sake. This human effort is why sake has long been seen as a sacred gift.

In 2024 UNESCO inscribed sake brewing with *kōji* mould on to the Intangible Cultural Heritage of Humanity list. Why is this significant? *Kōji* transforms rice starch into sugar, making sake possible, but it also underpins miso and soy sauce. UNESCO's recognition highlights that sake-brewing is not just technical skill – it's a living cultural practice preserved by master brewers and apprentices, passed down for generations.

Historically, why were women excluded from sake brewing – and is that changing? Brewing was once physically demanding work in hot *kōji* rooms, often performed by men bare-chested. Today, mechanisation and modern practices allow women to enter the industry as master brewers, presidents and innovators. Their finely tuned sense of smell is especially valuable, as contemporary sake emphasises fragrance even more than taste.

Many travellers assume sake only pairs with Japanese food. Is that true? Not at all. With styles ranging from fruity and sparkling to aged and cloudy, sake pairs beautifully with global cuisines. Fruity or acidic sakes complement herbs, citrus or cheese, while cloudy *nigori* and *doburoku* stand up to spicy Thai or Sichuan dishes. My signature pairings – like a blue-cheese and ham cutlet with *doburoku* – show its versatility.

What advice do you give those trying sake for the first time in Japan? Skip the jargon. Don't just ask for 'dry' sake – describe flavours you enjoy – like apple, peach or chocolate – and let staff guide you. Try the Japanese way of eating and drinking together: a bite of food, a sip of sake, letting flavours fuse in your mouth. That's where sake's true magic is revealed.

酒

Whisky

TOP Sampling whisky at the Suntory Yamazaki Distillery between Kyoto and Osaka.

BOTTOM Masataka Taketsuru, president of Nikka Whisky, at the company headquarters in 1964.

Japan produces some of the finest whiskies in the world, from the single malts and blends of major makers Suntory and Nikka to cult favourites made by small-batch producers such as Chichibu.

Japanese whisky production began in 1870, but the country's first commercial distillery (Osaka's Yamazaki) opened in 1924. Consumption was mostly domestic until the early 2000s, when Japanese whiskies started winning major international awards and garnering enthusiastic acclaim overseas. This success encouraged expansion in the whisky industry and saw a significant increase in the number of small-scale and regional craft distilleries, to the point that there are now more than 50 whisky producers Japan-wide and over 100 distillery sites in operation. With increased visibility overseas, a number of Japanese whisky companies are actively exporting their products.

The bulk of Japanese blended whisky is consumed in cocktails, notably in the popular and ubiquitous *haibōru* (highball; whisky and soda), which is also sold premixed in cans at *konbini* (convenience stores). Fine whisky is mainly ordered straight or *rokku* (on the rocks). It is often mixed with hot water (*oyu-wari*, a favourite in winter), or cold water (*mizu-wari*, popular amid the summer heat).

Some favourite whiskies include the Yamazaki 12 from Suntory, which is light with dry-spice notes and loads of fruity flavours; Nikka's Yoichi Single Malt, known for its subtle hint of smokiness; Suntory's Hibiki 17 blend; and the Akashi Single Malt from the White Oak Distillery.

In 2024, with issues such as imported foreign spirits being bottled in Japan and then labelled as 'Japanese whisky', a set of standards was established for 'authentic Japanese whisky'. To use that label, a whisky must be distilled in Japan using malted grains and water sourced in Japan, be matured in Japan for at least three years in wooden casks, and then bottled in Japan at a minimum of 40% alcohol. True Japanese whisky lovers are rejoicing.

WHISKY PIONEER

The main distillery of Nikka Whisky – one of Japan's top whisky producers – is located in the small town of Yoichi, on Hokkaidō Sea of Japan coast to the west of Sapporo. It was founded by Masataka Taketsuru, the renowned 'father of Japanese whisky', who went to Scotland in 1918 to study whisky-making techniques, came back with his Scottish wife Rita, and then set up his distillery in Yoichi in 1934.

Taketsuru chose Yoichi for its 'clear water, brisk air and rich peat', which he considered to be close to the conditions in Scotland and would therefore give him the best opportunity to recreate fine Scotch whisky in Japan. He also believed that being near the sea gave a 'briny hint' to the whisky during maturation. The processes he brought with him are still in use today; first sold in 1940, Nikka Whisky is a regular award-winner and today ranks among the world's best single malts.

Tea

LEFT A Japanese tea ceremony, circa 1900.

CENTRE Whisking matcha at Ippodo Tea Room in Kyoto.

RIGHT Matcha tea served with mochi at Ippodo Tearoom.

Japan's love affair with green tea dates back to its introduction from China. Yet no-one can really agree when tea arrived in the country: some suggest the 8th-century Nara period, while others credit its introduction to Buddhist saint Dengyō Daishi in 805.

In the 12th century the monk Myōan Eisai introduced the Rinzai school of Zen Buddhism to Japan. He also brought back both Chinese tea and the Chinese tea ceremony, a move that saw the drink really take off here. At the end of the 12th century, green tea was sowed at Uji, near Kyoto – where some of the best tea in Japan is still produced. The Japanese court and aristocracy soon took wholeheartedly to tea, and to its formalised drinking: the tea ceremony, with all of its carefully observed rituals. It took another half a millennium or so for the rank and file to pick up the habit, its popularity spurred on by the invention of a convenient, newfangled form: *sencha* (infused leaf tea).

The powdered form used in tea ceremonies is matcha, which (unlike the usual infusion style of tea) is whisked into a thick, deep-green emulsion and drunk unstrained. However, Japan's common, everyday tea of choice is *bancha*, a coarse teatea that's always drunk hot and is served free in restaurants. When it is roasted (the magnificent smell that pervades Japanese shopping arcades) it becomes *hōjicha* (roasted tea), which possesses a deep, wonderfully smoky taste; it has the lowest level of caffeine, and is good hot or cold.

The leafy green *sencha* is made from leaves that are reasonably tender and young, and is often served on special occasions. But when the most honoured of guests stop by, out comes the *gyokuro* – a magnificently fragrant, umami-rich, comparatively rare tea that is grown in bamboo cages that shut out much of the early spring light, resulting in extremely tender leaves that are only picked in a single harvest.

TEA CEREMONY: CHAJI

Kimono-clad guests assemble in a waiting room, select a member to act as the main guest, then proceed to the garden and the *tsukubai* (stone trough), washing hands and mouth to purify themselves of worldly concerns.

They then enter the teahouse, admire the calligraphy work in the *tokonoma* (recess) and greet the host before being treated to a light *kaiseki* meal, sake and a *wagashi* (Japanese sweet). Guests then retire to the garden/waiting room before re-entering the tearoom, stopping to admire the flower arrangement that has replaced the hanging scroll in the *tokonoma*. The thick *koicha* (opaque matcha) is passed in a single bowl from the host to the guest, who savours it before wiping the bowl and passing it to the next person. The host then rebuilds the coals in the brazier and prepares the thinner *usucha*, which he or she whips to a frothy consistency with the bamboo *chasen* (tea whisk), before passing it to each guest. Cultured conversation reigns.

LOCAL PERSPECTIVE  YAME TEA FARMER

Shinji Matsunobu

Shinji Matsunobu is a third-generation tea farmer and head of Yamayu Tea Farm in Yame, Fukuoka Prefecture, and chairs the Yame Tea Division of Japan Agriculture Cooperative. Tea growing in Yame began in 1423 with seeds from China.

Matcha is booming overseas, but how is it consumed in Japan? What teas are most common in daily life? Until recently, matcha was mostly enjoyed in tea ceremonies, whisked with a *chasen* (bamboo whisk) at formal gatherings or on special occasions. Today it appears everywhere – from lattes to ice cream and sweets. In daily life, however, *sencha* is the go-to tea, served with meals or to guests. Bottled teas, sold in vending machines and convenience stores, have also become part of daily life.

Yame is famous for *gyokuro*. How does it differ from other teas? *Gyokuro* is shaded as it grows, increasing chlorophyll and theanine and producing a rich umami with little bitterness. Yame's highest grade, Traditional Authentic Yame Gyokuro, has earned Japan's Geographical Indication (GI) status – a system that protects regional foods of exceptional quality, much like Champagne in France. It has also won first place at Japan's National Tea Competition for 25 years in a row. *Gyokuro*'s high levels of amino acids and caffeine sharpen the mind while calming the spirit. With less than 1% of Japan's total production, it is usually reserved for special occasions.

What makes Yame's natural environment so suited to tea? The balance of temperature, rainfall and fertile, well-drained soils is ideal. Yame averages 15.4°C [59.7°F] and 200cm [79in] of rainfall – perfect for continuous growth from spring through autumn. Tea roots extend more than 1m [3ft] into the ground, constantly drawing nutrients from the deep soil. Combined with Yame's six centuries of cultivation knowledge, these natural conditions produce teas of exceptional quality.

How is tea enjoyed in daily life? Tea is drunk after meals to refresh the palate, with catechins [antioxidants] providing benefits such as cavity prevention. Farmers keep the custom of 'three o'clock tea' during work breaks. In Yame, the Shincha Festival marks the spring harvest with tastings and celebrations.

Beyond Yame, where else should tea lovers explore? I'd start with Yame's *sencha* green tea for anyone new to Japanese tea. After that, Kagoshima – also in Kyūshū and now Japan's largest tea-producing region – offers a wide variety of teas to enjoy.

Miso

LEFT A warming bowl of miso ramen.

CENTRE Red, white and aged miso paste.

RIGHT Mixing steamed soy beans by hand to make miso.

A precursor of miso arrived on the Japanese mainland from China sometime around 600 CE, not long after Buddhism, and people here have been devouring it with gusto ever since – at lunch, dinner and even breakfast.

Made by mixing steamed soy beans with salt and *kōji* (a fermenting agent made from either barley, soy beans or rice, which works in a way somewhat akin to yeast), miso is integral to any Japanese meal, where it is most likely to be present as *miso-shiru* (miso soup) or as *dengaku* (a flavouring), where it's spread on vegetables such as *nasu* (aubergine/eggplant) and *konnyaku* (devil's tongue) or on *sake* (salmon).

Miso soup is made of a mixture of *dashi* (fish stock) and miso, plus other ingredients such as *shijimi* (freshwater clams) or *asari* (short-necked clams); assorted vegetables such as *daikon* (radish), carrot or *gobo* (burdock root; especially good for the digestion); pork in *tonjiru*; or simply tofu.

In preparation, miso should never boil, and it is often served with a topping of sliced *negi* (spring onion) or *mitsuba* (Japanese parsley). Good *shijimi-miso* soup combined with the aromatic pepper *sanshō* is a heavenly combination, and it's rumoured to be helpful in cleansing the liver should one happen indulge in too much sake.

The most common type of miso is *kome-miso*, fermented with rice *kōji*. *Mame-miso* made using soy-bean *kōji* is popular along the Tōkai (eastern) coastline of Honshū, while *mugi-miso* made using barley *kōji* is found throughout Kyūshū (except in Fukuoka, where they too make *kome-miso*).

One of the great delights of touring Japan is to sample miso's regional variations. Some would argue that you can recognise a person's birthplace by their choice of miso. *Sapporo-ramen*, which features a hearty miso-based broth, is a great way to keep the cold at bay during winter and has become a nationwide favourite.

REGIONAL VARIATIONS OF MISO

Sendai-miso is a dizzyingly salty miso that's said to have been developed by the lord Date Masamune in 1593, at his Sendai Castle. *Shinshū-miso*, meanwhile, hails from Nagano Prefecture; less salty, though still unmistakably rustic, it has a much-praised, slightly tart quality. Dark, fiery red *Edo-miso* is slightly sweet, and is named after the former capital before it became Tokyo.

Hatchō-miso was originally created in Okazaki, Aichi Prefecture, not far from Nagoya, and was first made in the town's Hatchō area (8th district), where it continues to be produced today. It was shipped to Tokyo (then Edo) by the ruling elite, the Tokugawa family, who came from the Okazaki area and were sorely proud of their homegrown product. The citizens of Edo were hugely underwhelmed, shipped it back and developed their own.

Kyoto shiro-miso is a delicate, sweet, aristocratic white miso that inhabits the rarefied world of *Kyō-ryōri* – Kyoto specialist cuisine. It's used in making *o-zōni*, a miso soup containing *mochi* (pounded rice cakes).

ART, C

AND
DESIG

RAFT
N

Architecture

ABOVE The Tōdai-ji is one of five Buddhist temples at ancient Nara.

From the rustic, asymmetrical beauty of a teahouse to the loveliness of Kyoto's Ginkaku-ji or the old-fashioned charm of a wooden, thatched-roof countryside *minka* (folk house), the popular image of traditional Japanese architecture is one of elegance and restraint. However, as scholars David and Michiko Young note in *The Art of Japanese Architecture*, there is also a less well-known side that's characterised by 'the appreciation of exuberant colours and complexity of form', and one which is flamboyantly displayed in Nikkō's opulent Tokugawa mausoleums and in most decorative trends of the Momoyama period. The fact that Japanese architecture can encompass these opposing qualities stands as testament to its dynamic nature.

Over time, Japan's architectural developments have mirrored the country's level of engagement with the wider world. Techniques, knowledge and practices from other cultures would be eagerly absorbed, then a period of inward retreat would give time for these influences to be thoroughly assimilated. This has occurred in cycles over the centuries, resulting in an overall oscillation between architectural restraint and exuberance. Nara-period rulers looked to Tang China for architectural cues, building large temples like Tōdai-ji after the introduction of Buddhism.

The following Heian period saw Japan distancing itself from China, developing architectural styles more suited to its climate and sense of aesthetics. The eighth Ashikaga shōgun, Yoshimitsu, reopened trade relations with China in 1401, and his penchant for Chinese culture is clearly reflected in the eclectic design of Kyoto's Kinkaku-ji.

STATUS, FUNCTION AND FORM

Even more so than it is today, Japan was a deeply hierarchical society for centuries, segmented into groups that adhered to strictly drawn class lines. These historical realities are expressed in the contrast between Japan's elite and commoner-class buildings and living spaces. Elite architecture often served to demonstrate status, power and authority. Although Nijō-jō in Kyoto was built as a residence by the first Tokugawa shōgun in the early 17th century and then maintained for centuries, the shōgun resided in Edo and rarely used the castle. Designed to impress, Nijō-jō's function was more symbolic and political: a physical reminder to the Kyoto aristocracy of the shogunate's reach and power.

Architecture for the common people was largely utilitarian, as exemplified by Edo-period merchant townhouses and communal bathhouses, both of which showcase urban life in Edo (what's now Tokyo) at the time. Up to

ABOVE Traditional screens at the temple of Takiguchi-dera in Kyoto.

three-quarters of the city's commoner population lived in *nagaya*, rows of single-storey, one-room tenements. Alongside public bathhouses, these fostered close community interaction and communication within Edo's commoner class.

There were also considerable regional variations in architecture. The heavy annual snowfall in Gifu and Toyama precipitated the development of *gasshō-zukuri* houses, with steeply angled thatched roofs that resemble hands pressed together in prayer. Under the Tokugawa shogunate, some farmers (especially landowners) began to diversify into manufacturing or selling sake and miso; the wealth generated by these alternative occupations was often channelled into the construction of larger, more sophisticated homes.

ARCHITECTURE IN TRANSITION

The 1868 Meiji Restoration signalled the demarcation between 'traditional' and 'modern' Japan. The ensuing rush to modernise had the greatest impact on public buildings, which were constructed in stone and brick and incorporated styles, techniques and materials adopted from the West. Many early Meiji buildings were destroyed by earthquakes and war, but some survived – such as Kingo Tatsuno's iconic red-brick Tokyo Station building.

The early 20th century saw a reconciliation of Western styles and design with Japanese aesthetic traditions, both in public-facing and residential architecture. A rare example of a Taishō-era property emblematic

TOP LEFT The steeply pitched thatched roofs of Shirakawa-go, central Honshū.

TOP RIGHT The exterior of a Christmas-themed love hotel in Osaka.

RIGHT The modern design of Tokyo's Nezu Museum.

BOTTOM LEFT The temple of Kinkaku-ji in Kyoto has a gold exterior.

of these transition years is the Kyū Asakura House in Tokyo. This wooden building is an exquisite example of Japanese carpentry but also features elements such as a Western-style living room, glass windows and a garage.

Rising nationalism during the 1930s saw a demand for major public buildings to express greater 'Japanese-ness'. One result was the Imperial Crown style of buildings such as Nara Station and the Kyoto City Kyocera Museum of Art, which combine Japanese-style roofing and decorative motifs with symmetrical Western-style facades.

With rapid economic growth, technological developments and a greater emphasis on individualism and self-expression, the postwar years were the perfect playground for Japan's architects – the major constraint was that structures should be fire- and earthquake-resistant. Modern Japanese architects had the freedom to develop highly diverse signature styles. Tadao Ando's exposed-concrete buildings are characterised by clever use of natural light and complex, maze-like pathways; designs by Kenqo Kuma – such as Tokyo's Nezu Museum – often feature intricate wooden or bamboo lattices.

Architects also played fast and loose with love hotels, which are as Japanese as any temple building. During the peak construction period in the late 1980s, a wide range of themes and fantasies played out in love hotel designs: castles with turrets, walls covered with biscuits, neon-lit spaceship interiors. These exuberant, escapist spaces highlight how Japanese architects continue to respond to the needs of modern society.

TRADITIONAL ARCHITECTURE

WOOD

A beautiful and durable natural material, wood is well-suited to Japan's climate.

TATAMI

Soft tatami mats made from rice-straw and rush are used as flooring in Japanese-style rooms

SHŌJI AND FUSUMA

Fusuma (moveable screens) and *shōji* (sliding doors) are used to partition spaces.

ENGAWA

Elevated verandas of bamboo or wood, *engawa* connect the inside and outside of a building.

GENKAN

Before entering a home, shoes are removed in the *genkan* (entryway or foyer).

Ceramics

ABOVE A dogū or clay figurine from the Jōmon period.

TOP RIGHT One of the ancient kilns as used in Seto.

BOTTOM The work of ceramic artist Yasumaro Ozawa in Seto.

Dating back to the Jōmon era, Japan's ceramic heritage is as ancient as the nation itself, and is one of the oldest pottery traditions in the world. Early ceramics were functional, reflecting the ways in which the hunter-gatherer, hut-dwelling Jōmon people lived their lives. Utilitarian, unglazed earthenware pieces – often deep jars – were made using coiled clay (without the assistance of a potter's wheel), then baked in open fires. As well as these everyday items, used for storage and for cooking over an open flame, the Jōmon also made ceramic pieces for ritual and spiritual use – including *dogū*, small humanoid or animal-formed figurines.

The Jōmon was an incredibly long era, and while early ceramics were simply crafted, Middle Jōmon–era pots were produced with decorative flame-like flourishes and the lips embellished with rope patterns. In fact, the period is named for these artistic ornamentations: 'Jōmon' means 'cord-marked'.

The culture of ceramics changed significantly with the onset of the Yayoi period in 300 BCE, an era characterised by the importation of Chinese and Korean innovations including agricultural practices such as rice farming. In terms of ceramics, *sueki* stoneware techniques introduced from Korea utilised both

BECKONING CATS

Visit any casual restaurant in Japan and you might be greeted by an ornate ceramic cat at the counter, greeting you with a waving paw. Cats were originally introduced to Japan via Chinese ships (where they served as a means to control mice), and are seen as having symbolic protective qualities. In the Edo era, Japan's culture of beckoning cats – called *manekineko* – proliferated, and they're a still popular today. There are two main types: those with a raised right paw are said to bring money and luck, while a raised left paw brings customers.

Manekineko are still made in historic ceramics regions. With its large cartoon-like eyes, the Tokoname *manekineko* is the most ubiquitous of these welcoming felines, and Baigetsu kiln is responsible for crafting around 80% of the market share. 'They are part of the Tokoname identity,' says Yoshitaka Ina, owner of specialist *manekineko* shop Yamatane. '*Manekineko* are not machine-made, industrial items; they are handmade with love.'

the potter's wheel and kilns that could be fired to temperatures over 1200°C (2192°F), so enabling the production of resilient tableware.

THE SIX ANCIENT KILNS

The Heian period saw the establishment of what are now known as the Six Ancient Kilns: Bizen, Seto, Tokoname, Echizen, Shigaraki and Tamba, which all remain prominent ceramics hubs today. The wares produced by these kilns are named for their respective regions, have distinct aesthetic sensibilities, and make use of different firing techniques. By and large, the formation of these districts was dictated by the availability of the natural materials needed to make ceramics,

LEFT The pottery of Kiko Ando, an artisan of Bizen ware.

RIGHT Ceramic artist Seiichi Otsuka working in his studio in Mashiko (see page 174).

which in turn impacted the style of the pieces. For instance, Tamba ware from the Sasayama and Tachikui districts of Hyōgo dates back some 800 years. The clay from this region is brownish, enriched with iron from the rice fields and mountains, and the pots produced from it are fired in multi-chambered climbing kilns set on slopes, in which ash blown on to the pots creates a unique glaze. Similarly, Bizen ware uses a local clay, *hiyose*, which contains iron and organic material, resulting in durable wares characterised by a brown-red hue. Each piece is fired at high temperature, and kilns are traditionally fuelled by red pine, which results in distinctive molten-ash patterns.

Seto ware, on the other hand, is known for its glazes and has an entirely different aesthetic. Aside from tableware, one of the biggest uses of Seto ware today is for *eto*, or zodiac animals. *Eto* has its roots in the Chinese calendar, with each year represented by one of 12 animals. Since the Edo period, the custom of decorating *eto* animals to display at home has proliferated. Chugai Toen is one of the largest Seto-ware makers in the region; PR department staffer Mika Inoue explains that 'At the beginning of the year people change their *eto* ornaments, but there are also people who keep the old ornaments and decorate them again in 12 years' time.'

FROM TEA TO WABI-SABI

The culture of ceramics was greatly impacted by tea culture during the Momoyama period, when the art of the tea ceremony began to flourish. In 1191, Japanese monk Myōan Eisai returned from China to establish the country's first Zen Buddhist temple. Alongside this temple came tea, which was used for religious practice. Tea-drinking became a hobby for aristocrats but was brought to the masses in the 1400s by another monk, Murata Jukō, who espoused a meditative tea culture. By the 16th century, tea master Sen no Rikyū had advocated a *wabi-sabi* aesthetic philosophy (p64) that flourished during the time. '*Wabi*' means a modest simplicity and 'sabi' literally means rust – and *wabi-sabi* sensibilities embraced

1 BIZEN
Bizen is known for its unglazed ceramics.

2 ECHIZEN
Ceramics from Echizen are notable for their simple forms and grey glazes.

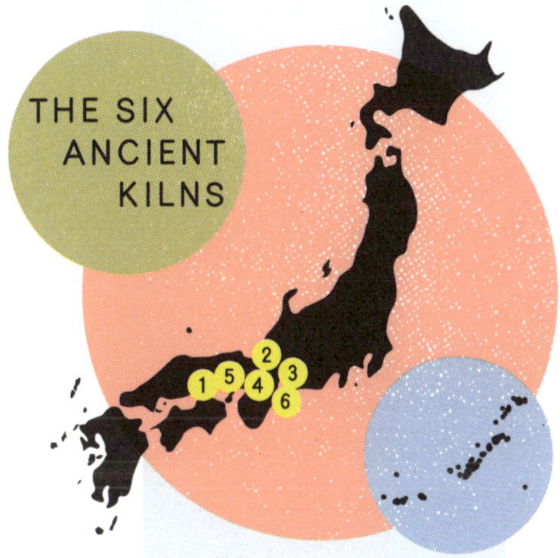

3 SETO
Seto ware exhibits a rich variety of glazes.

4 SHIGARAKI
Unglazed pottery from Shigaraki is known for its rough texture.

5 TAMBA
Rustic, unglazed wares from Tamba are traditionally fired in multi-chambered climbing kilns.

6 TOKONAME
This ancient pottery hub is famous for its *manekineko* (waving cats).

the idea that aged things are beautiful, and that imperfection is a value. *Wabi-sabi* was also imbued with the notion of the impermanence and transience of life – as evidenced by types of tea-ware such as Raku, which has a distinct, uneven texture that is somewhat rough. From the 18th century onwards, the proliferation of tea culture also saw the establishment of new ceramics hubs across Japan, each with their own distinct characteristics.

DIVERSIFICATION

Thanks to the Korean potters who, from the 17th century onwards, brought the technical ability to produce porcelain, the Edo period saw a major development in the evolution of Japanese ceramics. The discovery of porcelain stone in Arita resulted in the rise of Imari ware – instantly recognisable for its blue glaze and red, green and gold decorative features.

TOP LEFT Japanese master potter Shōji Hamada in Mashiko.

CENTRE A kutani porcelain plate from the Meiji period.

RIGHT The porcelain bridge made at the Nabeshima-clan kiln in the renowned ceramics village of Ōkawachiyama.

Other ceramics regions sprung up across Japan, outside of the established Six Ancient Kilns; even now, each town's identity remains intertwined with ceramics, from galleries and museums to artists' ateliers, kilns and outdoor art. Some districts – such as Kutani, in Ishikawa Prefecture – took on aesthetic sensibilities that were a departure from *wabi-sabi* aesthetics. Kutani ware is a hyper-decorative style, adorned to the degree that it is almost psychedelic, with dense floral motifs in vibrant colours.

The closest ceramics hub to Tokyo is Mashiko, just 100km (62 miles) north of the capital. The genesis of Mashiko as a pottery hub was kickstarted when potter Keizaburō Ōtsuka started making everyday items here during the Edo era. But Mashiko really rose to prominence amid the rise of the folk-craft Mingei Movement, which lauded the beauty of utilitarian, artisan-made everyday items as a backlash to the industrialisation of the Meiji era. In 1930, one of the movement's founders, Shōji Hamada, set up a kiln in Mashiko and used his clout to energise the region. Tatsuzō Shimaoka, one of Hamada's students, also worked in Mashiko from 1953 until 2007, and was designated a Living National Treasure in 1996.

Interestingly, the characteristics of Mashiko ware are hard to pinpoint, as all the potters work with a sense of freedom. The reason for this disparity is a lack of history, explains Noriyuki Tsukamoto, the manager of Mashiko ceramics store Toko: 'There is less of a rigid hierarchical structure and strict apprenticeships that are the norm for other pottery towns. The environment fosters openness and innovation. That openness is part of Mashiko's identity and allows for more independence.'

CONTEMPORARY CERAMIC STARS

BIZEN

Unglazed Bizen-ware pieces are fired at a high temperature using red pine.

MASHIKO

There are around 300 ceramicists working in Mashiko, a town known for being open to outsiders.

TOKONAME

The identity of Tokoname is completely defined by its beckoning *manekineko* cats.

SETO

Seto ware is quite diverse owing to the availability of a wide range of materials.

TAMBA

Young artisans like Tamba-ware potter Yuki Ogami may also have a background in fine art.

LOCAL PERSPECTIVE  MASHIKO POTTER

Seiichi Otsuka

Mashiko is a famed pottery town, known for its earthy stoneware and its influence on Japan's folk-craft Mingei Movement. Daisei Gama, the town's largest climbing kiln, is run by Seiichi Otsuka, whose family have been crafting traditional ceramics since 1861.

Why do ceramics continue to play such an important role in Japanese culture?
Pottery has always been part of daily life – from tea-ceremony utensils to the simplest rice bowl. There are pieces that are treasured like jewels, and others that quietly support everyday meals, yet both are essential. The variety reflects the depth of Japanese culture itself.

How do regional styles like Mashiko's remain alive today?
Each region developed its own way of working with local clay and fire. In Mashiko, the emphasis has long been on practical, everyday wares, a tradition we still carry on. Regional styles survive because they're rooted in the land and the rhythms of people's lives.

You continue to use traditional tools and processes. Why is that important?
We prepare our own clay, use a foot-powered potter's wheel, burn wood to make ash, turn that ash into glaze, and finally fire our pieces in a wood-fired kiln. These age-old practices connect us directly to nature. I value the power of the human body and the flame of wood fire – the dialogue between the maker and the natural world gives each work life. The unpredictable patterns created by the fire and ash bring a unique character to every piece, making each vessel both personal and alive.

How do you see the relationship between craft and nature?
Everything begins with nature – the clay, the wood, even the kiln itself. To create truly beautiful ceramics, we must be rooted in nature. When we work with it rather than against it, the result carries warmth and spirit that machines can never replicate. What I value most is continuing to live and work this way – immersed in soil, wood and tradition.

Lacquerware

ABOVE Incisions on a lacquer tree for harvesting its sap.

TOP RIGHT Wajima lacquerware is known for its fine finish.

BOTTOM Lacquerware maker Takaho Shoji at work in Wajima.

Go into any Japanese home or eat at one the country's restaurants and you are almost certain to encounter *shikki* (lacquerware). Also known as *urushi*, after the native word for the sap of the lacquer tree, this is both a craft and an artform with an exceptionally long history in Japan – 9000-year-old burial accessories coated in lacquer have been excavated on Hokkaidō.

Toxicodendron vernicifluum, the Latin name for the lacquer tree, hints at its dangerous nature: the sap contains urushiol, an oily compound that causes skin rashes. However, treated with care in its liquid state and left to harden, lacquer is one of nature's wonder products. When applied in coats to an object, lacquer acts as a highly durable, waterproof sealant. With regular use and polishing, this glossy coating can become even more beautiful over time. It is these preserving, utilitarian and eco-friendly qualities that have seen craftspeople down the centuries paint *urushi* onto carved wooden items such as bowls, plates and spoons, as well as other materials including basketry, metal, leather and paper.

Becoming a *urushi* artisan requires years of training. The precise and time-consuming nature of the work – it can take a month or more to carefully apply the many layers of lacquer needed for the desired finish – meant that,

historically, this was a craft patronised by the wealthiest and most exclusive levels of Japanese society.

Across Japan, a wide variety of styles of lacquerware have developed over the centuries, alongside techniques to achieve beautiful decorative effects that have raised the craft into an art. *Maki-e* – a compound word meaning 'sprinkling' (*maki*) and pictures (*e*) – is a technique in which designs are drawn on the surface of an object with clear lacquer; the piece is then dusted with metal powder such as gold or silver to create the image.

Hold such a piece of *shikki* and you will be appreciating the work of several craftspeople. Take Yamanaka lacquerware, for example, which has flourished in the hot-springs area of Yamanaka Onsen in Ishikawa Prefecture for over 450 years, and is characterised by its celebration of Japan's native woods. Woodworkers, underglazers, painters and *maki-e* artists combine their skills to create the final product.

BUYING LACQUERWARE

1 JŌBŌJI
Source of most of Japan's lacquer, and a centre of the craft for 1300 years.

2 KISO HIRASAWA
A town of artisans on the historic Nakasendō route, famed for its simple but elegant lacquerware.

3 KUROE
The red surface lacquer of distinctive *Kuroe-nuri* wears away in patches to reveal a black undercoat.

4 SABAE
Made in beautiful colour combinations, Sabae's *Echizen shikki* is known for its lustre and refinement.

5 WAJIMA
Wajima is famed for its high-class, durable lacquerware, incorporating powdered earth from the region.

Sculpture

LEFT A dogū clay figurine from the late Jōmon period.

CENTRE Burial statues at Haniwa Garden in Heiwadai Park, Miyazaki Prefecture.

RIGHT An 18th century netsuke of a mouse gnawing on a candle.

Around 10,000 years ago, the hunter-gatherer Jōmon people who lived on the islands of the Japan archipelago were creating small clay figurines known as *dogū*. No-one is entirely sure of their purpose, but to modern-day eyes their decorative and abstract features place them as the starting point of the story of Japanese sculptural art.

The next chapter in Japan's sculptural story begins in the 3rd century CE, during the Kofun period. Clay figures from this time, known as *haniwa*, are more obviously shaped like people and animals, as well as tools and houses. As they have typically been found on or next to burial mounds, it's assumed that their purpose was to guard the dead. But even before the arrival of Buddhism to Japan in the 6th century, material culture here was growing ever more sophisticated. Bronze, stone and wood were beginning to be crafted into sculptures – all of which can be found in the 3D art of Buddhist temples. Made in 609 CE by a master sculptor who had emigrated to Japan from the

Korean peninsula, the copper Asuka Daibutsu is believed to be the nation's oldest such Buddha statue.

The Guze Kannon – a 179cm-tall (70.4in) gilded statue enshrined at the Nara Prefecture temple of Hōryū-ji – was carved from a single piece of camphor sometime in the 7th century. The sculpture's longevity is thanks to it being carefully wrapped in cloth and kept out of direct sunlight for most of each year.

In subsequent centuries, under the patronage of imperial courts first in Nara and later Kyoto, sculpture became ever more elegant, sophisticated and refined. The Kei school of Buddhist sculpture, which emphasised realism, began in the 14th century and went on to become highly influential. Religion continued to be the driving force for sculptural inspiration and innovation.

During the Edo period, the arts flourished across the board and spread into daily life. Sculpture became something that could be secular rather than exclusively spiritual. This process accelerated after 1868, during Japan's Meiji-era opening to the world after centuries of seclusion. Just as non-Japanese were enamoured with the country's refined arts, so Japanese artists and craftspeople eagerly embraced Western styles, materials and processes.

NETSUKE

Sculpture in Japan took a turn towards the miniature in the 17th century, when decorative *netsuke* became all the rage. Part of the everyday attire of smartly dressed upper- and merchant-class men, netsuke are beautifully carved toggles once used to attach silk cord-strung pouches or *inro* (small cases) to an obi (the sash-belt of a kimono). Although they come in a wide variety of designs, it is *katabori netsuke* – three-dimensional figures carved in the round – that are the most common.

From the middle of the 19th century, as foreign traders began to arrive in Japan, the small and characterful *netsuke* became extremely popular as a collectable item. Some of the best examples of *netsuke* are held in museums outside of Japan – and one of the most famous is *The Hare with Amber Eyes*, which features in the book of the same name by British ceramicist Edmund de Waal.

ABOVE Pumpkin by Yayoi Kusama at Benesse Art Site on Naoshima.

TOP RIGHT Taking the ferry to Teshima island.

BOTTOM White Deer (Oshika) by Kohei Nawa is displayed on the Oshika Peninsula in Ishinomaki, Miyagi.

CONTEMPORARY SCULPTURE

A sculpture of a giant yellow pumpkin covered in irregular polka dots sits at the end of a pier on the island of Naoshima in the Seto Inland Sea. It was created by Yayoi Kusama, one of Japan's greatest living contemporary artists, and it draws visitors from around the world. Kusama is now in her 90s and has been creating art for seven decades in many mediums, but this sculpture is her most famous. It is one of many significant pieces exhibited on the islands of Naoshima and Teshima, run by Benesse Art Site Naoshima .

Her conceptual but accessible work forms part of a new wave of distinctly Japanese sculpture that has emerged since the 1970s. Other notable artists of the time include Tarō Okamoto, whose best-known sculpture is the 70m-tall (230ft) *Tower of the Sun*, made for Osaka's Expo 70. Okamoto's works, featuring bright colours and stylised images, take inspiration both from the primitive art of the Jōmon period and that of modern manga and anime.

The works of artists such as Yoshitomo Nara and Takashi Murakami also take cues from contemporary Japanese pop culture, while Murakami's 2008 *Oval Buddha* also reveals a connection to much older themes and traditions. It was inspired by a 10th- or 11th-century wooden statue of the historical Buddha Shakka (which is held in the collection of the Museum of Fine Arts in Boston, USA).

The influence of nature and of the ancient Japanese religion of Shintō is present in the works of Kohei Nawa and Toshikatsu Endō. Nawa's *PixCell-Deer#24*, in which a taxidermied deer is entirely covered in various-sized glass beads, carries echoes of the Kasuga Deer Mandala, a painted religious scroll that dates back to the 15th or 16th century. Endō's artistic process involves the scorching of wood black – as in a religious rite – for the creation of his minimalist, monumental sculptures and installations.

WHERE TO FIND SCULPTURE

1 BENESSE ART SITE NAOSHIMA
Major artworks displayed across Seto Inland Sea islands Naoshima, Teshima and Inujima.

2 HAKONE OPEN-AIR MUSEUM
Some 120 sculptures by leading Japanese and international artists in a beautiful highland setting.

3 ISAMU NOGUCHI GARDEN MUSEUM
Large granite and basalt sculptures at the Shikoku Island studio of the American-Japanese artist.

4 MOERENUMA-KŌEN
Noguchi designed this Sapporo park, where monumental, functional sculptures are part of the landscape.

5 KIRISHIMA OPEN-AIR MUSEUM
Kyūshū Island museum displaying works by Yayoi Kusama, Keiji Uematsu and Takashi Murakami.

Calligraphy

LEFT Calligraphy brushes, ink and inkstone.

RIGHT Seihan Mori, chief priest of Kyoto's Kiyomizu-dera, writes a kanji meaning 'bear' to symbolise the year 2025.

The origins of written Japanese go back to around the 6th century CE, when Chinese characters – *kanji* (p14) – were adopted to transcribe the language. There are around 50,000 *kanji*, each with one or several meanings depending on their combination.

Because Japanese is different to Chinese, two other phonetic syllabaries – *hiragana* and *katakana* – were added a few centuries later. The former is used for transcribing Japanese, the latter reserved for all foreign words and names. These three writing systems are the basis of *shodō*, the 'way of writing' that is the traditional form of Japanese calligraphy.

Created with brush and ink, *shodō* is taught to children at Japanese elementary and junior high schools, and many continue it in adulthood, either as a hobby or as an artistic practice. As with any kind of writing, there are different styles. *Kaisho* is the regular form of the script, most analogous to roman block capitals in written English. *Gyōsho* is semi-cursive script; *sōsho*, fully cursive script, is the most artistic but also the most difficult to read because of its fluid, expressive nature.

Zensho is brush calligraphy rooted in Zen Buddhism – writing as a meditation and a spiritual practice that express one's inner state. Hōryū-ji, one of Japan's oldest Buddhist places of

worship, is home to the *Hokke Gisho*, composed in 615 CE and considered the oldest written Japanese text. Through subsequent historical epochs, calligraphy developed and flourished with both royal and religious patronage.

The 8th-century monk Kūkai (known posthumously as Kōbō Daishi), alongside Emperor Saga and the government official Tachibana no Hayanari (both from the 9th century), are known collectively as the Sanpitsu (Three Brushes). Alongside other examples of *shodō*, their calligraphy has been revered since it was first committed to paper and ranks among some of Japan's most prestigious works of art, accorded national treasure status.

PERFORMANCE CALLIGRAPHY

Since 1995, the Japanese Kanji Proficiency Society has run an annual national ballot to decide the *kanji* that best sums the year. The result is announced at Kyoto's Kiyomizu temple on 12 December, where the head priest ceremonially writes the character live on television.

Calligraphy is also energised by performance *shodō*, developed about 30 years ago to engage schoolchildren. The writing of large-scale characters is choreographed in a routine with music – it's a team sport combining both athletic and artistic skills, with the ultimate contest being the Shodō Performance Kōshien held annually on the island of Shikoku. The contest has become the subject of a manga and TV series, as well as a movie. Contemporary performance calligraphers include Kōji Kakinuma and Shōko Kanazawa, the latter born with Downs syndrome – both regularly perform live *shodō*, and were the only calligraphers to contribute art to the official posters for the Tokyo 2020 Summer Olympics.

LOCAL PERSPECTIVE  CALLIGRAPHY ARTIST

Ouka

Based in the ancient capital Nara, Ouka brings the art of ink to every corner of Japanese culture. Blending traditional calligraphy with creative depictions of yōkai (spirits and supernatural beings), she shares her talent through workshops.

How would you explain Japanese calligraphy? Japanese calligraphy, or *shodō*, arrived from China around 1400 years ago and evolved into a distinctly Japanese art. It is not only about writing characters beautifully but about the movement of the brush, the balance of ink and empty space, and the rhythm within each stroke. Japan also created *kana* scripts, known for their soft, flowing lines, which add an elegance unique to Japanese calligraphy.

What role has calligraphy played in Japanese culture, and how has it evolved? Calligraphy was once essential knowledge taught in temple schools, where writing was central to education and communication. Over time it expanded into both a practical skill and a refined art. Today, almost all children learn the basics of brush and ink in *shūji* (brush-writing) lessons as part of the language curriculum. More advanced artistic calligraphy, *shodō*, is usually learned through clubs or elective courses, where students explore expressive, creative writing styles.

What is *kakizome*, and why is it important? *Kakizome* (literally 'first writing') is an annual New Year's event in Japan. Students, as well as adults, practise writing auspicious characters or phrases with brush and ink to welcome the new year. It is a nationwide event that combines learning, skill development and artistic expression, reinforcing the cultural importance of calligraphy.

Calligraphy is often described as calming or meditative. Why is that? Even a single line reflects one's state of mind. Writing becomes a dialogue with oneself, encouraging focus, patience and awareness. Practices like *shakyō* (sutra copying) continue as a meditative art, showing how calligraphy can calm the mind and foster concentration. The rhythm of the brush draws the mind into a peaceful space, allowing creativity and reflection to emerge naturally.

What makes the tools of calligraphy so important? Each tool – brush, ink, inkstone, paper – has its own character. All come from nature: animal hair, tree fibres, soot and stone. Because of this, calligraphy is a deeply tactile art. The feel of the brush, the absorbency of the paper and the richness of the ink all shape expression. Performances can be shared digitally worldwide, yet its cultural role – aligning mind and spirit – remains as vital as ever.

Theatre

LEFT Mayuko Kashiwazaki tries on her mask for a traditional noh drama.

CENTRE Noh at Tamba-Sasayama's Kasuga Shintō shrine during cherry blossom season.

RIGHT Mask artisan Hiroyuki Yamamoto paints a mask for a theatrical performance.

Traditional theatre is one of Japan's most revered art forms, replete with historical significance, symbolism and unique practices that have seen noh, kabuki and kyōgen inscribed on UNESCO's Intangible Cultural Heritage of Humanity list. Ranging from the ethereal experience of a noh play to the dazzling spectacle of kabuki, the repertoire, themes and aesthetic sensibilities within Japanese theatre forms are incredibly diverse.

NOH AND KYŌGEN

Noh is a form of masked theatre that uses speech, music and movement to express an allegorical and deeply emotional multidimensional realm. It expresses an animist worldview that encompasses non-human perspectives, crossing into the supernatural and the realm of gods. While noh is a form of traditional theatre that is performed today, scholar Diego Pellecchia says that 'To understand why noh looks the way it is right now, one

would need to look at the origins of noh – which are rituals to conjure spirits, to appease deities and to expel evil. In these rituals, masks were used for spirits to take some kind of form and appear in front of an audience. Noh really has this religious aspect, both in Shintō and Buddhist contexts.' Pellecchia describes an interplay between the audience and the actors, and a communication during the performance: 'Masks are like mirrors, really; we project our feelings, emotions and fears on them. With their the subtle movements, the actors leave enough room for the audience to imagine emotions.'

Developed in parallel with noh, kyōgen is a comedic theatre form that describes everyday life and is designed to be performed as light relief. Productions typically feature only a few actors, who perform without masks; movements are exaggerated and (just like Shakespeare plays) dialogue is deliberately archaic, typically voiced in Muromachi-era language.

KABUKI

Visually opulent kabuki theatre has its roots in the early Edo period, when it flourished in urban entertainment districts. Performances usually depict historic events or the lives of prominent people rather than having a didactic

BEHIND THE MASK

Masks are a crucial part of Japanese theatre, in particular noh; and there are over 200 types of noh masks alone. 'The mask is the tool through which the deities appear in front of the audience', says scholar Diego Pellecchia. 'It's a kind of shamanistic tool.' These hand-carved wooden masks are designed to create expressive shadows, which are enhanced or dissipated according to whether the actor is facing up or down.

'Japan's native religion of Shintō is connected to nature worship – every element of nature is divine, and inanimate things are considered to have a soul,' says renowned contemporary mask artist Hiromitsu. 'For example, lightning is said to occur when the god Kaminari-san is angry. In order to portray the stories of the gods that inhabit these everyday natural elements and occurrences, masks are used. Masks are also worn for traditional *kagura* dance performances, which are a kind of offering to the gods.'

the *mie*, the *tsuke* [wooden clapper-board] is struck.'

As in noh, all the roles are played by men. Kabuki is said to have originated around 1603 via the performances of dancer Izumo no Okuni, whose popularity in Kyoto saw many locals – including prostitutes – emulate her style. Fearing that kabuki was morally depraved, the Edo authorities banned women (and later young male actors) from performing it; casts of adult male actors (known as *onnagata* when playing female roles) became the norm.

purpose: kabuki is simply entertainment. There is an extravagance to the theatrics – the costumes, makeup and exaggerated poses are designed to provide a dazzling spectacle. Dressed in revolving sets with gorgeous scenes of snow or cherry blossom, kabuki stages feature *hanamichi* – a platform extending into the audience, which is used for dramatic entrances and exits.

Kabuki retains an enduring appeal. 'It has 400 years of history but the current kabuki is very sophisticated, developed and refined,' says kabuki expert Kazui Yabe. 'Everything is beautiful – even the fight scenes. The actors don't use a microphone, all the sounds are live. Kabuki training school involves learning acting, dancing, makeup, singing and playing the *shamisen*. Actors need to learn the traditional Japanese music because it has a very different rhythm and pitch.'

Yabe also describes the dramatic convention of *mie*, where an actor will adopt a striking pose, with hands extended and head turning dramatically, creating a kind of emotive pause. 'In the Edo period, the theatres were really crowded and noisy,' she says. 'It was considered OK to eat, drink and chat. The poses during emotional peaks are to garner attention; before

RIGHT Actor Hayato Nakamura in kabuki character.

BUNRAKU

Thematically similar to kabuki, and using the same scripts, bunraku is a form of expressive puppet theatre. Also from the Edo era, it's performed by half-life-sized puppets dressed in gorgeous outfits. Each is operated by three puppet-masters (one controlling the head, right hand and facial expressions; the others the left hand and legs), who perfectly coordinate the movements to create a lifelike effect. The story is narrated by way of a chanted *jōruri*, accompanied by a *shamisen* player.

RAKUGO

Less extravagant but equally as entertaining, rakugo also emerged among the commoner class during the Edo period. Performed in *yose* theatres by seated (usually) male actors, rakugo is form of sharp storytelling characterised by comedic monologues that are dense with verbal puns, double entendre and lyrical witticisms, and are usually capped off with a plot twist or dramatic punchline. Performers use only a fan and a small cloth as props.

Hayato Nakamura

Hayato Nakamura was born into one of Japan's most renowned acting families and made his stage debut at the age of nine. Praised for revitalising kabuki for new generations, he captivates audiences in Japan, alongside work in television and film.

Kabuki is performed entirely by men, with actors also playing female roles. Why? Kabuki began in the early 1600s with women performers, known as *onna-kabuki*. But the shogunate banned women on stage, citing 'corrupting public morals'. Young men briefly took over but they too were prohibited, leaving only adult men. That's how the tradition of men playing female roles – *onnagata* – was born. Most actors specialise either as *tachiyaku* (male roles) or *onnagata*. My family line excelled in *onnagata*, and until high school I only played women. But when I performed opposite legendary actor Bandō Tamasaburō, he told me, 'You suit *tachiyaku*.' With my tall build and voice, I switched to male roles, where I've remained.

What does it mean to inherit kabuki through your family? Growing up in a kabuki household doesn't automatically decide your path, but for me it felt natural. Beyond acting, I absorbed the traditions, manners and way of relating to people that have been passed down for centuries. When I step on stage, I don't feel I'm only performing; I carry the weight of history.

Costumes and makeup are such a striking part of kabuki. What role do they play? They're not just for show. Costumes and makeup communicate character – status, emotion, even temperament. Bold colours can suggest power or courage, while subdued tones convey calmness or inner conflict. In kabuki's early days, when stage effects were limited, these visual cues were vital to storytelling, and they remain central today.

Kabuki plays often draw on historical themes. What kinds of stories do audiences see? Kabuki stories range from *jidaimono* (period plays) about the world of samurai before the Edo period, to *sewamono* (domestic plays) portraying the lives of ordinary people during the Edo period. While classics remain central, new works are also inspired by contemporary pop culture. I've performed in kabuki versions of *One Piece* and *Naruto* – famous manga and anime series – which preserve kabuki's style while opening the door to new fans.

What would you say to someone watching for the first time? Kabuki has been performed for over 400 years, and yes, it can seem intimidating. But if you come to the theatre, I think you'll be struck by its beauty.

Ikebana

TOP An ikebana artist holds a nadeshiko (Japanese pink) flower prior to placing it in an arrangement.

RIGHT A side view of an ikebana composition.

Far more than just beautiful bouquets, ikebana is the Japanese art of flower arranging, and there is much philosophy behind it. Ikebana seeks to capture the beauty and the transience of the seasons and, like Japanese garden design and bonsai, it is strongly associated with the idea of landscape: it aims to bring the essence of a landscape indoors.

Flowers were originally arranged in Japan as altar offerings in Buddhist temples, but by the middle of the 15th century flower arrangements had become a major indoor ornament for the reception rooms of noble residences. There were already experts who specialised in this art, several of whom established traditions which are followed to this day. Very simple arrangements were also used to adorn the rustic-style rooms in which intimate tea ceremonies were conducted. However, during the 18th century, an influential style known as *seika* or *shōka* (depending on which traditional school of ikebana you belong to) was established, which centred on the idea of having three main pieces of vegetation (they don't all have to be flowers; they can include large leaves and branches) which respectively symbolise heaven, earth and humankind. The flower arrangement itself symbolises the harmony between all three.

The importance of the number three is reflected in the arrangement of these chief compositional elements. They are trimmed to different heights and placed in relation to each other so that together they suggest a shape of a scalene triangle (which has sides of different lengths). When the arrangement is seen from above, the tips of the three chief elements should also form a scalene triangle; this creates a sense of depth when the ensemble is viewed from the front.

Other styles of ikebana involve different number theories and ideas of space and form, but an important concept in most is that of asymmetry, which produces feelings of both tension and of a delicately achieved balance that unites all the elements of the arrangement. There was a time when emphasis was placed on the discipline of learning and mastering the principles of ikebana, and it was thought to play an essential role in moral upbringing – especially that of women. Ikebana is still treated as a serious lifelong study in Japan.

FIVE STEPS OF IKEBANA

THE STRUCTURE
The basic shape is a central stalk flanked by a secondary stem and a shorter third stem.

THE KENZAN
The stems of the flowers are fixed onto the sharp nail-like points of a *kenzan*.

THE FIRST STEM
The most important, central stem is always placed first when creating an ikebana arrangement.

BUILDING THE COMPOSITION
Other stems are added in a row, always placed before and behind the central stem.

THE FINISHED ENSEMBLE
From the front, the finished arrangement must appear to emerge from a single point.

Bonsai

LEFT A bonsai tree at Takamatsu Bonsai no Sato (see over the page).

RIGHT A bonsai grower tends to a tiny pine tree.

Bonsai is the art of cultivating a miniaturised but fully mature tree, usually in a wide and relatively shallow plant pot. Careful seasonal pruning of the branches and roots ensures that the tree gets sufficient nutrients to grow healthily, while maintaining a size that is proportionate to that of its pot. Bonsai conifers can live for hundreds of years when given loving care and attention.

The idea behind bonsai is to produce the illusion of an elegant, fully grown tree seen from some distance away. Of course, they are also an object of beauty when inspected up close, but fundamentally bonsai is one form of an ancient Chinese and Japanese tradition of creating miniaturised landscapes in a pot or tray.

Originally, these landscapes featured large stones representing mountainous islands, surrounded by white gravel symbolising the sea. Plants, such as pines, were added to enhance the overall appearance of the composition. Later on, in Japan, the focus gradually

shifted to the plant itself. By the 18th century, a form emerged that did away with stones altogether. At the same time, the practice became more popularised and accessible to the Japanese public.

Emphasis came to be placed on the art of pruning and shaping the bonsai tree so as to reveal the inherent beauty of its shape. To achieve this, side branches are thinned out. Techniques and conventions govern how to position certain branches (often using wire to secure them in place) in order to create a desirable overall shape that's well balanced and pleasing to the eye. Many bonsai fanciers begin with a sapling or a young grafted tree and shape it gradually over the years, potting it on into slightly larger containers until it finally achieves the desired size. The health of the plant always remains the paramount concern. Older trees may lose vigour in some of their branches, which may require pruning back. On the other hand, a dead branch is sometimes retained if it adds an attractive element to the look of the tree.

It is a great mistake to assume that just because a bonsai is small, it is happy indoors on a windowsill. They are trees, after all, and need to be outdoors, although in severe conditions they may require protection from wind and cold.

PERFECT PLANTS FOR BONSAI

PINES
Bonsai master Kunio Kobayashi trims a centuries-old bonsai pine at his Shunkaen Bonsai Museum, Tokyo.

JAPANESE APRICOT
Auspicious pink- and white-flowered *Prunus mume* bonsai trees are displayed in Kyoto.

JAPANESE MAPLE
This magnificent Japanese maple at the Omiya Bonsai Art Museum near Tokyo is in the *kabudachi* (multi-trunk) style.

PLUM TREES
Like this cherry plum (*Malus cerasifera*), even fruiting trees can be used for bonsai.

AZALEAS
Flowering shrubs, such as these colourful satsuki azaleas, are popular among bonsai enthusiasts.

Yusuke Hashimoto

Yusuke Hashimoto helped found Takamatsu Bonsai no Sato, home to one of Japan's largest public bonsai collections. He promotes bonsai through markets and workshops and runs Sakuya Kobo, offering bonsai sales and learning experiences.

Why is Takamatsu such an important place for bonsai?
Takamatsu, in Kagawa Prefecture, is known as Japan's 'Bonsai Kingdom'. The region produces over 80% of Japan's pine bonsai, thanks to its mild Seto Inland Sea climate, well-drained soil and abundant sunlight – ideal conditions for growing black pine. At Takamatsu Bonsai no Sato, visitors can see an incredible collection of over 10,000 miniature trees, nurtured with the expertise of around 50 local bonsai gardens.

How do you choose a tree when creating bonsai?
The word *bonsai* comes from *bon* (盆 pot) and *sai* (栽 to grow), so in principle, any tree can be made into a bonsai. Every tree has its own character. For example, a black pine should express the dignity and power of the species, while a maple should show a sense of seasonal beauty.

There are many styles of bonsai. Could you tell us about some representative ones and their characteristics?
Two of the most iconic are *moyōgi* (informal upright) and *kengai* (cascade). In *moyōgi*, the trunk curves gracefully from side to side, creating a sense of movement and rhythm that reflects the natural flow of a tree shaped by the wind. *Kengai*, on the other hand, has branches that extend below the edge of the pot, evoking the drama and resilience of a tree clinging to a steep cliff, enduring the harshness of nature.

Why do you think bonsai holds such deep meaning in Japanese culture?
Bonsai is a 'living artwork' that reflects the Japanese appreciation of *wabi-sabi* – the beauty of imperfection and simplicity. Within a single tree, beauty and decay coexist. Features like *jin* and *shari* – the bleached, deadwood areas – convey the passage of long years, capturing the full cycle of nature in miniature form.

What do you want people to feel when they look at bonsai?
I hope they sense the grandeur of ancient trees, the harshness of nature, and the quiet patience it takes to nurture them. Bonsai often has an image of being difficult or exclusive, but I want people to enjoy it more casually, appreciating it as a living artwork that anyone can connect with.

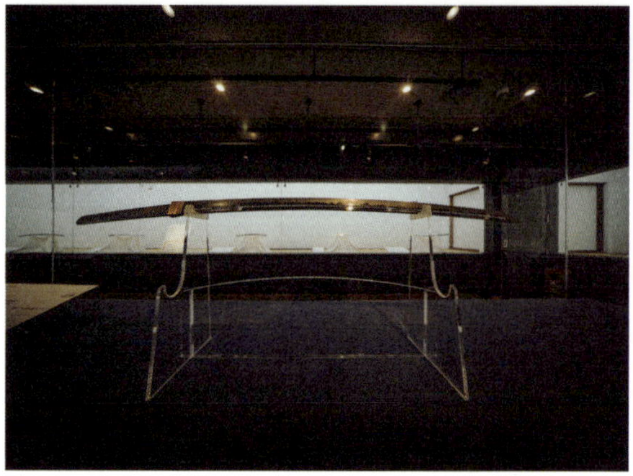

Swords and knives

ABOVE A sword displayed at Bizen Osafune Sword Museum in Okayama Prefecture.

TOP RIGHT Swordsmith Akihira Kawasaki holds steel over an anvil as apprentice Toru Watanabe hammers the metal to forge katana blades at Kawasaki's workshop in Misato.

BOTTOM A samurai in 19th-century Yokohama.

Created over 1000 years ago and handed down through generations of nobles and warriors, the Dōjikiri Yasutsuna is the greatest of Japanese swords. Displayed in Tokyo National Museum, this national treasure comes garlanded in legend. A study of its attributes – the graceful curve and razor-thin edge of the blade, the hardened core with its beguiling surface pattern, its carefully balanced length of 80cm (31.5in) – provides insights into what has long made Japanese sword-smithing so revered.

Commonly associated with samurai (and said to embody a warrior's soul), *nihontō* (Japanese swords) were developed as deadly weapons over the centuries, as rival clans battled each other across the country. In peacetime, as the blades became more ceremonial in nature, the craftsmanship involved in making swords continued to evolve.

Objects of authority and of sacred rites, Japanese swords are symbolic of the county's traditional culture. They are classed both by the period of their making (the oldest being *jōkotō*, made up until around 900 CE) and their school – meaning where they were made and the manufacturing traditions associated with that location. There are also several different types of blade, ranging from long *ōdachi* or *nodachi* swords to the *tantō* – a

dagger, either straight or slightly curved, which was the weapon of choice for *seppuku* (ritual suicide).

The blades are admired for the *hada* (grain) of the *tamahagane* (the special type of steel used to make them), and for the *hamon* (temper patterns) that ripple across their surface. The steel's strength is the result of a forging process, in which both high- and low-carbon steel are combined and impurities hammered away.

There remain roughly 300 swordsmiths practising the craft in Japan today. Because of the complex processes involved it may take months to make a single sword. Visitors to the workshop at Bizen Osafune Sword Museum in Okayama Prefecture can observe the various manufacturing processes, including traditional forging, blade engraving, polishing and sharpening.

This ancient art of honing the strongest and sharpest of blades also finds modern-day expression in knife-making, with Japanese kitchen knives treasured by chefs and home cooks the world over.

1 KAPPABASHI, TOKYO

The capital's kitchenware street, where Tsubaya, Kamata and Kamaasa are go-to shops for knives.

2 SAKAI, OSAKA PREFECTURE

Many Japanese chefs use Sakai knives, handmade in this town for centuries.

3 SEKI, GIFU PREFECTURE

An industry hub since the 14th century, home to some 100 blade manufacturers and 10 active swordsmiths.

4 MIKI, HYŌGO PREFECTURE

Kitchen knives and all kinds of blades are made in Japan's oldest blacksmithing town.

5 TAKEFU KNIFE VILLAGE, FUKUI PREFECTURE

Both museum and factory, housing a collective of local knife manufacturers.

Kawaii

LEFT Takahashi Hiroaki's early 20th-century woodblock print Shironeko (White Cat) radiates cuteness.

RIGHT Takeshita St in Tokyo's Harajuku is the heart of kawaii culture.

The word kawaii is a complimentary adjective implying that something or someone is cute, sweet, endearing and innocent. The traits of kawaii design are typically compositional roundness, pastel colours and a face with similar proportions to that of a child. In Japan, kawaii is the dominant pop-culture aesthetic – and it is present everywhere, from bus stops shaped like watermelons and construction signs that resemble rabbits to girls dressed in frilly outfits or bear-shaped parfaits in bakeries.

The Japanese notion of kawaii has developed thanks to the vision of some of Japan's most revered creators, from fashion designers to robotics scientists, but it has been cultivated over hundreds of years. During the Edo period, *ukiyo-e* woodblock prints already featured motifs that are undeniably kawaii, from goldfish using leaves for umbrellas to anthropomorphic cats visiting bathhouses. The work of famous painters from that era, such as Maruyama Ōkyo (1733–95), also featured kawaii-antecedent subjects such as adorable roly-poly puppies.

Kawaii culture took on its contemporary form at the start of the 20th century, during the beginning of the Taishō period. It owes much to the inherent cuteness of manga characters, and to the aesthetic that commercial illustrators brought to products targeted at a youth market,

often featuring charming-looking girls. Designer Takehisa Yumeji (1884–1934) made stationery and dolls with innocent, romantic patterns specifically marketed towards educated and affluent high school girls. Following on from Yumeji, illustrators such as Junichi Nakahara (1913–83) and Rune Naito (1932–2007) continued to produce all manner of sundries – from book illustrations to homewares and stickers – adorned with sparkly eyed, fashionable girls. In fact, Naito is credited with popularising the word 'kawaii' to describe this aesthetic.

THE QUEEN OF CUTE

Who is five apples high, a British girl, has whiskers – and yet is one of Japan's biggest cultural ambassadors? None other than the queen of kawaii herself, Hello Kitty. In kawaii culture, there is no other icon as ubiquitous nor as cherished, and since her 'birth' in 1974, there has been no other pop cultural phenomena that has so completely captured the hearts of Japanese people.

Keiko Nakamura, curator of the Takehisa Yumeji Museum in Tokyo, specifically attributes the proliferation of kawaii products in the 1970s to the oil crisis that was sparked by the 1973 Arab oil embargo. Nakamura explains that 'Until then, the manufacturing industry had been aimed at exports to the United States, but they had to

LEFT Shopping for cute Rilakkuma merch at the Kiddy Land store in Harajuku, Tokyo.

RIGHT Kawaii is all about the accessories.

focus on the domestic market instead because of the economic climate of the time.' Hello Kitty became the first large-scale pop-culture phenomena from Japan to take over the domestic market – and then the world.

One of the most striking features of Hello Kitty is that she has no mouth, although Kazuo Tohmatsu (PR for Sanrio, the company behind the ubiquitous feline) insists that 'It is not that Hello Kitty doesn't have a mouth, it is just that she doesn't have a mouth drawn in.' However, the fact that she has no visible mouth (and hence no definable 'mood') means that anyone can identify with her, however they themselves might be feeling – and this emotional ambiguity is a feature of many hit kawaii products. Bear character Rilakkuma is equally devoid of expression, but according to his maker, San-x, this means that fans can interpret him however they want.

KAWAII IDENTITIES

The meteoric rise of cute idols in the 1980s meant that girls not only wanted adorable things, but to *be* kawaii as well. Popular girls' manga of the time portrayed a female ideal that was cutesy sweet but also independent and self-actualised. Kawaii became an aesthetic quality tied to identity – and one that could be constructed visually through makeup and fashion.

While Japanese haute-couture luminaries flourished in the 1980s and '90s, subcultures also bloomed. In particular, *FRUiTS* – a street-style magazine established in 1997 by photographer Shoichi Aoki – showcased fashions worn by kids on the streets of Harajuku, in western Tokyo. The focus on everyday people, pre-social media, was fresh for the time. Kawaii subcultures like Gothic Lolita and *decora* sprang up, and Harajuku became the epicentre of cute-fashion communities. Kawaii became a globally recognised aesthetic, to the degree that the Ministry of Foreign Affairs appointed Lolita models as 'kawaii ambassadors'.

For its fans, kawaii culture is a positive outlook that champions diverse lifestyles. 'Kawaii fashion encourages people to dress based on how they feel and what they love rather than dressing to meet others' expectations', says popular kawaii model and artist RinRin. 'It helps grow self-confidence, as you learn to explore and embrace what you like. It's a great way to learn about your own style and connect with others who share similar creative outlets.'

KERNELS OF KAWAII CULTURE

LICCA CHAN DOLLS

Japan's saccharine Barbie equivalent, adorned with cute fashion.

KAWAII FASHION

Styled as innocent and sweet, typically pastel coloured and frilly with many layers.

HELLO KITTY

Loved by children to adults alike, Hello Kitty is the queen of kawaii.

TRANSPORT

Cute characters are emblazoned on planes, trains and bus stops, and around train stations and airports.

FOOD

For kawaii devotees, food isn't worth eating unless it's in the shape of a cute animal.

Textiles

ABOVE Members of a silkworm-farming family sort through cocoons in 1925.

Textiles have a storied history in Japan. This was one of the first places in the world in which hemp was cultivated, having been planted here as the primary fibre crop during the Jōmon era. Easy to grow and able to flourish in poor soil, hemp produced a strong, durable plant fibre that was used to make fishing lines and rope, while its nutritious seeds were a source of food.

Over time, though, the production and use of fabric in Japan was mediated through the filter of class and status: what people wore bore reflection to their social standing, and textiles were crafted accordingly. In the Edo period, sumptuary laws mandated that clothing for the commoner class was to be modest in nature, in terms of both material and design. Hemp and cotton were textiles for the lower classes, whereas silk in its multitudes of woven and dyed forms were fabrics for the aristocracy and samurai.

Particularly in northern Japan, which was historically poor and had sparse access to textiles, peasants wore what was known as *boro*: clothing made of hemp, which was restitched continuously to reinforce the cloth rather than being thrown out. This created somewhat surreal-looking patchwork garments that are now exhibited in museums across the world as 'sustainable textile art'.

Cotton only flourished in the 16th century, when the commoner class began producing domestic quantities of raw cotton, which was often dyed with indigo; by 1890, when European writer Lafcadio Hearn visited Japan, the ubiquity of indigo cloth led him to dub the colour 'Japan blue'. Yukihiro Fujisawa, a contemporary *aizome* (indigo-dyeing) artisan based in Kyojima, says that 'Indigo dye comes from *ai* [the Japanese word for the indigo plant], so when the cloth is also a plant-derived material such as hemp, they are compatible and produce a beautiful colour which has longevity.'

In the 18th century onwards, cotton was produced as a cottage industry in the south Kantō region; a hierarchical distribution model was developed, with wholesalers placed at the top. The first mill was built at the end of the Edo, in the former Satsuma domain, using spinning machinery imported from England. By the Meiji period, the government was subsidising the growth of cotton as an industry, and as Japan's textile industry moved towards modernisation, cotton became the first sector to achieve mass production.

ABOVE TOP A silk haori jacket from the 1920s featuring red and white cranes in flight.

BOTTOM Chieko Kakino, who has been weaving for some 60 years, operates her loom as she weaves a silk kimono at her Tatsugo studio in 2020.

FROM SILK TO DENIM

As a luxury item and the preferred fabric for higher-class kimonos, silk has had a different trajectory to cotton and hemp. The former province of Joshū

LEFT A worker at the traditional Pure Blue Japan denim factory in Okayama.

RIGHT A design of irises is painted on denim by Kyoto's Denim Dosu brand.

(now Gunma) was the centre of Japan's silk industry, and silk exports surpassed that of China by the early 1900s. Japan became a leader of silk production, and rising the demand meant that homesteads could raise silkworms. Women were at the forefront of silkworm farming, spinning thread and weaving cloth even after modernisation in the Meiji period. Following WWII, the rise of new textiles such as nylon, made using synthetic materials, meant that silk became a rare commodity – and with fewer people now wearing kimono, silk production has dropped out of everyday Japanese life.

Ironically, as Japan's textiles industry continues to modernise – with new technologies enabling larger-scale production, and the rise of synthetic textiles and global trade meaning it's cheaper to use foreign fabrics than those produced domestically – there has also been a shift in the other direction: towards natural, domestically produced denim. Comfortable, casual and cool, jeans are a wardrobe staple across the world, loved for their versatility and durability. But not all denim is the same, and some of the world's best-quality denim is produced in the Okayama Prefecture district of Kojima.

In the 1940s, Kojima became a manufacturing hub for heavy-duty cloth, which was used to make sails,

military uniforms and traditional *tabi* footwear. During the postwar occupation, American soldiers unwittingly became ambassadors for US fashion. In the 1960s, a company that was later to become Big John (one of Japan's largest denim brands) started to stitch jeans for US companies. By the 1970s, they were producing their own textiles as well.

Today, Kojima has around 40 premium denim companies, utilising vintage shuttle looms to produce 40% of Japan's total denim output. These arcane machines must be operated by skilled, expert artisans, but the resulting cloth is of outstanding quality; brands such as Momotaro and Evisu are highly regarded for their thick, textured denim.

DENIM TIMELINE

EDO ERA Okayama becomes a base for cotton production.

1930s Okayama's cotton industry is going strong, with its fabrics primarily used to make uniforms.

POST-WAR During the occupation, US soldiers sell off their denim on black-markets.

1960s American style becomes hugely popular in Japan, and remains in vogue through to the 1980s.

1973 Okayama company Big John makes the first domestic denim

1991 Denim brand Evisu is established in Osaka, producing products showcase flashy Japanese street style.

2000 Japanese denim gains greater global attention into the new millennium.

Ukiyo-e

TOP The Great Wave off Kanagawa, from the series Thirty-six Views of Mount Fuji by Katsushika Hokusai.

BOTTOM A woodblock print from 1762 by Suzuki Harunobu.

Ukiyo-e is a form of woodblock-printed art that flourished during Japan's Edo era, in the 17th to the 19th century. The prints were made by artists from the commoner class, working for clients who were predominantly wealthy merchants – but while ukiyo-e prints are now exalted as fine art and displayed in museums the world over, they were akin to tabloid media during the Edo period. They depicted daily life with a focus on urban entertainment culture – such as kabuki theatre actors and sumo wrestlers – as well as ephemeral pleasures, from erotica to portraits of famous courtesans. The scenes portrayed were a reflection of the times: the Edo era was characterised by peace and prosperity, even amid the lower echelons of society. Live-for-the-moment spirit and hedonism are abundant in the works.

The first ukiyo-e master is said to have been Hishikawa Moronobu (1618–94), who was born in present-day Chiba Prefecture. He is known for his prints of beautiful women,

and his upbringing in a family of textile makers is evident in the meticulous details and patterns of his subjects' kimonos. The earliest ukiyo-e were monochrome, printed only using black *sumi* ink until artist Suzuki Harunobu (1725–70) pioneered colourful *nishiki-e* prints, made with multiple woodblocks, during the mid-Edo period.

Edo-era woodblock printing required the work of four parties: an artist, a carver, a printer and a publisher (the latter often acted as an artist's patron, and commissioned the works they produced). The artist would first draw the composition on paper; this artwork was then pasted to a cherry-wood block, and the carver engraved the wood so that lines were raised. Ink was then applied to the block for printing. Colours were carved on separate blocks, with up to 20 made for a single artwork. They were printed on *washi*, fibrous Japanese paper made from mulberry-tree bark. This form of mass production meant that thousands of prints could be made from a single set of blocks, until the wood degraded.

THE GRAND MASTERS OF UKIYO-E

Several superstar artists ascended, each excelling at particular genres. Kitagawa Utamaro (1753–1806) depicted beautiful, stylised women, capturing their feminine allure.

Katsushika Hokusai (1760–1849) and Utagawa Hiroshige (1797–1858) popularised landscapes and renditions of animals, which were a departure from the prevalent portraits. Arguably the most famous singular artwork to come out of Japan is Hokusai's 'The Great Wave off Kanagawa', rendered in striking Prussian blues; his 'South Wind, Clear Sky' (commonly known as 'Red Fuji') shows the majestic mountain from a different vantage point. Both prints are from Hokusai's *Thirty-six Views of Mount Fuji* series, which cemented his position as a landscape master.

In 1856, Hiroshige published another famous landscape series, *One Hundred Famous Views of Edo*, which focused on urban life through the seasons, with scenes such as Kinryūzan temple blanketed under snow, Kameido shrine adorned with wisteria and the adjacent plum park in bloom.

Perhaps the most subversive of all the artists, Utagawa Kuniyoshi (1798–1861) is known for his prints of warriors, mythical creatures and supernatural beings. Each of his

ABOVE Two prints from Hiroshige's 19th-century ukiyo-e series One Hundred Famous Views of Edo.

TOP RIGHT Crafting a woodblock print by hand at Takezasado workshop.

RIGHT Japanese tattoos may feature designs derived from ukiyo-e.

works are powerful and vivaciously alive. When an official decree was put in place to ban the popular pictures of courtesans and kabuki actors, Kuniyoshi – who was anti-authoritarian to begin with – created comical pieces showing animals in their likenesses (such as anthropomorphic cats in kimono) to get around the laws.

UKIYO-E TODAY

During the Meiji period, though exquisite prints were still being made by apprentices of the Edo-era legends, advances in print technology and the use of mass-produced paper meant that ukiyo-e culture declined. Today, Motoharu Asaka is one of few remaining professional ukiyo-e artists. Working from his Shinjuku studio, Asaka produces reproductions of Edo-era work as well as new commissions. He believes that the materials are what makes ukiyo-e so exceptional: 'Handmade things have a warmth, your soul shows in the work,' he says. 'The *washi* has warmth. Rather than just painting on top of the paper, you get the feeling that the ink has seeped inside. The pigment is made of things from nature such as plants and minerals, so humans feel an affinity to it. I use mountain cherry wood that is 200 years old, and because it comes from trees that were alive, I feel that the wood breathes and adjusts to my work. It feels like a partnership and together I can produce good work.'

TATTOO PRINTS

While there are tattoo traditions all over the world, the designs produced by Japanese tattooists are certainly some of the most impactful, often covering entire bodies with narrative and symbolic artwork. Perhaps surprisingly, the ukiyo-e, tattoo and kabuki theatre cultures of Japan are inextricably intertwined, having flourished simultaneously during the Edo era. Famed ukiyo-e artists such as Utagawa Kunisada, Tsukioka Yoshitoshi and Toyohara Kunichika featured tattooed protagonists in their work – but it was Utagawa Kuniyoshi's series *The 108 Heroes of the Suikoden* (commissioned in 1827) that really created a tattoo craze. Featuring a parade of warriors covered in full-body tattoos, the prints inspired members of the commoner class to emulate these designs on their own bodies. In turn, ukiyo-e masters made the tattoos in their artworks ever more complex, and their designs served as the genesis of the Japanese decorative tattooing that's still practiced today.

LOCAL PERSPECTIVE  CARVER & LACQUER ARTIST

Kaoru Kamo

Based in Inami, Toyama – Japan's largest centre of woodcarving – Kaoru Kamo is a fifth-generation woodcarver and lacquer artist. She also offers hands-on woodblock print workshops at Inami's Bed and Craft boutique hotel.

What is Japanese woodblock printing? It began in the 8th-century Nara period with Buddhist texts, but flourished in the Edo period with ukiyo-e. These prints were the popular media of the time, depicting kabuki stars, geisha, sumo and landscapes. After the Meiji era, they declined with the arrival of Western printing. In the 1900s artists like Hasui Kawase and Shikō Munakata revived the craft for a global audience. Studios still use Edo-era techniques.

How do Hokusai and Hiroshige still matter today? Their bold compositions and colours resonate in modern painting, design and even anime. Hokusai's *Great Wave off Kanagawa* is recognised worldwide. In Japan, children still carve wood or linoleum blocks at school, and some families make New Year's cards this way. While professional printmakers are fewer, the artform remains an enduring part of Japan's cultural life.

Why is Inami so important to Japanese art and heritage? Inami traces its skills back to the carving of Zuisenji Temple, whose ornate Buddhist sculptures and intricate carvings shaped the town's identity as a centre of master carvers. Some 100–150 carvers still work here, with many workshops lining the streets and the town itself decorated with carvings. Inami's woodcarvers contribute to heritage restorations across Japan, including Nagoya and Shuri Castles. My father helped restore Izumo Taisha, one of Japan's oldest and most important Shintō shrines. Work included creating and repairing the decorative horizontal panel above the treasured Yatsuashimon Gate, and I assisted him on site.

Can you share about your work and what inspires it? I practice *chōshitsu* (carved lacquer), layering coloured lacquer many times before carving with chisels. I leave tool marks visible, without polishing. This comes from Banzan Kamo, my grandfather, a pioneer of contemporary *chōshitsu*. Few continue the craft today, as it is time-consuming and expensive, but I hope my work conveys even a little of the sense of wonder my grandfather's work had on me.

How do workshops keep these crafts alive? By carving themselves, visitors understand the time, skill and beauty of the craft. Workshops inspire future artisans and conversations with participants also give me fresh ideas. I encourage everyone to visit, watch the carvers at work, and try carving for themselves.

NATU

LAND-

RE
AND
SCAPE

Seasons and climate

TOP LEFT A wave of cherry blossom arrives in Tokyo by April.

TOP RIGHT Discover the Izu Peninsula, southwest of Tokyo in Shizuoka Prefecture.

Japan sits in the northern hemisphere, so it's warmer in the south, colder in the north and the seasons run the same as in Europe and North America. Place a map of Japan over that of the eastern seaboard of North America and the Japanese archipelago stretches from Miami to Montreal, spanning some 22 degrees of latitude.

SPRING (MARCH TO MAY)

The season of *sakura* (cherry blossoms) is a highlight in Japan. It all kicks off in Kyūshū – Okinawa doesn't get the same blooms as the rest of the country – in mid- to late March, moving northward and hitting the major cities of Honshū (such as Kyoto and Tokyo) as early as late March; the season in northern Honshū starts in mid-April and in Hokkaidō in late April. Exact dates change by the year, so Japanese keep a track of the blossom forecast in the daily news and online. *Mankai* (full bloom) is the peak, about a week after the buds start to open. The weekend nearest to *mankai* is when the biggest crowds gather for *hanami* (blossom-viewing parties). Over the following week or so, the petals start to fall, covering parks and rivers in carpets of pink.

It's not just about the *sakura*, however – *ume* (Japanese plum) blossoms mark the start of spring as they are the first to bloom, usually

in February and March. Later, a few weeks after the cherries, come azaleas and wisteria. It's greening up in the mountains too. Rural inns serve dishes with foraged *sansai* (mountain vegetables; page 124) – fresh shoots and fern fronds served atop noodles or fried in tempura.

SUMMER (JUNE TO AUGUST)

A concept that the Japanese are immensely proud of, *shiki* (meaning 'four seasons') is deeply woven into the country's culture and art, and into daily life. The concept does, however, forget to mention an extra season called *tsuyu* – the rainy time. For a month to six weeks, from June to mid-July, Japan swelters with wet, humid, stickily uncomfortable weather, not ideal for travel. *Tsuyu* doesn't usually reach the far north, so cooler, drier conditions prevail in Hokkaidō.

True summer kicks in from mid-July – as do the summer school holidays, which last through to the end of August and see families and students heading out to enjoy themselves. Hikers believe the best weather is at *tsuyu-ake-tōka*, the first 10 days following the end of the rainy season, and mountain huts are packed over this period.

This time of year, the typical greeting is *'Atsui desu ne!'* (Hot, isn't it!). The cities in particular are scorching and many locals head to the hills or

BOTTOM LEFT Stroll the banks of the cooling Kamo-gawa in Kyoto.

BOTTOM RIGHT Blossom envelops Yoshino-yama in Nara Prefecture.

beaches to cool off, but not everyone can get away. City dwellers have come up with their own strategies to beat the heat: beer gardens on department store rooftops do a roaring trade, while in Kyoto, restaurants along the Kamo-gawa set up *kawayuka*, terraces for al fresco dining suspended on stilts out over the riverbanks.

AUTUMN (SEPTEMBER TO NOVEMBER)

Autumn leaves draw phenomenal crowds to the many resort areas, temples and gardens known for their colourful displays. Most prized are the *momiji* (maples), which turn a fiery red. The opposite of the cherry blossom front, which moves northward in spring, the change of colour in autumn foliage gradually spreads southward from Hokkaidō, and from higher elevations down to the coasts and cities. Just as Japanese keep track of the blossom forecast in spring, so they track autumn's turning leaves with a yellow foliage forecast and a red foliage forecast (with the yellows turning before the reds). The leaves generally start to change as early as late September in Hokkaidō and high-mountain areas, and then move south; trees in cities like Tokyo and Kyoto don't turn until early November, later in some years. Tokyo's autumn tree, the *ichō* (gingko), becomes resplendently gold in early December.

Autumn is also the time of *tsukimi* (moon-viewing parties) and raucous harvest festivals, time-honoured events that historically thanked the gods for a bountiful harvest.

LEFT Autumn foliage of red maple trees around Kiyomizu-dera temple.

CENTRE The festivities of Hachiman Matsuri are staged each October at Sakurayama Hachiman-gū in Takayama, Gifu.

TOP RIGHT Winter snow on cedars in Oku-no-in cemetery at Kōya-san.

BOTTOM RIGHT Hitting powder snow in Hokkaidō.

WINTER (DECEMBER TO FEBRUARY)

Winters are cold, with gardens, temples and shrines stripped of their vegetation and sometimes taking on a forlorn appearance. But there are many clear days, and this time of year is also conducive to the kind of private moments that can be had in destinations such as Kyoto, Kanazawa and the mountain monastery complex at Kōya-san. Foodies love winter as prime time for seafood and sake.

The ski resorts are also buzzing, with winter-sports enthusiasts (both Japanese and from around the globe) taking advantage of the abundant falls of fresh powder in Japan's *yukiguni* (snow country). More than 500 ski areas are spread across Honshū and Hokkaidō, from Hakuba and Nozawa Onsen to Myōkō Kōgen and Zaō Onsen. The city of Sapporo also makes the most of the winter weather, hosting its legendary annual Yuki Matsuri (Snow Festival) in early February.

1 YOSHINO, NARA PREFECTURE

Some 30,000 cherry trees cover the mountain in a sea of blossoms at this famous viewing spot.

2 SAPPORO, HOKKAIDŌ

The Yuki Matsuri (Snow Festival) in early February is Japan's top winter celebration.

3 KAMIKŌCHI, NAGANO PREFECTURE

This mountain retreat and hiking trailhead is a popular escape from city heat in summer.

4 NIKKŌ, TOCHIGI PREFECTURE

Vivid autumn colours at the World Heritage–listed shrines, temples and Lake Chūzen-ji.

5 UENO PARK, TOKYO

The capital's top cherry-blossom-viewing site, with over 1000 trees and a festive atmosphere.

Volcanoes and thermal sites

RIGHT Driving towards the snowy volcano of Yōtei-zan near Niseko ski resort.

Sitting on the Ring of Fire – a horseshoe-shaped chain of vigorous volcanic activity around the Pacific Ocean, which is the site of some 75% of the world's volcanoes – the Japanese archipelago is located in one of the most geologically active areas on the planet.

The Shintō creation myth tells that Japan came into being through a cosmic union (and a stirring of the ocean with a jewelled spear) between the gods Izanami and Izanagi – which resonates with the more prosaic reality that the islands emerged from the sea millions of years ago. Since then, they have been uplifted through tectonic movement, in which heat in the Earth's core drives 100km-thick (62-mile) plates to float and move on a virtual (if infinitely slow) conveyor belt of molten rock. Japan sits where four tectonic plates meet, and when these plates slide under and over each other, huge amounts of friction are generated. This friction is the source of earthquakes and of a tremendous amount of heat, which melts the surrounding rock; this rises to the surface as magma and forms volcanoes. Volcanoes can also be formed at 'hot spots', where heat rises in the form of a mantle plume – a particularly hot area in the Earth's mantle, rising and pushing through cracks in the Earth's crust to break out as a volcano.

JAPAN'S VOLCANOES

The Japan Meteorological Agency (JMA) continuously monitors 50 of Japan's 111 active volcanoes, and there are around 15 'volcanic events' here each year. The most famous volcano (and Japan's highest) is, of course, 3776m (12,388ft) Mt Fuji; snowcapped for six months of the year, this incredibly symmetrical cone last erupted in 1707. On the Nagano–Gifu prefectural border, the second-highest volcano is 3067m (10,062ft) Ontake-san; its last eruption occurred in 2014, killing 63 hikers. In Kumamoto Prefecture on Kyūshū, Aso is one of the largest calderas in the world, with a diameter of about 25km (16 miles), a

FUJI'S LOOK-ALIKES

For hundreds – if not thousands – of years, Mt Fuji has been the talk of the country. Its perfect shape and dominating height made it the undisputed, and at times unifying, symbol of Japan, even for many Japanese who had never seen it with their own eyes. Such was the awe of Mt Fuji's beauty that villagers and townsfolk throughout Japan began creating their own local version of Fuji to worship, admire and be proud of. Today, there are at least 30 well-known mountains the length of the country called 'something-or-other Fuji', often attached to the old nameheld by the province before the new prefectural names were adopted in the early 1870s. Hokkaidō's spectacular Yōtei-zan, a huge drawcard for the alpine resort of Niseko, is known as Ezo-Fuji; Kaimon-dake in Kagoshima Prefecture is Satsuma-Fuji; Iino-yama in Kagawa Prefecture is Sanuki-Fuji – and so on.

ABOVE Noboribetsu jigokudani (hell valley) on Hokkaidō is created by the thermal activity of Hiyori-yama.

TOP RIGHT Japanese macaques warm up in the hot springs at Nagano City.

BOTTOM RIGHT Ibusuki Onsen in the south of Kagoshima is famed for its sunamushi (hot-sand spas).

circumference of more than 100km (62 miles) and the active Naka-dake crater at its centre.

In southern Kyūshū, Sakurajima is an incredible sight. Sitting out in Kagoshima Bay, it's Japan's most active volcano, smoking almost constantly and having minor eruptions regularly. It also sits just a few kilometres from what feels like the very precarious city of Kagoshima, where daily weather reports include an 'ash forecast' predicting the amount of ash billowing up from Sakurajima, as well as wind directions; if easterlies are forecast, washing isn't hung outside and local people take umbrellas to work to fend off falling ash. The *kanji* for Sakurajima mean 'Cherry Island' – and an island it was, until 1914, when a massive eruption spewed enough lava to connect it to the mainland on the eastern side of Kagoshima Bay.

VOLCANIC LANDSCAPES

Along with volcanic areas come *jigokudani* (hell valleys): barren, brown areas of steam vents, bubbling hot springs, mud pools and sulphurous streams. Many are popular with visitors (local authorities rope off dangerous spots) – there are spectacular *jigokudani* at Noboribetsu Onsen in Hokkaidō, and at Murodō, the highest point of the Tateyama–Kurobe Alpine Route in the Northern

Alps. And Jigokudani Monkey Park in Nagano Prefecture is known for its 'snow monkeys', Japanese macaques that come to bathe in the hot-spring waters.

At Iō-zan (Sulphur Mountain) in Hokkaidō's Akan Mashū National Park, it's possible to walk right up to smoking, yellow sulphurous vents and eat eggs cooked in the boiling water. In southern Kagoshima Prefecture, you can take a 'sand bath' on the geothermally heated beach at Ibusuki City, while offshore to the south, Yakushima's Hirauchi Kaichū Onsen is a hot spring in the sea: it's only possible to bathe two hours either side of low tide, as the rest of the time it's covered by the ocean. Mizunashi Kaihin Onsen, east of Hakodate in Hokkaidō, is a similar spot.

1 MT FUJI

This symmetrical cone is the highest mountain in the country and a symbol of Japan.

2 SAKURAJIMA

Japan's most active volcano sits just a few kilometres east of the populous city of Kagoshima.

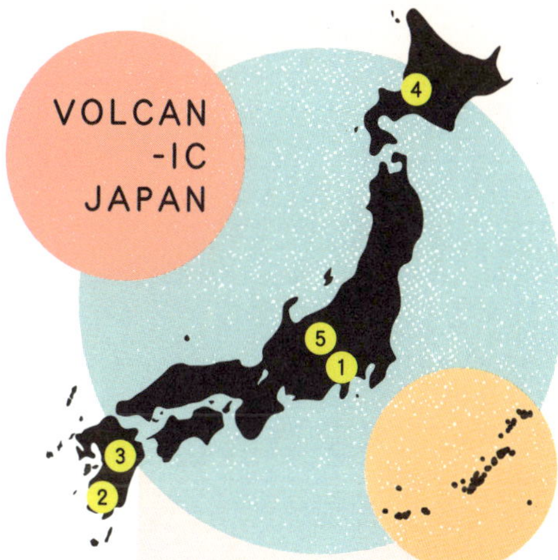

3 ASO-SAN

With a diameter of some 25km (16 miles), Aso has one of the largest calderas on Earth.

4 YŌTEI-ZAN

Hokkaidō's spectacular Mt Fuji lookalike, near the alpine resort of Niseko, is known as Ezo-Fuji.

5 JIGOKUDANI MONKEY PARK

Home of the 'snow monkeys', Japanese macaques that bathe in the natural hot springs.

Coasts

ABOVE Fuji from the Miho Peninsula.

TOP RIGHT Yurigahama Beach off Yoronjima in Kagoshima.

BOTTOM A tsunami drill at Hiyoriyama in Ishinomaki, Miyagi Prefecture, in 2025.

Comprised of its four main islands alongside some 14,000 smaller ones, Japan has the sixth-longest coastline in the world – more than much larger nations such as the USA, China and Australia. With the Pacific Ocean to the east, the Sea of Japan to the west, the East China Sea to the southwest and the Sea of Okhotsk to the north, no point in Japan is further than 150km (93 miles) from the sea.

PROTECTING JAPAN

Anticipating enjoying Japanese aesthetics, beauty and the love of nature, visitors to Japan are often shocked to see the amount of concrete along the country's coasts. Much to the dismay of conservationists (but to the great joy of construction and concrete companies), the government has opened its purse-strings – particularly in the economic boom times of the 1980s – ostensibly to make Japan and its populace 'safer'. Today, it's estimated that about half of the coastline has been altered in some way, mostly with

concrete breakwaters and piles of the ubiquitous tetrapod – a wave-dissipating, interlocking concrete structure with four legs that is stacked up to protect the country's shoreline.

There are two big worries along the coast. The first comes via the typhoons (20–25 annually) that barrel into the region between June and October. They come from the southeast, from warm parts of the western Pacific Ocean, and all Japanese watch weather forecasts for each typhoon's projected level of growing intensity, estimated date of arrival and potential trajectory. Besides pounding the coastline, typhoons cause flooding, landslides and play havoc with flights, trains and ferry timetables. Okinawa is right in typhoon alley, while the southwestern and southern coasts of Kyūshū, Shikoku and Honshū are also regularly in the firing line. Besides large amounts of concrete along the coasts here, road cuttings and rivers have also been heavily concreted to make them 'safe'.

The second concern along the coast is far less predictable. Footage of the tsunami that hit the Pacific coastline of Tōhoku, in northern Honshū, following the 2011 Great East Japan Earthquake is impossible to forget. With a maximum wave height of 40m (131ft), the tsunami caused an estimated 20,000 deaths, and also triggered a meltdown at the Fukushima Daiichi nuclear plant.

ABOVE The floating torii gate of Miyajima.

TOP RIGHT Aharen beach on tropical Tokashiki Island in Okinawa.

BOTTOM The Hotaluna water bus moored at the Odaiba Island marina in Tokyo Bay.

Given there's a 70–80% chance of a magnitude 8–9 earthquake occurring within the next 30 years in the Nankai Trough (to the south of Honshū, Shikoku and Kyūshū), disaster preparedness is omnipresent. Shikoku's Kōchi Prefecture has 126 purpose-built tsunami evacuation towers along its coastline for members of the public who don't have time to reach higher ground in the event of a tsunami. Residents regularly participate in evacuation drills. This is not a question of if, but when; a big tsunami is coming.

CELEBRATED COASTAL VIEWS

In 1643, scholar Hayashi Gahō announced his picks for the Nihon Sankei (the Three Great Views of Japan), and they have been celebrated ever since. All are on the coast and great efforts have been made to protect them.

The three comprise the floating *torii* (shrine gate) at Itsukushima-jinja at Miyajima, not far from Hiroshima city in the Seto Inland Sea; the pine-clad bay of islands of

CREATING NEW COASTLINES

Umetate-chi is the Japanese word for land reclamation, changing the coastline and creating new land from the sea. Japan's main cities, with limited flat land, have constructed a slew of artificial islands. Tokyo Bay has a number of them, the best-known being Odaiba, over the Rainbow Bridge, known for its shopping, dining, entertainment facilities and a replica of the Statue of Liberty. Toyosu holds the relocated Tsukiji Fish Market, which reopened as Toyosu Market in 2018.

Osaka city has a number of *umetate-chi* islands in its port area in Osaka Bay, while Kansai International Airport to the southwest was opened on its own *umetate-chi* island in 1994. Similarly, Chūbu Centrair International Airport has been operating on an artificial island, 35km (22 miles) south of Nagoya city in Ise Bay, since 2005. Kōbe's airport, opened in 2006, is also on a purpose-built island.

Matsushima, near Sendai in Miyagi Prefecture; and the 3.6km-long (2.2-mile) sandbar, Amanohashidate, on the Sea of Japan coast of Kyoto Prefecture, known as the 'Bridge to Heaven'. All are popular destinations for travellers.

Depicting a wave looming over a fishing boat, with Mt Fuji in the background, Hokusai's 1831 woodblock print *The Great Wave off Kanagawa* is equally iconic, and is arguably the most reproduced image in the history of art.

PRISTINE SHORES

Japan does have some relatively untouched beaches, but they're off the beaten track and require effort to reach. In southwest Shikoku, near the cape of Ashizuri-misaki, Ōkinohama (also known as Ōki Beach) is a 2km-long (1.3-mile) stunner, popular with surfers, clam divers and egg-laying sea turtles. In the Amami Islands southwest of Kyūshū, Yoron Island has magnificent white-sand beaches, a huge array of turquoise hues within the surrounding reef and the 'phantom beach' of Yurigahama, a sandy islet only visible off the east coast at low tide.

Known as one of the most beautiful of Okinawa's islands, Kume-jima, some 90km (56 miles) west of the main island, features spectacular Hatenohama, a 7km-long (4.3-mile) sandbar in the sea that can be accessed on day trips.

Islands

ABOVE Iturup is one of the southern islands of the Kuril chain.

TOP RIGHT The waterbound district of Dotonbori in Osaka, Honshū.

BOTTOM RIGHT The northern island of Hokkaidō is the heartland of Japan's Ainu people.

To the Japanese, their homeland is a *shimaguni* (island country), very distinct and different from the other main players in Northeast Asia – China, Russia, Korea and North Korea. Japan is proud of its *shimaguni-konjō* (island mentality), often thought of as guts, grit and determination (and also, possibly, stubbornness). With no land borders and a population that is 97% ethnically Japanese, Japan is made up of over 14,000 islands, 430 of which are inhabited. From around 20,000 to 10,000 years ago, however, when sea levels were lower, Japan was connected to the Asian continent via land bridges to the Korean peninsula in the west and via Sakhalin and the Kuril Islands in the north. These allowed both humans and animals to cross and populate what is now the Japanese archipelago. As the glacial period ended and sea levels rose, the land bridges submerged, isolating Japan and its four main islands.

HONSHŪ (本州)

By far Japan's largest island, Honshū covers 60% of the country's total land area and is home to the biggest cities and some 80% of Japan's population. The Kantō region (関東地方) around Tokyo has a population of around 45 million, while the Kansai region (関西地方) around Osaka and Kyoto numbers some 25 million – combined, these

two great metropolises are home to well over half the country's (declining) population of 124 million.

Honshū is long and narrow, with mountainous spine that separates the Sea of Japan coast – known for its harsh climate and heavy winter snowfalls – from the Pacific coast, where milder conditions prevail.

HOKKAIDŌ (北海道)

Japan's big northern island only officially became part of the country in 1869, when the Meiji government recognised its strategic importance and colonised it to counter Russian regional expansion. The colonisation of Hokkaidō was then promoted, and this included forced assimilation of the island's Ainu people, who came close to losing their language, religion and customs; they were only legally recognised as an Indigenous people of Japan in 2019.

While Hokkaidō covers over 20% of Japan's land area, it has only 5% of its population and is still viewed by many as an undeveloped 'land of opportunity'.

1 HONSHŪ (本州)
The largest island, with 60% of Japan's land area and 80% of its population.

2 HOKKAIDŌ (北海道)
Became part of Japan in 1869, with 20% of the land area and 5% of the population.

3 KYŪSHŪ (九州)
Third-largest island, with 10% of Japan's land area and 10% of its population.

4 SHIKOKU (四国)
The fourth-largest island, with 5% of the land area and 3% of the population.

5 OKINAWA (沖縄)
This long string of islands was annexed by Japan in 1879.

ABOVE An Okinawan holding a shisa or lion-dog statue.

CENTRE An active volcano steams on Kyūshū Island.

TOP RIGHT Ōkuboji marks the end of Shikoku's 88 Temple Pilgrimage trail.

BOTTOM Aniva Lighthouse was built by the Japanese off Sakhalin Island.

KYŪSHŪ (九州)

Known for its semi-tropical climate, active volcanoes and onsen (hot springs), the country's third-largest island covers 10% of its land area and holds some 10% of its population. During Japan's period of *sakoku* – from 1633 to 1854, when the Tokugawa shogunate isolated Japan from foreign influence and Christianity – Dejima in Nagasaki, northwest Kyūshū, was the only port in Japan open for international trade, mainly with the Dutch and Chinese.

Kyūshū is frequently in the firing line for the 20–25 typhoons that approach Japan from the southeast each year, between June and October.

SHIKOKU (四国)

Fourth in size is the island of Shikoku, making up 5% of Japan's land area and hosting around 3% of the population. It's known for the 88 Sacred Temples of Shikoku pilgrimage – the route by which Buddhist saint Kōbō Daishi achieved enlightenment; pilgrims have been following in his footsteps for some 1200 years.

Through the centuries, Shikoku has been thought of by Japanese as as remote and difficult to reach. However, three bridge systems linking the island to Honshū, which were opened between 1988 and 1998, have brought the island much closer to mainland Japan in the minds of most.

ADDING AND LOSING ISLANDS

Japan's land area has undergone many changes in the last 160 years, including the addition of Hokkaidō in 1869 and the Ryūkyū Islands in 1879. After winning the Russo-Japanese War in 1905, Japan also took control of southern Sakhalin Island – Russia kept the northern part – giving Japan its first land border with another country. The prefecture of Karafuto was established, but Russia took back southern Sakhalin at the end of WWII; around 400,000 Japanese immigrants had to be repatriated.

Still in dispute with Russia are the four southernmost islands in the Kuril chain, between Hokkaidō and the Kamchatka Peninsula, seized by the Soviet Union at the end of WWII. At their closest point, Japan and Russia are a mere 3.7km (2.3 miles) apart here, and the unresolved dispute means that the two countries are technically still at war – they never signed a peace treaty to end WWII.

OKINAWA (沖縄)

The string of islands stretching southwest between Kyūshū and Taiwan is known collectively as the Ryūkyū Islands (琉球列島) or the Nansei Shotō (南西諸島), the 'Southwest Islands'. While northern isles in the arc are part of Kagoshima (Kyūshū's southernmost prefecture), those southwest of Okinawa (the main island) to Yonaguni (which is 110km/70 miles east of Taiwan) make up Okinawa Prefecture.

In 1879, Japan annexed the archipelago, and Okinawa became the country's 47th prefecture. After WWII, however, the US controlled the islands from 1945 until they were returned to Japan in 1971. There are still numerous (and controversial) American bases in Okinawa.

LOCAL PERSPECTIVE

YAKUSHIMA RESIDENT

Noriko Uchimuro

Born in Kōbe, Noriko Uchimuro moved to Yakushima in search of 'a place blessed with sea, mountains, and rivers, where the water and air are delicious.' Now a certified eco-guide, she helps visitors understand the island's bond between people and nature.

What makes life on Yakushima different from the mainland? One of the biggest differences is the strength of community. Village life is punctuated by festivals that connect people to each other and the seasons. In spring, the island celebrates the Mori Mizu Biraki (Mountain and Water Opening), a Shintō ritual welcoming the outdoor activity season and praying to the gods of mountains and rivers for safety and abundance. Summer brings lively festivals, including dragon-boat races and music and dance concerts, where people of all ages participate; autumn features tug-of-war competitions that keep ancient customs alive, even winter brings uniquely Yakushima rites.

Can you explain these winter rituals? On 7 January, the Nanakusa Celebration marks a rite of passage for seven-year-old children. Families dress them in festive clothing, visit neighbours and enjoy a seven-herb rice porridge for health and growth. That same day, the Onibi Fire Ceremony lights large bamboo and wood pyres to drive away evil spirits and pray for safety in the year ahead. Both traditions connect villagers to the community and the natural world.

How do islanders interact with nature in daily life? Children swim in rivers and the sea every summer. Clean water to drink and play in is normal, and from a young age, they feel part of nature.

Yakushima is known for heavy rainfall – how do people live with it? When it rains, it pours. When it doesn't, we miss it. Even when ferries are cancelled for days, we accept it as part of life. Nature sets the rhythm here. The Studio Ghibli film *Princess Mononoke* is said to be inspired by Yakushima.

How do you view sustainability on the island? Walking through these ancient forests inspires a deep connection with nature and a desire to protect it. Sustainability here is about living in harmony with the seasons and respecting our place in the natural world, so every visit can plant a small seed of conservation.

What can Yakushima teach the world? Locals halted large-scale logging in the 1970s to protect the forests. A saying captures island life: 'Ten days in the mountains, ten days at sea, ten days in the village.' It reflects a humble, sustainable life, intimately tied to nature.

Wildlife

ABOVE A wild brown bear prowls the rocky shore of Shiretoko Peninsula, Hokkaidō.

With over 14,000 islands spread over 22 degrees of latitude, Japan's incredible variety of habitats play host to a diverse wealth of wildlife.

KUMA *(bears)*

There are two species of bear found in Japan: the *tsukinowa-guma* (Japanese black bears) that inhabit Honshū and Shikoku, and *higuma* (Ussuri brown bears) of Hokkaidō.

While bears have already been declared extinct on Kyūshū and are critically endangered on Shikoku, black bear numbers are increasing on Honshū, despite habitat destruction and human encroachment. These relatively small *higuma*, a subspecies of the Asian black bear, generally live in mountain and forested areas; they have a body length of to 1.4m (4.6ft) and weigh up to 120kg (265lb).

Weighing up to 400kg (882lb) and with a body length of 2m (6.6ft), Hokkaidō's *higuma* are much bigger and more aggressive, and can be a danger in the case of an unexpected encounter. While *higuma* are found all over the island, World Heritage–listed Shiretoko Peninsula is home to Hokkaidō's largest concentration of them. Japanese hikers carry a *kuma-yoke* (bear repeller) in the form of a bell attached to their backpack, but it is *sansai-tori* (wild-vegetable foragers) who are more likely to have bear

encounters, given they're sharing the bears' food supply.

NIHON-ZARU *(Japanese macaques)*
Known as *Nihon-zaru* (Japanese monkeys), usually shortened to *saru*, the Japanese macaque is the only species of monkey in Japan, living on Honshū, Kyūshū and Shikoku, but not north of the Blakiston Line (p240) in Hokkaidō. As they often inhabit areas that see snowfall in winter, they're also known as 'snow monkeys'; the *saru* bathing in hot springs surrounded by snow at Nagano Prefecture's Jigokudani Monkey Park is an oft-photographed image. Living as far north as the Shimokita Peninsula at the northern tip of Honshū, the Japanese macaque is the furthest-north-living non-human primate on Earth. A subspecies of the *Nihon-zaru*, the *Yaku-zaru* live on the island of Yakushima, off the southern tip of Kyūshū, and are Japan's southernmost population of monkeys.

Monkeys (of a kind) are also found in Nikkō, where the famous Three Wise Monkeys, who 'see no evil, hear no evil and speak no evil', are carved over the door at the grand shrine, Tōshō-gū.

ABOVE Tanuki are misleadingly known in English as Japanese raccoon dogs.

TOP RIGHT A figurine of Tanuki the Tipsy Trickster in a Japanese garden.

TANUKI *(Japanese raccoon dog)*
Often mistranslated as being a badger, the *tanuki* is also known in English as the Japanese raccoon dog, but it isn't

ABOVE A Japanese serow, unique to the country.

RIGHT The city of Nara is famous for its free-roaming roe deer.

a species of raccoon or dog. A type of canid endemic to Japan, *tanuki* are more closely related to foxes than domestic dogs, and are likened to racoons for their grey-brown colouring and face markings.

Tanuki can climb trees using their curved claws, and are mostly nocturnal and reclusive; they're rarely seen in the wild, except as roadkill. But they have a long history in Japanese legend and folklore. Thought of as mischievous tricksters and lovable buffoons, *tanuki* often feature in statues outside bars. Depicted with big bellies and huge testicles, the straw-hat-wearing statues grasp flasks of sake and invite customers in for a good time.

INOSHISHI *(wild boar)*

Japan's ferocious *inoshishi* are found on Honshū, Kyūshū and Shikoku, but not on Hokkaidō. Predominantly inhabiting mountains and forests, *inoshishi* are sometimes found in suburban areas near their home habitats on garbage days, attacking residents' bins.

With *Inoshishi* revered for their fearlessness, people born in the Year of the Boar are similarly believed to be courageous, determined and honest. *Inoshishi* are also associated with good fortune and prosperity, and during the Meiji era, the boar was featured on the ¥10 note. Boar also form the basis of *inoshishi-nabe*, a hotpot cuisine.

KAMOSHIKA *(Japanese serow)*

The *kamoshika* is a serow, a goat-antelope endemic to Japan, known and respected for its speed, strength, agility and sure-footedness on mountain cliffs. It tends to be solitary or live in a small family group and can be seen in the wild in the mountains of Honshū, Kyūshū and Shikoku, most often by hikers. While it was nearly hunted to extinction in the mid-20th century, mainly for its meat, in 1955 the *kamoshika* was protected as a Special National Monument and numbers have grown to the point where it's no longer threatened.

Revered as a 'living treasure of the forest' by local conservationists, the wild *kamoshika* is held in such high esteem that in 1973, when the Chinese government gifted Japan a giant panda, the Japanese responded by sending them two *kamoshika* in return.

1 KUSHIRO SHITSUGEN NATIONAL PARK, HOKKAIDŌ

Japan's largest undeveloped wetland is home to the *tanchō-zuru*, the red-crowned white crane.

2 JIGOKUDANI MONKEY PARK, NAGANO PREFECTURE

The place to photograph 'snow monkeys' bathing in hot springs surrounded by snow.

3 NARA PARK, NARA

Some 1300 deer roam freely here, and are regarded as divine messengers of the Shintō gods.

4 IRIOMOTE ISLAND, OKINAWA PREFECTURE

Iriomote is the only habitat of the endangered *yama-neko* wildcat.

5 KŌNOTORI-NO-SATO PARK, TOYOOKA

Wetland habitat for the Oriental white stork, successfully brought back from near extinction.

KITSUNE *(fox)*

Two subspecies of the red fox are found in Japan, the *kitsune* (Japanese red fox) on Honshū, Kyūshū and Shikoku; and the slightly larger *kita-kitsune* (Ezo red fox) on Hokkaidō. *Kitsune* are highly adaptable and while they generally live in rural and mountain parts, they have increasingly been found in suburban and even urban areas.

Foxes are believed to have supernatural abilities (such as shapeshifting) within the realms of Japanese myth and, as the messengers of Inari – the Shintō *kami* (god) of rice, sake, fertility, prosperity and business – they also feature at the estimated 30,000 Inari Shintō shrines across Japan. Kyoto's Fushimi Inari Taisha is the head Inari shrine, known for its thousands of vermilion *torii* gates – and for its countless fox statues.

SHIKA *(deer)*

While deer are known as *shika* across Japan, there are several subspecies. The *Ezo-jika* of Hokkaidō is the largest, while the *Yaku-jika* of Yakushima off southern Kyūshū is smaller, with short legs. Known for swimming between islands, the *Kerama-jika* of Okinawa's Kerama Islands are Japan's most southerly population of deer, and also the country's smallest.

Famously, around 1300 deer roam freely around Nara Park, where they are regarded as divine messengers of the *kami* (gods) of the grand shrine Kasuga Taisha. Carefully protected here for over 1000 years, deer in the park are said to be descended from an ancient deer species and are designated Natural National Monuments of Japan.

LEFT The Ezo red foxes of Hokkaidō have especially bushy tails.

YAMA-NEKO *(Iriomote cat)*

Found only on Iriomote Island in the remote Yaeyama group of Okinawa Prefecture, the Iriomote *yama-neko*, as it is called in Japanese (it's referred to as *yamamayaa* in the local Yaeyama dialect) is a subspecies of the leopard cat, a small wildcat commonly found on the Asian continent (though it was only established as a separate subspecies in 1965). Recognised as a Natural Monument of Japan in 1972, it is listed as critically endangered today, with a total population estimated at fewer than 250.

Mostly active during the twilight hours, the Iriomote *yama-neko* is about the same size as a domestic cat, but with shorter legs, a longer body, a fatter tail and a longer, narrower skull. Its coat is dusky brown, patterned with rows of dark spots.

KURO-USAGI *(Amami rabbit)*

A member of an ancient species of rabbit that lived on the Asian continent but became extinct there, the Amami rabbit is often called a living fossil. The dark-furred *kuro-usagi*, with their bulky bodies and short hind legs, are found only on the islands of Amami Ōshima and Tokunoshima (between Kyūshū and Okinawa), where an estimated population of between 3000 and 5000 live mainly on Amami Ōshima. Designated as endangered, they are a Special Natural Monument of Japan.

ABOVE Watch out for the endangered Iriomote wild cat.

RIGHT Red-crowned white cranes perform courtship dances in winter on Hokkaidō.

The Amami rabbit's biggest threats have been fast cars, feral dogs and cats, plus the Indian mongoose, which was introduced to Amami Ōshima in 1979 as a means of controlling venomous snakes. Once it was determined how destructive the mongoose had been to the Amami rabbit population, a mongoose eradication program was instigated in 2005; it was declared a success in 2024 – good news for the Amami rabbit.

TANCHŌ-ZURU *(red-crowned white cranes)*

The elegant *tanchō-zuru* is a symbol of luck, loyalty and longevity in Japanese culture; fable accords that it can live for 1000 years, and it features on the tail of every Japan Airlines plane. In the early 20th century, however, the cranes were thought to be extinct due to overhunting and habitat destruction. In 1926, some 20 birds were rediscovered in the marshlands north of Kushiro in Hokkaidō, and following concentrated conservation efforts, they now number around 2000.

Cranes, which stand up to 1.5m (5ft) in height, with a wingspan of up to 2.4m (7.9ft), can be seen year-round, but the best time to spot them is during winter when they gather at feeding spots. There are various viewpoints around the wetlands of Kushiro Shitsugen National Park,

between Kushiro and Akan Mashū National Park. They are a huge draw for nature photographers, especially during winter courtship dances.

ŌWASHI *(Steller's sea eagle)*
Japan's largest bird of prey and one of the most impressive-looking raptors in the world, this huge fish-hunting eagle boasts a wingspan of up to 2.5m (8.2ft). Native to Russia's Kamchatka Peninsula and northern parts around the Sea of Okhotsk, they fly south for the winter to eastern Hokkaidō.

Both *ōwashi* and white-tailed eagles can often be seen perching on drift ice in the Sea of Okhotsk from ice-breaker cruises that depart Abashiri from late January to early April. They're also often spotted hunting for fish at wetlands around the lake of Fūren-ko, near Nemuro.

THE BLAKISTON LINE

An English naturalist who lived in southern Hokkaidō between 1861 and 1884, Thomas Blakiston was the first person to notice that many of the island's native animals are different species to those on the southern side of the Tsugaru Strait, which separates Hokkaidō and Honshū. This is usually attributed to the fact that Hokkaidō once had land bridges with north Asia, while Honshū and southern Japan were connected to the Korean Peninsula. At 20km (12.4 miles) across at its narrowest point, and with extremely deep waters and strong currents, the Tsugaru Strait is a formidable boundary between the two.

Bears found on Honshū are Asiatic black bears, while Hokkaidō's are Ussuri brown bears. Japanese macaques live on Honshū, but not Hokkaidō. Other species found north of what is called the 'Blakiston Line' are Siberian chipmunks, Hokkaidō red squirrels, *Ezo-jika* (Hokkaidō deer), *kita-kitsune* (northern fox), Ezo salamander and Blakiston's fish owl, the largest living species of owl, named after the man himself.

KŌNOTORI *(Oriental white stork)*
Widespread in Japan through the 19th century, the *kōnotori* was on the verge of extinction by the 1920s due to overhunting, deforestation and habitat destruction. The final straw came after WWII via a huge increase in the use of pesticides in agricultural production, especially in rice fields; the *kōnotori* became extinct in the wild in 1971.

Fortunately, the city of Toyooka, in northern Hyōgo Prefecture near the Sea of Japan, had proactively started a captive breeding programme in 1965 to save this magnificent bird. *Kōnotori* were acquired from Russia, and the programme to save, breed and eventually reintroduce them to the wild was successful – some 350 birds now freely fly in local skies. Standing around 1.3m (4.2ft) in height, with a 2m (6.6ft) wingspan, the *kōnotori* is, as in other countries, considered a bearer of happiness. Toyooka has endeavoured to preserve and create an optimal wetland environment, and Kōnotori-no-Sato Park, 10km (6 miles) south of Kinosaki Onsen, is a good place to see them.

TOP RIGHT A Steller's sea eagle delights birdwatchers on Hokkaidō.

BOTTOM RIGHT Habu snakes are preserved in jars of local liquor.

BOTTOM LEFT The Japanese pit viper has potent venom.

ŌSANSHŌ-UO *(Japanese giant salamander)*
Endemic to Japan, the *ōsanshō-uo* is found in fast-flowing mountain rivers and streams in western parts of Honshū, northern Kyūshū and on Shikoku. It is a mammoth salamander, growing to 1.5m (5ft) in length, and is third-largest amphibian on the planet. With a lizard-like appearance, salamanders have slender bodies, blunt snouts, short limbs and a tail. Because it doesn't have gills, the *ōsanshō-uo* needs fast-flowing, cool, clear water where there is plenty of oxygen, which it absorbs through its skin.

Considered a vulnerable species, its main threats are pollution and habitat loss. In folklore, the *ōsanshō-uo* is known as the *hanzaki*, based on the belief that it could survive being cut in half (*'han'* means half, *'zaki'* means cut). Novelist Masuji Ibuse published *Sanshōuo* in 1929, a popular story about a large salamander who lives in a cave, but grows so big that it cannot get out.

SNAKES
Japan has two species of poisonous snake that have become notorious, especially among hikers. The *mamushi* (Japanese pit viper) is found on the four main islands. Rarely reaching over 80cm (31in) in length, it is a beige colour and stocky. Around 10 people per year die from *mamushi* bites, so it's important to seek attention quickly if bitten.

The *habu* (Okinawan pit viper) is found in the southwest islands of Kagoshima and Okinawa Prefectures. It is more slender and longer (up to 2.4m/7.9ft) than the mainland's *mamushi*. While bites must be taken seriously, the *habu* is most likely to be seen in souvenir and alcohol shops with its jaws propped open in a glass jar of the local firewater, *habu-shu*.

National parks and reserves

ABOVE Wild deer populate Yakushima National Park.

While the world's first national park, Yellowstone, was established in the USA in 1872, Japan didn't join the party for another 62 years, designating its first such reserves in 1934. The concept had been discussed in Japan for decades, but it was hard to implement. Unlike in the USA, where large tracts of government-owned land could easily be designated as parks, the areas targeted for protection in Japan had been populated and in private ownership for generations.

Today, the Japanese national park system is based on mixed ownership of the land among private individuals, businesses and local and prefectural governments. National parks here encompass farms, villages, small towns and all sorts of tourism infrastructure. A good example is the hot-springs resort of Jōzankei in Hokkaidō, which is within both the administrative boundaries of the prefectural capital of Sapporo and of Shikotsu-Tōya National Park.

In many cases, it's unclear where Japan's national parks begin and end due to a lack of signage – further complicated by the fact that a number of them are non-contiguous, split up into areas well apart from each other. As tourism has grown in importance to the Japanese economy, however, there has been significant investment in infrastructure, from walkways to visitor centres with extremely knowledgeable

ABOVE The rugged Kamikōchi highlands dominate Chūbu-Sangaku National Park.

and helpful staff. In general, there are no entry fees to Japan's national parks, although charges for specific activities such as climbing Mt Fuji are becoming more common.

Below the 35 national parks (*kokuritsu kōen*; 国立公園), managed by the Ministry of the Environment, are 58 quasi-national parks (*kokutei kōen*; 国定公園), run by the prefectures under supervision of the ministry, plus a network of prefectural parks managed by the local prefectures.

NATIONAL PARKS

Japan's 35 national parks can be found the length and breadth of the country. Northernmost is Rishiri-Rebun-Sarobetsu National Park at the northern tip of Hokkaidō. It includes the offshore islands of Rishiri and Rebun, along with the Sarobetsu Wetlands on mainland Hokkaidō. Conical, volcanic Rishiri is also the northernmost of Japan's famous *Hyakumeizan* (as chosen in mountaineer Kyūya Fukada's 1964 book *On Hundred Mountains of Japan*), and is a prime goal for '100-mountain' hikers who turn up from July to September to tackle its 1721m (5646ft) summit. The southernmost national park is Iriomote-Ishigaki, at the southwestern end of the Okinawan island chain, only some 200km (124 miles) east of Taiwan. Its subtropical

islands are known for their diverse wildlife, coral reefs, mangrove forests and traditional Okinawan culture.

Southwest of Tokyo, Fuji-Hakone-Izu National Park includes Mt Fuji and Hakone in the north, and the Izu Peninsula and Izu Islands to the south. Fuji is at the forefront of efforts to balance environmental needs with the boom in numbers of international tourists. With a climbing season of 1 July to 10 September, daily numbers have been capped at 4000 and climbers must pay a fee.

The high mountains of the northern Japan Alps are in Chūbusangaku National Park, with spectacular bases at Kamikōchi and on the Tateyama–Kurobe Alpine Route, while the more remote South Alps are in Minami Alps National Park.

Established in 1934, and comprising some 3000 Seto Inland Sea islands, Setonaikai National Park is bounded by Honshū, Shikoku and Kyūshū. Itsukushima-jinja, with its floating shrine gate, is at Miyajima near Hiroshima, while Naoshima has become renowned as an 'art island'. The 70km (43-mile) Shimanami Kaidō cycling course connects six islands between Onomichi on Honshū and Imabari on Shikoku.

TOP LEFT The torii gate on the crater-lake of Ashi-no-ko near Hakone.

CENTRE The Shimanami Kaidō cycling route connects the islands of the Seto Inland Sea.

TOP RIGHT Spinner dolphins play off tropical Chichijima, part of Ogasawara National Park.

BOTTOM The forests and ravines of Shiratani Unsui Gorge inspired the acclaimed Studio Ghibli movie Princess Mononoke.

UNESCO-LISTED NATURAL SITES

Japan has five natural World Heritage–listed sites, chosen for their unique ecosystems and biodiversity. The island of Yakushima in Kagoshima Prefecture was inscribed in 1993 for its ancient rainforest and giant *yaku-sugi* (Japanese cedar), some said to be over 1000 years old. Listed the same year,

Shirakami-Sanchi, in Aomori and Akita Prefectures in northern Honshū, claims to be the largest remaining virgin beech forest in East Asia.

Eastern Hokkaidō's spectacular Shiretoko Peninsula was inscribed on UNESCO's World Heritage list in 2005, for its marine life, coastal forests and mountains. Drift ice fills the Sea of Okhotsk here in winter, while the forests are home to the largest population of *higuma* (brown bears) in Japan.

Some 1000km (620 miles) south of Tokyo in the Pacific Ocean, the Ogasawara are a Galápagos-esque archipelago of over 30 subtropical islands, listed in 2011 for their unique flora and fauna. The only way to reach them is by a 24-hour ferry ride from Tokyo.

In 2021, four subtropical islands in the Nansei Shotō (Southwest Islands) were listed as a single World Heritage site. The landscapes of Amami-Ōshima, Tokunoshima, Northern Okinawa and Iriomote Islands include subtropical rainforests and mangroves, while unique and rare species include the Amami rabbit and the Iriomote cat.

1 RISHIRI-REBUN-SAROBETSU NATIONAL PARK

Japan's northernmost national park includes two remote islands.

2 IRIOMOTE-ISHIGAKI NATIONAL PARK

Subtropical islands make up the most southerly of Japan's parks.

3 FUJI-HAKONE-IZU NATIONAL PARK

Mt Fuji is a symbol of Japan, and a focal point of the park.

4 SETONAIKAI NATIONAL PARK

With 3000 islands in the Seto Inland Sea, this extensive park is spectacular.

5 YAKUSHIMA NATIONAL PARK

Both a national park and one of Japan's UNESCO World Heritage–listed natural sites.

Japanese gardens

TOP RIGHT The temple complex of Daitoku-ji in Kyoto has Zen gardens.

RIGHT A tsukubai (stone basin) offset by autumn colour in a Kyoto Zen garden.

The term 'garden' can be applied to a plot of land where plants are grown or, more generally, to a pleasantly ornamental space, usually featuring plants. In Japan, these two have traditionally been differentiated – and in the latter, the focus is on the creation of a landscape rather than the cultivation of plants (although plants are still important).

Reflecting Japanese perceptions of the country's native landscape, where mountains sweep down into the sea and rugged islands dot the coastline, many formal gardens here feature ponds and lakes, usually as a means of representing the sea. These frequently have islands (though the 'islands' may be merely a cluster of rocks or just one large stone), and are usually irregularly shaped, with jutting outcrops, spits of land, coves and inlets that reflect the varied, sinuous shoreline of this volcanic archipelago. This relationship between gardens and the sea was so important that, during the 7th century, Japan's landscape gardens were referred to as *shima* (islands).

MOUNTAINS AND STONES

Mountains are represented by clusters of boulders, or by hillocks and mounds that have been constructed in the garden for that purpose – although many famous ancient

gardens do have natural mountain scenery as a backdrop. Fortunately, the construction of a mountain feature in a Japanese garden does not necessarily require building an actual peak. Often the representation of a panoramic mountain scene offers a sufficient suggestion of this landscape in a relatively small space. The strategic placement of objects (often stones) of differing sizes in relation to each other is designed to play with perspective, creating the illusion of a very large thing – a mountain – that is very far away.

The aesthetic appreciation of the texture and natural shapes of stones and rocks is something the Japanese share with the Chinese. However as the geology (and thus the landscapes) of the two countries is so vastly different, the types of stone found and prized in each also differs. The Chinese are drawn to the fantastical shapes, wrinkled surfaces and perforations hewn out of porous limestone by the action of water. The Japanese favour boulders, mostly igneous or metamorphic, with sharp edges worn smooth by the current of a river or gradually weathered on a mountain slope. The Chinese stack their boulders high, whereas the Japanese bury them in the ground, sometimes so deeply that only a fraction of a boulder is exposed.

In Japanese gardens, boulders are frequently used to fashion a 'waterfall' down the slope of a hillock, in order to represent a mountain waterfall or a series of cascades. It is also important that real ponds in gardens should look as though there is a natural flow-through of water – even if a pump is actually doing the job of keeping the pond fresh. And if there is no running water, a dry stream-bed or an artificial waterfall feature – such as that in the gardens of the Adachi Museum of Art – can create the illusion of a lush water-fed mountainside – an effect achieved through the strategic placing of waterside plants.

LEFT An artificial waterfall in the gardens of Adachi Museum of Art in Shimane Prefecture.

RIGHT A mini Mt Fuji in Suizenji Jojuen Garden near Kumamoto Castle.

DRY-LANDSCAPE GARDENS

During the 14th and 15th centuries, the Japanese began to focus on the creation of landscape gardens that didn't feature any real water at all, with stones alone used to represent vast mountain ranges. Gardens of this type began to be constructed in Kyoto utilising small plots of land adjacent to buildings, such as within Zen Buddhist temple complexes. Not much is known about these gardens, as a civil war that broke out in the imperial capital in 1467 destroyed the city's major temples and aristocratic palaces. There are, however, some surviving 16th-century examples of the style, in which bodies of water – a

river, or even the sea – are symbolised by way of fine granite gravel that is artfully raked to represent currents of water.

This style of landscape garden is commonly referred to in the West as the 'Zen garden', because so many examples can be seen at Zen Buddhist temples. In Japan, however, it is known as *kare-sansui*, 'dry-landscape garden', with no reference to a specific religion or its related imagery. Thus, there was – and is – no inappropriateness in the style being used for secular domestic gardens.

GARDEN MOTIFS

Religious imagery does appear in many traditional Japanese landscape gardens, and is not restricted just to those in the

1 CHIRAN SAMURAI RESIDENCE, MINAMIKYŪSHŪ
Landscape gardens dating to the 18th and 19th centuries.

2 JŌEI-JI, YAMAGUCHI
A 16th-century temple garden with dry-landscape and pond gardens, and a seven-tier dry waterfall.

3 TŌFUKU-JI, KYOTO
Dry-landscape gardens begun by eminent 20th-century garden designer Mirei Shigemori.

4 KIYOSUMI TEIEN, TOKYO
Large landscape garden established in 1878 by the founder of Mitsubishi and featuring fine stones from around Japan.

5 GENKYŪ-EN, HIKONE
Spectacular 17th-century garden backdropped by Hikone-jō.

dry-landscape style. One of the most frequently seen motifs is a group of three stones, with the largest in the centre. This symbolises Buddha flanked on either side by an attendant Bodhisattva, but can simultaneously represent a waterfall. Daoist symbols also remain very popular today, particular the crane and the sea turtle, both representing happy longevity (cranes were said to live for 1000 years, sea turtles for 10,000). In the garden, cranes are symbolised by a triangular wing-shaped stone or a long rectangular one, signifying the birds' outstretched neck in flight. The turtle is frequently a low oval mound with an oblique stone at one end representing its raised head, and another stone at the other end representing its tail. It may have further stones to outline its carapace or to indicate its flippers, and it often has a pine tree growing on its back (pines being another symbol of longevity and endurance).

TEA GARDENS

Japanese tea gardens also usually represent a landscape. The very rustic style of tea ceremony developed in Japan during the 16th century involved having a small garden designed to suggest a path through a mountain forest (implied by the selection of trees and shrubs) which lead to a humble cottage (the tea-ceremony room) that symbolised the simple hut of a reclusive ascetic. Stone lanterns were introduced to these gardens to provide illumination, as were stone basins (*tsukubai*) at which guests could draw water to rinse their hands and mouths, so purifying themselves of worldly concerns before the start of the tea ceremony.

The idea of such tea gardens was that guests should put aside their day-to-day concerns as they proceeded along the path. Flowering plants were generally avoided, as they were thought to be distracting.

GARDENS THROUGH THE SEASONS

This emphasis on greenery, along with stone lanterns and water basins, was also adopted in domestic gardens where, rather than a plethora of blooms, the changing seasons are announced by a shrub or two – say a camellia and azaleas in the springtime, or a crepe myrtle tree in the summer. Even the number of deciduous trees producing wonderful autumn colour tends to be restrained in traditional domestic gardens. An enkianthus shrub with flaming orange leaves or a fiery-red winged spindle can serve as a foil for pruned conifers and broadleaf evergreens.

But whether located outside a private home, a temple or a teahouse, Japanese gardens are designed to shine year-round. Plants die down or lose their leaves, but that is a reflection of the cycle of the seasons. Through it all, the image of a natural landscape – a slice of the natural world – endures, holding the whole concept of a garden together through the passage of time.

LEFT A tea ceremony house and garden at the temple of Nanzen-ji, Kyoto.

LOCAL PERSPECTIVE  GARDEN JOURNALIST

Shinobu Sawada

Shinobu Sawada is editor-in-chief of Niwa, Japan's leading garden magazine. Having studied Japanese gardens and environmental design at Kyoto University of the Arts, she brings insights into historical and modern Japanese gardens.

How have Japanese gardens evolved, and what cultural ideas influence their design? We Japanese have cultivated gardens for over 1000 years, adapting styles to the social conditions of each era. At their core, gardens reflect a sense of nature worship rooted in Shintō, connecting people to the spiritual and natural world.

What meanings do elements like stones, water and bridges hold? Stones, water and plants are used through *mitate*, or symbolic representation. A small rock arrangement might represent a famous mountain or an island at sea – the garden invites the viewer to complete the scene mentally. Bridges often carry spiritual symbolism. Pure Land gardens, such as Mōtsū-ji (Iwate), Eihō-ji (Gifu) and Shōmyō-ji (Yokohama), are designed to evoke the Buddhist paradise, with ponds representing the ocean or river separating the human world from the Pure Land, and bridges providing a symbolic passage between them.

What classical principles guide gardeners today? Texts like the 12th-century *Sakuteiki* (Records of Garden Making), considered the oldest gardening manual in the world, and the Edo-period *Tsukiyama Teizōden* (Illustrated Traditions of Hill and Pond Garden Construction) codify how to arrange hills, ponds, islands and stones. *Tsukiyama Teizōden*, a woodblock-printed manual aimed at gardeners and builders rather than elites, made traditional garden knowledge accessible. These works shaped the aesthetic principles that continue to define Japanese gardens today.

How does seasonality shape gardens? Seasonal changes guide design and maintenance. In snowy regions, gardeners use *yukitsuri* (conical ropes supporting pine branches) and wrap tree trunks with straw mats to help control pests. Seasonal events – from cherry blossom to firefly-viewing – influence layout. Gardens such as Kyoto's Katsura Imperial Villa are designed so these spectacles are experienced in harmony with architecture and landscape.

Any advice for visitors? Japanese gardens are best appreciated with some knowledge of history and culture. Guided tours can help visitors notice that stones, wells, lanterns and pathways are not merely decorative – they are objects of contemplation. Gardens are spaces for quiet reflection as well as aesthetic enjoyment.

Mountains

ABOVE Hiking the Tateyama-Kurobe Alpine Route.

TOP RIGHT Trekkers take in the view from Kitadake in Minami Alps National Park on national Mountain Day (11 August).

RIGHT Japanese pilgrims ascending Mt Fuji in 1904.

If Japanese culture has been influenced by its isolation, it has equally been shaped by its topography, with mountains accounting for some 75% of the country. Japan sits at the complicated and turbulent intersection of four major tectonic plates. The Pacific Plate subducts beneath the North American Plate along the Japan Trench, while the Philippine Plate subducts beneath the Eurasian Plate along the Nankai Trough. Plate movement is frequent, though unpredictable, and mountainous Japan is constantly trying to prepare for the unexpected in terms of natural disasters.

ALPINE HISTORY

Drawing on nature worship in Japan's native Shintō religion, and on the pursuit of enlightenment in Buddhism (which was introduced to Japan in the 6th century), the syncretic religion of Shugendō came to the fore in the 8th century. It was based on the idea of its followers, *yamabushi* (mountain priests), attaining magical powers

by following harsh ascetic practices in the remote mountains. Legends grew, with stories such as those of *yamabushi* walking on fire, pouring boiling water over themselves or climbing ladders of swords.

During the Edo era, when the country was run by the Tokugawa shogunate and isolated from the rest of the world, some 95% of the Japanese population were peasants, whose lives consisted of eking out a living, producing food and paying taxes. Most were farmers or fishers, and had no reason to go to the mountains – which were viewed as uninviting and inhospitable and still the realm of the mystical holy men.

With the Meiji Restoration of 1868, many foreigners came to Japan to aid in the modernisation of the country. Englishman William Gowland is among those credited with naming the Japanese Alps in the 1880s, when comparing them to the European Alps; another Englishman, Walter Weston, is considered the 'Father of Japanese Alpinism'. Weston climbed many peaks here and spurred an interest within Japan in hiking and climbing as an outdoor pursuit and a source of enjoyment. In 1896 he published *Mountaineering and Exploration in the Japanese Alps*, which described his adventures and introduced Japan's mountains to the world.

ABOVE Trekkers and tourists must book a slot to tackle Mt Fuji.

CENTRE A yamabushi splashes water on the bonfire at the Takao-san fire-walking festival.

RIGHT The summit of Ishizuchi-san, Shikoku's highest peak.

Interest in the mountains and outdoor pursuits grew, especially once railway expansion made the hinterland more accessible from the early 1900s. Following WWII, when Japan was rebuilding, few had the means for leisure activities, but by the 1970s, with Japan's economy growing and an increase in private car ownership, the mountains became a potential destination for nearly everyone. The 1980s and 1990s brought an outdoor boom, which saw Japanese not only clambering all over their own mountains, but travelling the world to hike and climb overseas.

Today, Japanese mountains are popular with everyone, not just the locals. The tourism boom of the 2020s has seen keen hikers from all over the world experiencing the high life here. While many foreign hikers are fixated on Mt Fuji, other Japanese peaks present an opportunity to get behind that *tatemae*, the public face that Japan shows the outsider. To glimpse the *honne* – the private face that few foreigners are privileged to see – watch the sun rise on a summit with

30 others, share a beer in a mountain hut or soak naked in an onsen after the hike with Japanese you met on the track.

THE 'BIG MOUNTAINS' OF CHŪBU

Cutting through the middle of Chūbu (central Honshū), at right angles to the coasts, is the Itoigawa-Shizuoka Tectonic Line; this has produced Japan's highest mountains, linking the Sea of Japan and the Pacific Ocean. These include the peaks of the North, Central and South Alps, all 21 of Japan's 3000m-plus (9842ft) peaks, and the country's highest three volcanoes in the form of Fuji, Ontake and Norikura-dake.

The Chūbu region is also home to Japan's three great spiritual mountains – Tateyama, Hakusan and Fuji – as well as half of Japan's '100 Famous Mountains' and an array of hiking tracks, mountain huts, camping areas and hot springs that make it the country's most popular hiking region. While Mt Fuji is a great climb (limited to 4000 people per day from July to September), climbers don't get great views of this iconic volcano while they're ascending it. Seasoned Japanese hikers have the North Alps at the top of their bucket list – in particular the three Tateyama peaks, accessed by the spectacular Tateyama Kurobe Alpine Route; and the peaks above secluded Kamikōchi, the trailhead for climbing Hotaka and Yarigatake.

100 FAMOUS MOUNTAINS

In 1964, noted alpinist and author Fukada Kyūya released his book *Hyakumeizan*, in which he chose his '100 Famous Mountains of Japan' – selected for their height, history, shape and character. Hoping to encourage Japanese outdoor enthusiasts to discover more of their homeland, it was his wish that Japanese hikers would choose their own 100 and set out to climb them in their lifetime. It didn't quite work out that way. Kyūya's 100 are the accepted 100, and they stretch from the island of Yakushima (off the southern tip of Kyūshū) to Rishiri-tō, a remote isle off the northern tip of Hokkaidō. There are now lists that pick out Japan's 200 and even 300 'Famous Mountains', as well as selecting 100 Famous Flower Mountains. But the peaks selected in *Hyakumeizan* remain the top of the lot, and summiting them all is a target for many Japanese hikers – whether it takes them five years or 30.

LOCAL PERSPECTIVE  FUJI MUSEUM DIRECTOR

Nobuko Inaba

Nobuko Inaba is the director of the Mt Fuji World Heritage Centre, Shizuoka, a museum to mark Mt Fuji's designation as a UNESCO World Cultural Heritage Site. It explores the volcano's geological, artistic and spiritual significance.

Mt Fuji has been revered for centuries and is often described as a sacred mountain. Why does it hold such deep spiritual importance in Japan? Mt Fuji has long inspired both awe and reverence. For ancient people, its eruptions symbolised nature's power – something to be feared yet respected. When the volcano quietened, it became a place of ascetic training for *shugenja* [*yamabushi*], mountain monks who practiced rigorous physical and spiritual discipline, and later a destination for pilgrimages by ordinary people. Even today, its elegant, solitary form evokes a spiritual connection. It embodies harmony between people and nature – a relationship at the heart of Japanese belief.

What led to Mt Fuji's designation as a UNESCO World Cultural Heritage Site in 2013? While Fuji is a natural wonder, UNESCO recognised it for its cultural value – the centuries-long interaction between people and the mountain. Shrines, pilgrim routes and artworks all testify to this shared human history shaped by nature. The designation reflects the wisdom of living alongside, not akjlOpart from, the natural world – an idea that's vital for a sustainable future.

Artists and writers have long been captivated by Mt Fuji. What makes it so creatively inspiring? Its perfect symmetry, visible from afar, exerts a magnetic pull. Artists across generations have sought to capture it. Katsushika Hokusai's [*ukiyo-e* series] *Thirty-Six Views of Mount Fuji*, especially 'The Great Wave off Kanagawa', made Fuji an icon worldwide. Its image continues to inspire modern art, design and photography – it is a timeless muse.

For visitors today, what are meaningful ways to experience the spirit of Mt Fuji? Climbing can be rewarding, but it is crowded. I recommend exploring the shrines at the base, walking historic pilgrimage trails or visiting our centre's observation deck – all allow reflection on the mountain's beauty and meaning.

What do you hope visitors will take away from their encounter with Mt Fuji? That Fuji is more than a scenic landmark. It reflects how Japanese people have lived with nature – with humility, respect and creativity. Understanding Fuji offers a glimpse into something essential about Japan itself.

Forests

ABOVE Cedar trees line a path at Shiratani Unsui Gorge on Yakushima.

Throw away that image of Japan as simply an urban jungle. With 70% of its land area covered in forest, it is one of the most forested countries in the world – compare that to the 40% in Canada, 35% in the USA and just 13% in the UK. Natural forest accounts for about half of Japan's coverage, including old-growth forest and woodlands that were cut, but then left to naturally regrow. The other half has been planted for logging.

Japan stretches over 22 degrees of latitude, and has an incredibly wide diversity of regions within the East Asian temperate zone. In the south, the islands of Okinawa and the Ogasawara Archipelago fall in the subtropical zone – Okinawa's Yaeyama group, for example, features mangrove forests. In contrast, northern Hokkaidō, in the subarctic zone, has trees such as the Ezo spruce. Japan also has high-altitude alpine zones in the mountains of central Honshū, where pine trees flourish.

PLANTED FORESTS

During and after WWII, Japan suffered a significant period of deforestation due to the need for rebuilding materials and fuel; much of the old-growth forest was decimated. This large-scale deforestation was followed by the mass cultivation of fast-growing

sugi (Japanese cryptomeria, known in English as cedar), and *hinoki* (cypress), tracts of which eventually covered about half of Japan's forested land.

By the time these planted forests were ready for harvesting in the late 1960s, cheap imported timber had flooded the market; there was little profitability in domestic forestry, and many areas that had been planted as lumber forest were left unharvested and unmanaged, creating unforeseen issues. The *sugi* and *hinoki* plantations may have been fast-growing, but these are also shallow-rooted trees and, when planted on steep hillsides, are prone to causing landslides during typhoonal rain, so causing huge scars on the landscape.

1 SHIRAKAMI-SANCHI

This World Heritage-listed region is home to the last virgin beech forests in Japan.

2 KASUGA-YAMA PRIMEVAL FOREST

Hunting and logging has been prohibited in the 'Forest of the Gods' since 841 CE.

3 IRIOMOTE ISLAND

Subtropical jungle including, banyans and mangrove swamps, that are ripe for exploration.

4 YAKUSHIMA

The ancient Japanese cedars here include the Jōmon Sugi, said to be over 2000 years old.

5 ARASHIYAMA BAMBOO GROVE

These soaring stalks of bamboo in western Kyoto are like another world.

Much to the chagrin of many, as the unharvested *sugi* and *hinoki* plantations thickened and aged, they also produced large amounts of pollen – and this has lead to a severe pollen allergy problem (*kafunshō*) which affects some 40% of the Japanese population. The pollen season moves across Japan from south to north from mid-February to mid-April, and the Japanese media tracks the pollen the same way it tracks the cherry blossom. A significant proportion of Japanese wear face masks whenever outside during this period. Hay-fever-suffering tourists should keep this in mind when visiting Japan over this period.

TOP LEFT The aged Jōmon Sugi cedar prompted efforts to protect Yakushima.

TOP RIGHT Japan's largest mangrove swamp is in Iriomote-Ishigaki National Park.

BOTTOM Arashiyama Bamboo Grove of Kyoto's Sagano village was established as a retreat for the nobility.

NATURAL FORESTS

Introduced in Japan in the 1980s, *shinrin-yoku* (aka 'forest bathing'; p96) is based on the idea that time spent in forests has benefits for both mental and physical health, from lowering stress and blood pressure to raising cognitive abilities such as creativity and focus. *Shinrin-yoku* is, of course, likely to be much more enjoyable and beneficial when performed in natural forests than in lumber plantations – and there are plenty of places to choose from.

Behind the grand shrine Kasuga Taisha in Nara, and part of the Historic Monuments of Ancient Nara World Heritage Site, Kasuga-yama Primeval Forest is known for its virtually untouched 'Forest of the Gods'. Hunting and logging have been prohibited here since 841 CE, preserving much of the area's flora and fauna, including a mix of ancient evergreen and deciduous trees.

South of mainland Kyūshū, the UNESCO World Heritage–listed island of Yakushima (90% of which is covered in forest) is known for its spectacular ancient *yaku-sugi* (Japanese cedar trees). The most famous of these is Jōmon Sugi, said to be somewhere between 2000 and 7000 years old.

A trip to Iriomote Island in the Yaeyama group (which lies at the southwestern end of the Okinawan chain of islands) offers the chance to explore dense subtropical jungle, either on foot, by stand-up paddleboard or by kayak. Banyans (and birds) abound here, while the largest untouched mangrove swamps in the country harbour a rich array of marine life.

Shirakami-Sanchi in northern Honshū is home to the last virgin beech forests in Japan, for which the region became one of the country's first World Heritage–listed Natural Sites in 1993. Hiking trails in the mountain range, which straddles the Aomori and Akita prefectural boundary, lead through pristine forests to waterfalls, lakes and mountain peaks.

The Arashiyama Bamboo Grove is one of Kyoto's best-known attractions, and while throngs of visitors may make it less peaceful than anticipated, standing amid these soaring stalks of bamboo is like being in another world. It's quietest in the early mornings and evenings.

AND
TECHN

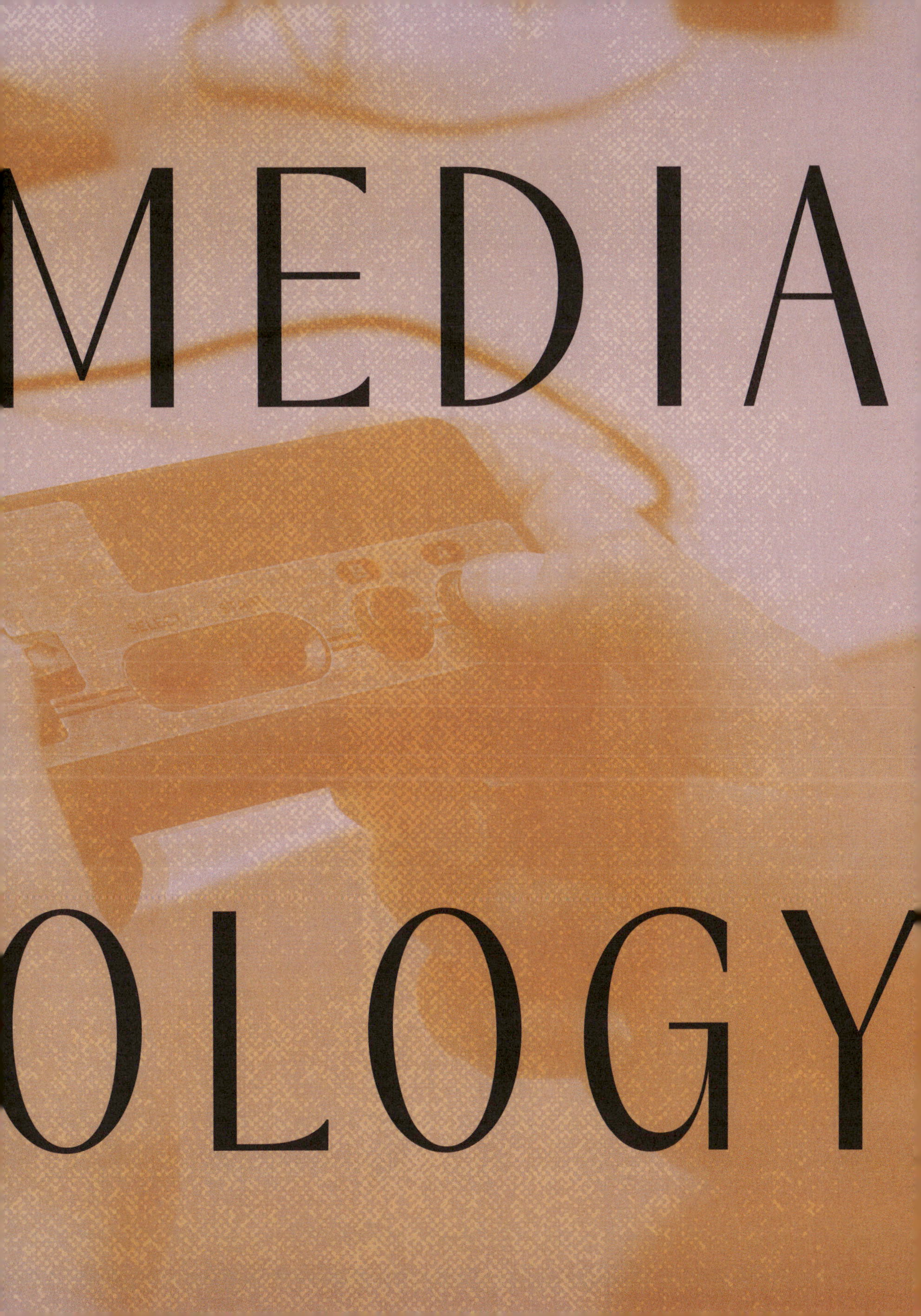
MEDIA
OLOGY

Literature and poetry

ABOVE A woodblock print by Okumura Masanobu of 18th-century courtesans.

RIGHT Text from Sei Shōnagon's The Pillow Book of observations of the Heian court.

Japanese literature traces its beginnings back to the 5th or 6th centuries. Early texts were first written in Classical Chinese and, later on, a hybrid Chinese/Japanese creole. The most significant of these are the *Kojiki* (712) and *Nihonshoki* (720), compilations of oral histories, Japanese myths and folk songs; and the *Man'yōshū* (759), the oldest existing anthology of Japanese *waka* poetry.

Literature, particularly poetry, was central to life in the imperial court during the Heian period, considered a golden age for Japanese art and literature. Poetry was an essential component of aristocratic correspondence and court life, not to mention moon-watching and sake-drinking gatherings. As such, the quality of one's verse was directly connected to one's social standing and rank. Narrative fiction and prose also blossomed during Heian Japan. This era birthed major works such as Murasaki Shikibu's *The Tale of Genji*, often called the world's first novel; and Sei Shōnagon's *The Pillow Book*, a poetic collection of essays and observations that's also valued as a historical document.

The effects of numerous civil wars between the late 12th and 17th centuries were reflected in literature. One of the most representative works of the Kamakura period is *The Tale of*

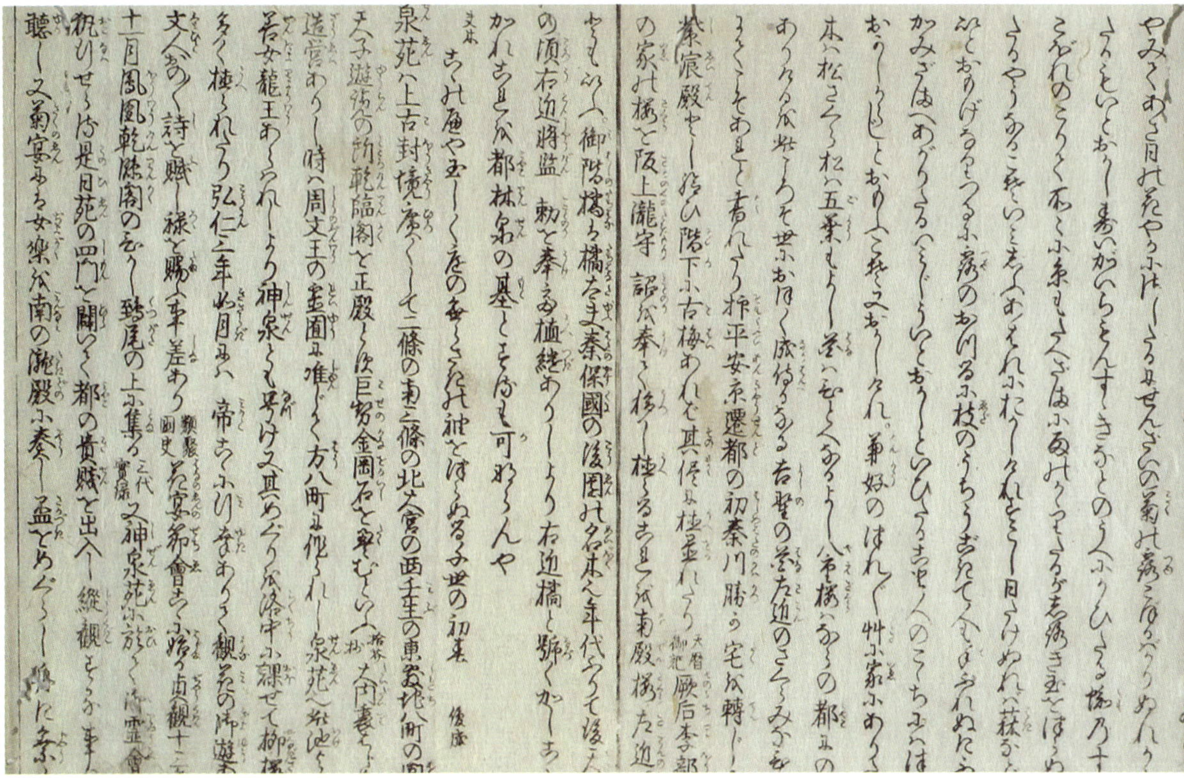

the Heike, an epic account of the five-year Genpei War in which the Taira and Minamoto clans struggled for control of Japan.

During the Muromachi period, aristocratic literature was gradually de-centred from wider Japanese culture as cultural and literary activities spread to all levels of society. Traditional tales took on new life in noh theatre, popularised by 14th-century playwright Zeami. Renga, a type of collaborative poetry involving multiple poets, was elevated to a literary genre in its own right. The opening stanzas to renga are what we know today as haiku, short-form poetry associated with Japan's most well-known poet, Matsuo Bashō.

The Edo period saw Japan achieve the highest literacy rates in the world relative to other nations at the time. All members of the samurai class could read, as could 50-60% of the merchant and peasant classes thanks to temple schools established throughout the country. To satisfy this increasingly literate populace, the publishing industry produced an unprecedented volume of printed materials in a staggering variety of genres – from satirical novels to fortune-telling guides. Booklenders would loan books to readers for a fee, typically around a third of the cost of the product. *Ukiyo-zōshi*, popular fiction that tended toward the racy and

salacious, was particularly sought after – a notable example is Ihara Saikaku's *The Life of an Amorous Man*.

EVOLVING IDENTITIES

With the reopening of Japan to the West, the Meiji period witnessed an influx of new ideas, artistic schools and literary forms – which Japanese writers eagerly absorbed into their work. Written in the first person, popular *shishōsetsu* (aka 'I-novels') shared similarities with autofiction, exploring characters' inner lives in ways that corresponded to the authors' own experiences, and highlighting conflicts between the 'enlightened' new Japan and traditional society.

ABOVE LEFT A depiction of Sei Shōnagon.

ABOVE RIGHT The Japanese author Yukio Mishima.

RIGHT Literary translator Yuki Tejima.

A striking feature of the 1920s and '30s is the coexistence of multiple literary and cultural movements. Jun'ichirō Tanizaki's *Naomi*, focused on a sexually liberated modern woman, illustrates the rapidly changing role of women in 1920s society. The proletarian literary movement produced politically radical novels and anarchist poetry, highlighting the challenges faced by underrepresented classes of people. The concurrent escalation in militarism resulted both in works that glorified war and those that condemned it.

Much of postwar literature grapples with Japan's defeat in WWII, with recurring themes of disaffection, despair and loss of purpose. Notable writers associated with these concerns include the far-right author Yukio Mishima; and Osamu Dazai, whose stories tend to involve anguished, self-destructive protagonists.

A shift happened in the late 1980s and '90s, when several women writers emerged and became visible in Japan's male-dominated literary establishment. Literary scholar Grace Ting comments that 'This partial achievement in gender equality has allowed the literary brilliance of more women to attract attention in Japan and abroad.'

LITERARY TRANSLATORS

As late as the mid-2010s, mainstream knowledge of Japanese literature in the Anglosphere was largely limited to Haruki Murakami, or canonical male writers such as Kenzaburō Ōe and Yasunari Kawabata. Japanese literary translations were usually published by academic presses, with little effort made to market to a wider audience.

This state of affairs shifted in 2017 with the unexpected success of Sayaka Murata's *Convenience Store Woman* (translated by Ginny Tapley Takamori); it opened the floodgates for novels by openly feminist writers like Mieko Kawakami and Aoko Matsuda who showcase a different side of society. 'Women writers in Japan have always had bold, distinctive voices,' says literary translator Yuki Tejima, 'but English readers have been able to see for themselves just how unique these minds are only in the past decade or so.' Looking to the future, Grace Ting anticipates that there will be 'more overtly queer Japanese literature out in English from well-established authors such as Rieko Matsuura and Kaho Nakayama, who have been largely overlooked'.

LANDMARK JAPANESE NOVELS

THE MAKIOKA SISTERS
Jun'ichirō Tanizaki's poignant portrait of a once-great Osakan merchant family.

TOKYO EXPRESS
This is a cerebral, thoroughly riveting murder mystery by Seichō Matsumoto.

THE WIND-UP BIRD CHRONICLE
Haruki Murakami's masterpiece of magical realism.

CONVENIENCE STORE WOMAN
Sayaka Murata's feminist novel is funny and unsettling.

BREASTS AND EGGS
Mieko Kawakami's frank portrait of contemporary Japanese womanhood.

Manga and anime

TOP LEFT The Ghibli Museum opened in 2001 in Mitaka, Tokyo.

RIGHT Manga artist Yumiko Igarashi signs books for her fans.

With captivating protagonists, complex stories and visuals that spark the imagination and provide vivid windows into other worlds, Japanese manga has an abiding appeal both here and around the globe – whether in printed form or when brought to life as anime. And from pop culture to the arts scene, fashion and tech to design, manga and anime have had a profound and enduring influence on Japanese society.

Though some Edo-era art might be said to have manga-like qualities, the term 'manga' (which loosely translates as 'sketches') was popularised in the early 19th century via the *Hokusai Manga*, a collection of woodblock prints by famed *ukiyo-e* artist Hokusai, many of which had a comical tone. The form of manga as it appears today emerged in the 1920s, via serialised cartoon strips in magazines and newspapers. Much like Western comics or graphic novels, there is limited use of text (which usually appears by way of speech bubbles); narratives are not limited to one particular theme, ranging from politics or WWII history to slices of contemporary life. While they might seem to be simple comics for kids, manga series are often sophisticated enough to captivate adult readers.

Popular modern manga falls under *shōjo* (meaning 'young female') and *shōnen* (young male) categories, but though these are pitched to their

respective genders, the titles usually have universal appeal – and that appeal is huge. The *shōnen* series *Dragon Ball* has sold more than 300 million copies worldwide, *One Piece* over 520 million and *Naruto* 250 million. Adult-orientated *gekiga* manga is equally popular, with classic series such as *Golgo 13* selling some 300 million volumes. Manga is both an influence on and a reflection of Japanese social values and norms. For readers of *shōnen* manga, its themes of friendship and camaraderie provide models of friendship, loyalty and human relationships, and the vast array of titles and themes offers a wide pool of aspirational figures.

SHŌJO MANGA

Japan's print media is highly gendered, and manga is no exception – but though the target audience for *shōjo* is girls and young women, it's read by all ages and genders. Series like *Sailor Moon* and *The Rose of Versailles* are beloved for their strong female protagonists, who go against social norms. Manga artist Yumiko Igarashi, whose *Candy Candy* manga features a female nurse, comments that 'During the economic bubble there were many female protagonists who wanted to be professionals.'

The first magazines for girls that featured manga were published in 1903. 'The audience has become very diverse,' says Noriko Inomata, researcher at the Kyoto International Manga Museum. 'Until the 1950s, most readers were elementary school students. Since the 1970s, more manga magazines aimed at older readers have been published, and the average age has gone up. Female university students started reading manga.'

FAR LEFT Manga artist Osamu Tezuka in 1963.

LEFT An early manga from 1926.

RIGHT A scene from the popular Dragon Ball anime series.

FAR RIGHT Tokyo's Nakano Broadway is the place to shop for manga and anime.

Dubbed the 'Godfather of Manga', Osamu Tezuka was one of the genre's most influential artists, whose complex work covered metaphysics and robotics, Buddhism and Shintō, war history and science fiction. Centred on the ramifications of the relationship between humans and technology, his manga reflected the wider themes of postwar philosophy, championing the notions that existence is precious and life in all its forms is to be cherished. Another seminal early artist was Shigeru Mizuki, who used *yōkai* (supernatural beings from Japanese folklore) in manga such as his popular *GeGeGe no Kitarō* series. His postwar-era *Shōwa: a History of Japan* is a strong example of didactic manga that goes beyond children's entertainment.

ANIME

In Japan, the word 'anime' refers to all kinds of animation, whether hand-drawn or computer-animated. While the first piece of Japanese animation – an unattributed 50-second fragment entitled *Katsudō Shashin* – was made in 1907, the contemporary style of anime was established by Osamu Tezuka in the 1960s, and used production techniques borrowed from Disney. During the 1970s, Japan's anime industry expanded alongside that of manga, with popular manga series adapted in cartoon form. The acclaimed 1988 cyberpunk epic

Akira (based on the 1982 manga of the same name) brought anime to an international audience; it utilised the talents of 68 animators, and each of the 172,000 frames were hand-painted. Recent popular anime adaptions include *Dragon Ball* and *Demon Slayer*.

Japan's most celebrated anime director is Hayao Miyazaki of Studio Ghibli, whose sophisticated work – including *My Neighbour Totoro* and *Princess Mononoke* – touches on themes of animism and existentialism. Many of Miyazaki's anime films have Shintō undertones, and his characters' relationship with nature, the environment and the spiritual world is described with complexity and compassion. Captivating audiences globally, despite its esoteric themes, his *Spirited Away* won the Academy Award for best animated feature in 2001.

ANIME TIMELINE

1910s Japan's first anime, *Namakura Gatana* (The Dull Sword), is released in 1917.

1930s Animators begin producing full-length anime, some tinged with political propaganda.

1960s Osamu Tezuka creates *Astro Boy*, Japan's first major anime TV series.

1970s Anime genres such as *mecha* (which feature often-benevolent robots) flourish.

1980s Cyberpunk anime peaks with 1988's *Akira*; series such as *Dragon Ball* define an era of *shōnen* manga adaptations.

1990s Female-orientated anime hit *Sailor Moon* airs; experimental anime such as *Ghost in the Shell* rise in popularity.

2001 Studio Ghibli masterpiece *Spirited Away* becomes the first anime film to be awarded an Oscar.

Kaijū

LEFT A still of Mothra from the 1961 film.

RIGHT A model of Godzilla towers over the Toho Building in Shinjuku, Tokyo.

Kaijū (monster) movies are not inherently Japanese. The 1933 US film King Kong pioneered the genre, but the release of Japanese-made *Godzilla* in 1954 cemented kaijū in Japan's popular consciousness. Translating as 'strange beast', kaijū is used to refer both to the creatures and the movies in which they feature – and the most famous Japanese kaijū is Godzilla.

Synonymous with the genre and the star of 38 films (both Japanese and American), this dinosaur-like reptile was created by director Ishirō Honda and brought to life by special-effects director Eiji Tsuburaya via the 'suitmation' technique – essentially an actor in a monster suit destroying a miniature set. While the results look somewhat absurd by today's CGI standards, they caused a sensation at the time. The *Godzilla* franchise – and kaijū in general – remain perennially popular, with Takashi Yamazaki's 2023 *Godzilla Minus One* grossing over US$115 million worldwide.

Following their success with Godzilla, production house Toho went on to create a huge range of kaijū characters; many starred in their own movies as well as making appearances in Godzilla films, in which monster battles between the characters as they obliterate cityscapes featured heavily. However, the films often had political undertones, too: the original *Godzilla* movie was an analogy for the trauma that followed the atomic bombs dropped on Hiroshima and Nagasaki; pterodactyl-like kaijū Rodan, with its irradiated eggs and nuclear-attack powers, appeared two years after the crew of tuna-fishing boat *Lucky Dragon 5* suffered radiation sickness following the US's 1954 nuclear test at Bikini Atoll.

The evolution of kaijū has also reflected Japan's changing society. Hedorah (sludge monster) was created in the 1970s, when industrial pollution and environmental degradation became a prominent concern in Japan; 2016 film *Shin Godzilla* offers a satirical view of official responses to disasters. Kaijū visuals have come of age, too: the clunky analogue effects of yore are long gone, and *Godzilla Minus One* won an Academy Award for its visual effects. With more Godzilla movies in the pipeline, the kaijū craze shows no sign of waning.

CLASSIC KAIJŪ CHARACTERS

MOTHRA

Highly popular, the Toho-created Mothra is a giant flying insect often depicted as female, and has benevolent qualities.

GAMERA

A fire-breathing flying turtle, Gamera emerged in 1965 as a malevolent force but developed protective qualities in time.

KING GIDORAH

Three-headed dragon King Gidorah first appeared in 1964, and is usually portrayed as the enemy of Godzilla and Mothra.

MEGALON

Insect-like, horn-headed Megalon stands on two feet, can travel at high speeds and deploys explosive powers.

MECHAGODZILLA

A robotic invader created by aliens, 1974's Mechagodzilla came to earth to destroy Godzilla via laser-beam eyes.

Music

ABOVE LEFT Vinyl albums from 1970s Japan.

Japanese culture is predicated on seasonality and sensitivity to nature, and music is no exception. *Hōgaku* is a blanket term for traditional Japanese music that has its roots in any time before or during the Edo period (the last era of traditional Japan). There are many forms, from religious prayers to theatre or court music. One of the most evocative aspects of traditional music – from the primordial beat of *taiko* (drums) to the haunting sounds of the *shakuhachi* (bamboo flute) – is that it can be used to symbolically emulate the sounds of nature, such as the clapping of thunder or the flow of water.

Japanese *min'yō* (folk music) is multifaceted and can be spiritual, ritualistic, didactic or simply an accompaniment to performances, dance and work. *Min'yō* also has distinct regional characteristics. Known for its heart-wrenchingly beautiful ballads, Okinawan folk music is particularly popular and has enjoyed commercial success. 'While the history of Okinawa may not stretch as far back as mainland Japan or China,' says ethnomusicologist Nathanael Ling, '*min'yō* stand as the cornerstone of the Ryūkyū heritage, an irreplaceable testament to their identity.'

In the Nara period, a significant music culture developed based on the importation of Buddhist music from other parts of Asia; Chinese court

music and dance was particularly influential as the government became centralised. *Shōmyō* (Buddhist chanting) and its lively intonations also influenced traditional storytelling.

RYŪKŌKA TO J-POP AND BEYOND

Meiji-period modernisation and Westernisation heralded a new era for Japanese music. During the genesis of Japan's recording industry in the 1920s and 30s, *ryūkōka* (an amalgamation of blues, jazz and classical, fused with Japanese traditional music) emerged and flourished. After WWII, though, the pop industry exploded, albeit with Japanese characteristics. *Ryūkōka* was eclipsed by *enka* (a modern Japanese sound characterised by sentimental and emotional vocals) and by *kayōkyoku*, Western-influenced Japanese pop that was the precursor of today's J-pop.

Commercially viable, catchy J-pop beqan as an emulation of Western girl groups, boy bands and rock acts. Artists paired rock sounds with Japanese melodies and localised Eurobeat-esque dance music to create a distinctly Japanese sound, often with romantic themes. Club culture also blew up during this period. Female J-pop artists often started out as teen idols producing simple, saccharine songs delivered via high-pitched vocals. Female singers such as Ayumi Hamasaki and Hikaru Utada became

ABOVE RIGHT Playing a shakuhachi (bamboo flute) in Kyoto.

ABOVE Yojiro Tatekawa, Yamantaka Eye and Yoshimi P-We of art-noise band Boredoms.

TOP RIGHT Pioneering multi-genre DJ Krush.

BOTTOM Neon-splashed nightlife abounds in Tokyo's Shinjuku district.

icons and were representative of the positive, outgoing era that defined Japan prior to the bubble-economy crash of the early 1990s. Loved for her *kawaii* look and her versatility (having dabbled in house, R&B and ballads), Namie Amuro was one of the greatest idols of the Heisei era, selling over 40 million records during a career that spanned the early '90s to the mid 2010s.

The 1990s also saw subcultures emerge (often via clubs and dive bars) as a counterpoint to mainstream pop. Japan is notorious for importing and re-appropriating aspects of global culture – as evidenced by early attempts at hip-hop, with local artists shamelessly mimicking American rappers while dismissing the less fraught socioeconomic realities of their own backgrounds. This did evolve into something more inherently Japanese, however. 'As the years went on, people started developing a sense of originality, an individuality that only they had', says pioneering Japanese hip-hop artist DJ Krush. 'Not only DJs, but also rappers were rapping in Japanese, and reflecting on things that were actually happening in their own country, not just copying gangs with guns.' Artists like Krush and the late Nujabes used Japanese instrumental elements in their hip-hop, creating fresh sounds and an authentic musical landscape that spoke of their own experiences.

KARAOKE

If there's one musical form that all Japanese people can get behind, it is karaoke. Literally meaning empty (*kara*) and orchestra (*oke*), the national pastime has become a global one as karaoke has spread across the world. The inventor of the karaoke machine is a point of contention: Tokyo engineer Shigeichi Negishi named his 1967 creation Sparko Box, while Daisuke Inoue created the more commercially viable Juke 8 in 1971. Both had a selection of songs that middle-aged salarymen felt an affinity with, and were distributed to bars.

The 1986 introduction of the karaoke box (a private karaoke room) proved immensely popular, and still dominates today; rather than embarrassing oneself in front of strangers, karaoke in Japan is more of a private affair. Chains like Manekineko rent out karaoke boxes by the hour, and it's not unusual for karaoke fans – groups or individuals – to visit weekly for a fix.

Occupying the most extreme end of the music-subculture spectrum is the abrasive underground genre known as 'noise'. Defying all norms of what could be called music, noise incorporates static, distortion and a general mish-mash of harsh sounds. From its epicentre in Kansai, the scene flourished in the '90s, with many noise-specialist labels releasing music and artists performing anarchic live shows in multiple venues. Female noise artist Doddodo explains: 'I sample children's songs, old folk songs, Indigenous music, hip-hop, rock and hardcore – anything goes'. The music's avant-garde and conceptual bent gave noise a type of academic cache – and while Japan's noise scene is niche, akin to a community of friends enjoying improvised chaos, it has picked up unexpected attention abroad; acts like Boredoms, Merzbow and Masonna have performed at international music festivals.

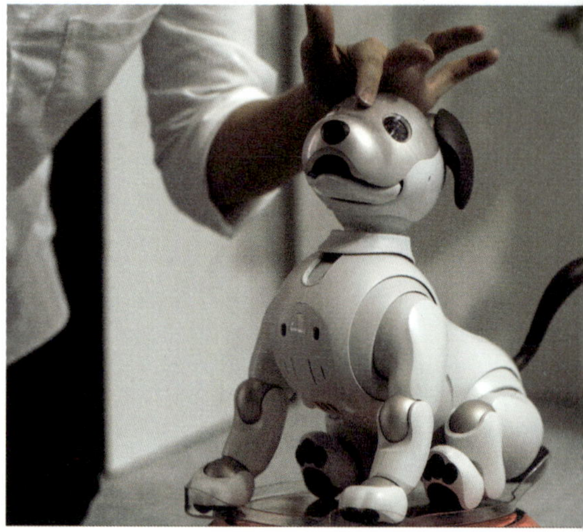

Robotics

LEFT Aibo the robotic dog, designed by Sony.

RIGHT Robot dinosaurs work the reception desks at Henn Na's chain of hotels.

From restaurants to care homes, mechanical helpers are deeply immersed in contemporary Japanese society. But long before modern innovations in robotics reached healthcare and customer services, the country's future scientists and engineers were being deeply influenced by early manga such as *Astro Boy* and *Mazinger Z*. These mechanical dreams cemented the presence of robots within everyday Japanese life, and inspired the work of researchers, designers and entrepreneurs – including Masayoshi Son, whose SoftBank Group released Japan's first mass-produced, commercially available humanoid (ish) robot, Pepper, in 2014.

The precursor to such front-facing robots, however, is Japan's excellence in industrial robotics. Companies such as Fanuc and Yaskawa Electric have long been global leaders in precise automated manufacturing, delivering robots that can assemble cars, electronics and consumer products efficiently. Such technological advances paved the way for robots designed for use outside of the factories, which were a lot more communicative. Launched in 1999, Sony's iconic dog-shaped Aibo became a global hit – a pet robot that could recognise its owner and express feelings by wagging its tail and moving its ears. (Aibo dogs returned in 2018 equipped with cloud-based learning,

which allowed them to develop colourful personalities and coexist with humans in a sophisticated manner.)

In 2000, two humanoid robots made their debut: Honda's Asimo and Sony's Qrio. Despite enthusiastic responses to their futuristic look and smooth movements, their high cost and limited capabilities meant they remained more of a novelty than a practical partner. But Japan's innovation in friendly robots continued. Tomotaka Takahashi and the University of Tokyo launched robot astronaut Kirobo in 2013, while Groove X's penguin-looking Lovot arrived in 2018; devotees can meet and take photos of these mechanical pets at Tokyo's Lovot Museum and Lovot Café. With a fluffy coat and a more affordable price, Casio's Moflin (released in 2024) offers reactive behaviours that some find calming.

EVERYDAY ROBOTS

Amid the heated, highly competitive robotics market, Japan blends cutting-edge technology with fresh perspectives. Friendly robots interact with visitors to Tokyo's National Museum of Emerging Science and Innovation – and bobots are also a part of daily Japanese life. Elmo's cat-faced BellaBot serves dishes and assists human servers in big-city restaurants; KDDI's office-delivery robots help busy professionals make purchases at *konbini* (convenience-store) chain Lawson by ordering on their smartphone and letting the robot fetch the products for them. SoftBank's Pepper welcomes guests at Tokyo's Pepper Parlor cafe, while Henn na is the world's first hotel chain to be staffed by robots. It's also possible to dive into immersive experiences: the robot-fight attraction at RED° Tokyo Tower offers a unique opportunity to wear a robot suit and throw a punch like a character in popular manga *Mazinger Z*.

Tomotaka Takahashi

Founder and CEO of Robo Garage, visiting professor at Osaka Electro-Communication University and founder of Marine X, robotics innovator Tomotaka Takahashi created energy-efficient Evolta robots and Kirobo, the world's first robot astronaut buddy.

Robots have fascinated Japan for decades. *Astro Boy* is famous, but are there other influences? *Doraemon*, *Mazinger Z*, *Gundam* and *Macross* are well known [manga series]. But for many researchers, engineers and hobbyists, the work that inspired them to make robots was *Plastic Model Wrestling Sanshiro*, a 1980s anime about miniature remote-controlled robots battling in elaborate wrestling matches – a concept that sparked many young people's interest in building and controlling their own robots.

Japan has a long tradition of *karakuri* (mechanical dolls). How do they connect to modern robots? European automata are sophisticated, so *karakuri* aren't entirely unique. Still, some surpass them – like the Stepping Doll and Archery Doll. The Archery Doll can pick up an arrow and shoot it, a skill even modern robots struggle with. Its creator, the founder of Toshiba, shows how genius inventors continue to shape daily life – much like Edison with GE.

Humanoid and animal-shaped robots are common in Japan. Why? Humans have extraordinarily delicate sensitivities toward living things – especially toward other humans. This isn't unique to Japan; it's instinctive. For example, very few people could bring themselves to cut off a Barbie doll's head with scissors, even though they know it's just an inexpensive PVC toy. If we apply this sensitivity in design or function, we can create compelling, appealing products. Japanese people of all ages also embrace character culture – unlike in the West, where characters are often seen as for children.

How do you see robots shaping Japanese culture in the coming years? Japan is conservative and slow to adopt new technology, but strong social conformity and high customer loyalty mean that once a technology reaches a certain level of acceptance, it spreads quickly – like the iPhone.

Do you have any personal thoughts or hopes for robots? A global robot boom is underway, but the consumer robot market is only about 50% likely to materialise. AI has made remarkable technical progress, but 'physical AI' – robots – are attracting attention as a vision to sustain investment. Talent, technology and capital are converging, and perhaps one day robots – ideally one of my own creation – will finally become part of daily life.

Inventions

LEFT Shigetaka Kurita, who designed the 176 emojis released by NTT Docomo in 1999.

RIGHT Osaka's Cup Noodles Museum showcases Japan's fast-food global innovation.

Japanese inventions often stem from a strong desire to improve everyday life, and the spirit of innovation has both shaped consumer products at home and set global trends. One of the most ubiquitous contemporary innovations is Toto's Washlet, which redefined Japanese bathroom culture. Back in the 1970s, when Western-style loos began to overtake traditional squat toilets, people covered the cold seat with socks. Toto employees were determined to deliver the perfect warm-seat toilet with a washing feature, and their Washlet is now used in over 80% of Japanese households. As demonstrated by the displays at Fukuoka's Toto Museum, engineers have kept refining the product; recent innovations include a spherical water-jet that maximises cleansing power with minimum water usage.

The world also has Japan to thank for another seemingly everyday product. Amid the tumultuous period after WWII, Momofuku Andō's efforts to give people better access to a hot bowl of ramen resulted in the invention of Chicken

Ramen (precooked instant noodles) in 1958. During a promotional trip to the US, Momofuku saw Americans eating noodles in a mug with a fork – so inspiring him to rethink his ramen. Produced since 1971, Nisshin's Cup Noodles are now available in a myriad of iterations, while Cup Noodles Museums in Yokohama and Osaka showcase Nisshin's history and Ando's visionary thinking.

Japan's contributions to the world of music include Sony's Walkman, which launched in 1979 and revolutionised the listening experience by taking music beyond the home and the car (boomboxes excepted); the first Walkman model, TPS-L2, has become a collector's item. Karaoke (page 281) also has a global reach. Invented in Japan during the 1970s, it has evolved from basic setups in bars to slick karaoke boxes, as well as translating to smartphone apps and Nintendo's handheld Switch.

Perhaps the most pervasive Japanese invention is the emoji. The precise origin of these pictograms remains debatable, but the best-known roots are the set of 176 icons released by Japanese mobile-phone operator NTT Docomo in 1999. The simple 12×12 pixel emojis encouraged phone users to insert colourful pictograms into emails as a way to replace entire words and add nuance; New York's Museum of Modern Art preserves the original set as a milestone in digital communication. Today, there are more than 240,000 emoji available on the Japanese app LINE.

JAPANESE INGENUITY

WASHLET

High-tech toilets that come with warm seats and a washing function.

CUP NOODLES

The mealtime choice of students and the time-poor across the globe are a Japanese invention.

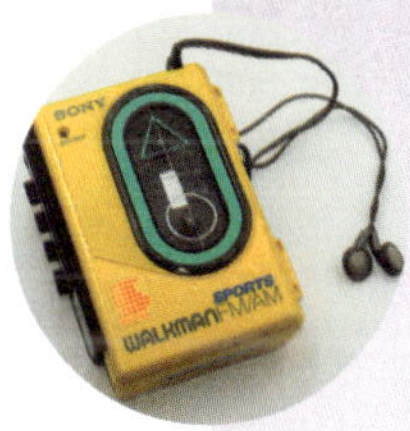

WALKMAN

This iconic pocket device was the world's first portable music player.

KARAOKE

From public singing sessions to today's swish private booths, karaoke is still supremely popular in Japan.

EMOJI

These perky, now all-pervasive pictograms originated in Japan in the late 1990s.

Trains

LEFT A woodblock depiction of the Takanawa Railway in the 19th century.

RIGHT The Tōkaidō Shinkansen speeds past Mt Fuji.

Japan's meticulously built railway network has done much to shape the growth of nation. Around Tokyo, residential and commercial development radiates outwards from the circle of the JR (Japan Railways) Yamanote Line, surrounding the Imperial Palace and the National Diet building at its centre. 'Japan's highly advanced system of interconnected railway lines is rarely found overseas,' says Meiji University's Professor Emeritus Hiroo Ichikawa, 'but this railway network is what has enabled Tokyo's rise as the world's largest metropolitan area.'

THE RISE OF SHINKANSEN

Back in 1872, Japan's first railway line opened between Tokyo and Yokohama, a bay area south of the capital. After this initial revolution in transportation, many other lines followed – including the first line in western Japan, linking Osaka and Kōbe, which opened in 1874. In those early years, steam trains chugged through ports and

small towns, but gradually, as the network expanded in the postwar years, rail became the backbone of Japan's industrial modernisation. In 1987, Japan National Railways was divided and privatised, giving birth to six regional passenger companies and one freight division. This ignited a competition among them and brought high service standards alongside clean, accessible and punctual operations.

In 1964 – just in time for the first Tokyo Olympics – Japan's first bullet-train line, the Tōkaidō Shinkansen, began transporting passengers from Tokyo to Osaka. This 500km (310-mile) journey initially took four hours, but thanks to technological advances, it's now been reduced to a mere 2½. By 2024, when the Tōkaidō line celebrated its 60th anniversary, total passenger numbers had surpassed seven billion – all of whom can enjoy picturesque through-the-window views of Mt Fuji as they speed through the countryside. Similarly, journey time on the San'yō Shinkansen line from Osaka to Hakata in Fukuoka Prefecture has almost halved since the line opened in 1975, shrinking from nearly four hours to just over two. Today, bullet trains run through the mainland of Japan, seamlessly linking east and west, and the network is set to expand further.

TRAIN-SPOTTERS' JAPAN

The Railway Museum in Saitama, just north of Tokyo, showcases the history of Japanese railways, from early steam locomotives to shinkansen simulators. In western Japan, Kyoto Railway Museum houses everything from commuter trains to the first shinkansen, from 1964.

Trainspotters may also appreciate the railway views from Ginza Sky Lounge, on the 15th floor of the Tokyo Kōtsū Kaikan building near Yurakuchō Station, where diners can enjoy French cuisine and the view of shinkansen trains gliding in and out below. Just a one-minute walk from Tokyo Station, the Kitte shopping mall affords close-up views of the station and its trains from an open garden on the 6th floor.

Eating food on trains is generally considered poor etiquette in Japan, but the shinkansen is an exception. Before hopping on board, many travellers pick up *ekiben* (literally 'train station bentō'), which are sold inside main stations such as Tokyo and Shinagawa and sometimes feature dishes representative of regional cuisine.

TOP LEFT Enjoy ekiben aboard the shinkansen.

TOP RIGHT A test run of a shinkansen through Tokyo in 1964.

SLEEPER TRAINS

While business travellers appreciate the shinkansen's lightning speed, some prefer to travel slowly by tucking themselves into a compact bed on an overnight service. The long-cherished sleeper line was the Blue Train, which connected Tokyo to Aomori in the north. Blue Train services ceased operations in 2015, but they're expected to make a comeback in 2027, with more technologically advanced trains (dressed in the original deep-blue livery) running from Tokyo to northern Japan. But there are still two sleeper services operating out of Tokyo: the Sunrise Seto (to Takamatsu in Kagawa Prefecture), and the Sunrise Izumo (to Izumo in Shimane Prefecture).

GO LUXURY AND LOCAL

In recent years, many luxury and unique train lines have opened up, designed to offer travellers greater comfort alongside scenic views.

Operated by JR Kyūshū, the Seven Stars in Kyūshū service is the epitome of luxury with its classic, wood-panelled interiors and exquisite cuisine offered at the restaurant carriages.

In western Japan, the Kintetsu Shimakaze trains travel from Osaka or Kyoto to Ise-Shima in Mie Prefecture. The cafe carriage's seats are all window-facing, designed to make the most of the dazzling ocean views.

Another well-known line, Kyoto's Sagano Romantic Train glides through lush Hozu River Valley, offering stunning mountain panoramas – particularly in autumn when the *momiji* (maple) leaves turn scarlet.

In the northern Noto Peninsula, the Noto Railway's Storytelling Train is staffed by attendants who share their experiences of the devastating 2024 Noto earthquake with passengers. Noto Railway resumed operation of this route just three months after the quake, so as to assist nearby residents' everyday lives – and this heroic effort was commemorated when the Storytelling Train service received the Special Award at the 2025 Japan Railway Awards.

CENTRE The Sunrise Seto sleeper train.

BOTTOM The luxe Seven Stars in Kyūshū service.

Computer games

RIGHT Super Nintendo World at Osaka's Universal Studios Japan theme park.

Japan's place at the epicentre of computer gaming was kickstarted in the late 1970s, when amusement company Taito produced the classic arcade shooting game Space Invaders. Before then, arcade-game machines had been installed randomly, but Space Invaders' popularity led to a rise in dedicated arcade game centres. In 1980, Bandai Namco released the iconic dots-eating game Pac-Man, later described as the Mickey Mouse of the 1980s.

As children's attention gradually shifted from board games to digital games, Nintendo made a significant pivot. Having originally manufactured the traditional card game Hanafuda, Nintendo pioneered the new market for home video games in the 1980s with the Family Computer, aka Famicom. This innovation brought popular arcade-game titles like Donkey Kong into households, but the Famicom was considered a luxury at first; children often gathered after school at the homes of families who owned one to play in turn – so creating the first generation of gamers.

GAMING GOES MAINSTREAM

In 1985, Nintendo released Super Mario Bros, and this masterpiece took the Famicom boom to the next level. Packed with innovative commands and hidden features, it made its designer Shigeru Miyamoto a legendary figure in Japan's gaming history. An inspiration to countless young game designers and programmers, Miyamoto later became the first game creator to receive Japan's Person of Cultural Merit award. But despite producing myriad megahit titles – including Donkey Kong and The Legend of Zelda – Miyamoto labels himself a game editor rather than a creator or designer, as he believes no-one creates something from zero.

Miyamoto's creations have transcended the gaming industry, and are now integral to Japan's wider cultural milieu – just as the gaming scene mirrors broad trends in Japanese culture, technology and the things that people value and cherish. But though trends constantly shift as technology evolves, the beloved retro games that originated here remain alive. Osaka's Universal Studios Japan welcomes game enthusiasts with themed Super Mario and Donkey Kong rides at Nintendo Super World; Nintendo Museum in Kyoto is often fully booked months in advance, with fans flocking in to see its collection

INFLUENTIAL COMPUTER GAMES

SUPER MARIO BROS

Since its 1985 release, this classic has seen millions direct Mario in his quest to rescue Princess Peach.

THE LEGEND OF ZELDA

Fantasy action-adventure series The Legend of Zelda is perennially popular.

DRAGON QUEST

Dragon Quest (aka Dragon Warrior) is the quintessential RPG series, with characters designed by Akira Toriyama.

POKÉMON GO

This multimedia phenomenon sees players capturing, training and trading wild Pokémon.

ANIMAL CROSSING

Animal Crossing's charming life-simulation series has become a massive hit.

of Nintendo products and play old Famicom games as well as experience cutting-edge immersive attractions.

FROM STEALTH-ACTION TO RPG

Hideo Kojima is another game-industry icon. His Metal Gear series established the stealth-action genre, in which players must sneak past enemies. Kojima says movies have shaped 70% of his identity, and he has incorporated cinematic storytelling techniques and dramatic effects into games – as well as heavy themes such as war, life and death.

As young game designers and producers who played Super Mario in their childhood entered the industry, Japanese computer games became more flexible and diverse. When Nintendo launched Game & Watch consoles in 1980, the market wasn't fully ready for handheld gaming gear, but their 1989-released Game Boy cultivated the future demand for portability which is now realised in Nintendo's Switch devices. Sony's PlayStation series also swept the global market, with its original PS2 console going on to sell some 160 million units. Released in 2005 for PlayStation and centred on Japan's gang groups, Sega's RPG (role-playing) game Yakuza was particularly outstanding in terms of depicting Japan's dark side.

RIGHT Japan's original 'Electric Town', Akihabara (aka Akiba) is the hub of games, gadgets and anime.

VIRTUAL PETS AND REAL-WORLD GAMING

For those who grew up playing them, computer games are part of everyday life – so it's no wonder that Pokémon and Tamagotchi (Bandai's mini pet-growing game toy) have proved so successful with adults as well as children and teens – in 1997, Bandai and Tamagotchi creators won the satirical IG Nobel Prize in economics for their success in luring fans to spend millions of hours caring for virtual pets. Nearly three decades after their initial release, both Pokémon and Tamagotchi remain commercially successful thanks to their constant updates. This socialising game genre was especially embraced during the Covid-19 pandemic. Nintendo's 2001 social simulation game Animal Crossing also helped players find solace in the virtual world, with over 48 million copies sold.

While classic Pokémon games are still popular, apps like Pokémon Go have provided a new, blended experience of monster-hunting and exploring the real world. Currently, 28 million active users head outside to catch a Pokémon in the 'wild'; places like Akihabara and another 'Electric Town', Nakano, are popular destinations. Other fans try to find footage of their favourite games in real life. The industrial areas of Kawasaki and Yokohama cities in Kanagawa Prefecture are famous among Final Fantasy fans, who hop on night cruises to take in views of illuminated riverside factories that evoke their (virtual) gaming memories.

HOBBY PARADISE
ボークス秋葉原ホビー天国
買取り
まっくす
アキバ駅前店
Laox
Duty Free
Flagship Store
Laox
Home Electronics Store
オノデン
免税 TAX FREE
冷蔵庫 洗濯機
都内・近郊 送料無料
お見積り無料です
加湿機 カーペット ストーブ エアコン
4F
TAX FREE 免税店 特売中!!
テレビ 冷蔵庫 エアコン 特売中!!
Panasonic
ONODEN
TAKARADA
TAX-FREE 免税商店
歓迎光臨
日本武道館
4th LIVE 開催決定
DISCOUNT COMPUTERS

Index

I

J

K

L

M

N

O

P

R

S

T

U

V

W

Y

Z

Credits

4: Cris Foto/Shutterstock; 6(t): Rintaro Kanemoto for Lonely Planet; 6(m): Kapi Ng/ Shutterstock; 6(b): Lia_t/ Shutterstock; 9(l): Malcolm Fairman/Alamy; 9(r): Album/ Alamy; 10(l): Print Collector/Getty Images; 10(r): Uchida Kuichi / Wikimedia Commons; 11: Mary Griggs Burke Collection, Gift of the Mary and Jackson Burke Foundation, 2015/The Metropolitan Museum of Art; 12: Keystone/Stringer/Getty Images; 13(t): Ezra Shaw/Getty Images; 13(b): The Asahi Shimbun/Getty Images; 14: Jonathan Gregson for Lonely Planet; 16: KPG-Payless/ Shutterstock; 17(l): MMpai/ Shutterstock; 17(r): Klaus Vedfelt/ Getty Images; 18: tagu/ Shutterstock; 19: Markus Mainka/ Shutterstock; 20: Lottie Davies for Lonely Planet; 23(l): Wolfgang Kaehler/Alamy; 23(r): Anadolu/ Getty Images; 24(l): Matt Munro for Lonely Planet; 24(r): Matt Munro for Lonely Planet; 25: Chris Willson/Alamy; 26: Courtesy of Hiromi Isori & Keiko Saito; 29(l): b-hide the scene/ Shutterstock; 29(r): Jonathan Stokes for Lonely Planet; 30: Courtesy of Engakuji Chief Abbot Yokota Nanrei; 32: JGalione/Getty Images; 34(l): Robert Gilhooly/ Alamy; 34(r): Anadolu/Getty Images; 35: Rintaro Kanemoto for Lonely Planet; 36: Courtesy of Tomokiyo Tanaka; 38: Katsushika Hokusai/Amorozov/Wikimedia Commons; 39(t): National Museum of Japanese History / Wikimedia Commons; 39(b): Pump Park Vintage Photography/ Alamy; 40(t): Heritage Images/ Getty Images; 40(b): Heritage Image Partnership Ltd /Alamy; 41(l): Soma Nomaoi Association; 41 (right, from top to bottom): Universal Images Group North America LLC/Alamy; Peter Horree/Alamy; brandstaetter images/Getty Images; Pump Park Vintage Photography/Alamy; KAZUHIRO NOGI/Getty Images; 42: Courtesy of Ayano Uehara; 44: Alla Tsyganova/Shutterstock; 45: thirawatana phaisalratana/ Shutterstock; 46: Courtesy of Kohei and Manami Yamada; 48: Nasu Tourism Association; 49: Bloomberg/Getty Images; 51(t): Niigata City Tourism; 51(b): Sabino Parente/Shutterstock; 52(l): Fletcher Fund, 1929/The Metropolitan Museum of Art; 52(r): davidf/Getty Images; 53: The Asahi Shimbun/Getty Images; 54: DI Palette; 56: BJ Warnick/ Newscom/Alamy; 57: Christian Kober/robertharding/Alamy; 58: IamDoctorEgg/Shutterstock; 59: The Asahi Shimbun/Getty Images; 60(l): Jonathan Stokes for Lonely Planet; 60(r): mapman/ Shutterstock; 61: BJ Warnick/ Newscom/Alamy; 62: J. Henning Buchholz/Shutterstock; 64: Penta Springs Limited/Alamy; 65(t): CPA Media Pte Ltd/Alamy; 65(b): Photo Japan/Alamy; 66(t): Rei Imagine/ Shutterstock; 66(b): leungchopan/ Shutterstock; 67: Courtesy of Otani Sanso ryokan; 68: Courtesy of Kazuhiro Otani; 71: Carl Court/ Getty Images; 73(l): Matt Munro for Lonely Planet; 73(r): Ladanifer/ Shutterstock; 74: Kengo Tarumi; 76: Jonathan Gregson for Lonely Planet; 77: Sanga Park/Getty Images; 78: RDNR/Shutterstock; 79(l): WildSnap/Shutterstock; 79(right, from top to bottom): Adam Loader/Shutterstock; TodorDinchev998 /Shutterstock; WildSnap/Shutterstock; RICHARD A. BROOKS/Getty Images; NurPhoto/Getty Images; 80: Courtesy of Fumihiko Kondo; 83(l): Yagi-Studio/Getty Images; 83(r): The Asahi Shimbun/Getty Images; 84: Courtesy of Susumu Hara; 87(t): Wang Jui-Lin/ Shutterstock; 87(b): Mayumi.K.Photography/ Shutterstock; 88: petesphotography/Getty Images; 89: The Asahi Shimbun/Getty Images; 90(t): Irene M M/ Shutterstock; 90(bl): petesphotography/Getty Images; 90(br): Jacob Wackerhausen/Getty Images; 92: Courtesy of Kenjiro 'Kenny' Ueda; 94: ZUMA Press, Inc./Alamy; 95: Xinhua/Alamy; 96: Iryna Makukha/Shutterstock; 97(l): Matt Munro for Lonely Planet; 97(right, from top to bottom): Brown PS/Shutterstock; west/Getty Images; metamorworks/Shutterstock; topimages/Shutterstock; MMpai/ Shutterstock; 99(l): Matt Munro for Lonely Planet; 99(r): visualspace/Getty Images; 100: The Asahi Shimbun/Getty Images; 101: Ritsu Miyamoto/Shutterstock; 103(tl): Richard Whitcombe/ Shutterstock; 103(tr):Kinstory/ Shutterstock; 103(m): MH0646 / Shutterstock; 103(b): Jonathan Stokes for Lonely Planet; 104(t): The Asahi Shimbun/Getty Images; 104(b): The Asahi Shimbun/Getty Images; 105: Daniel Shirey/ Stringer/Getty Images; 106: Aya Tiffany Sato; 107: Aya Tiffany Sato;109: Matt Munro for Lonely Planet; 111(l): masary78/ Shutterstock; 111(r): yamasan0708/Shutterstock; 112(l): Said Karlsson for Lonely Planet; 112(r): loreanto/Shutterstock; 113(l): yu_photo/Shutterstock; 113(right, from top to bottom): usukkey/Shutterstock; Torjrtrx/

Shutterstock; YUMIK/ Shutterstock; umaruchan4678/ Shutterstock; riphoto3/ Shutterstock; 114: Image Source Limited/Alamy; 115(l): Lottie Davies for Lonely Planet; 115 (right, from top to bottom): flyingv3/Shutterstock; naoima/ Shutterstock; Pongphan Ruengchai/Alamy; karins/ Shutterstock; KPG_Payless/ Shutterstock; 116: Rintaro Kanemoto for Lonely Planet; 117: Courtesy of Naruki Takimoto; 118: Courtesy of Naruki Takimoto;121(t): M Andy/ Shutterstock; 121(b): The Washington Post/Getty Images; 122: Hayashi Kisara/Shutterstock; 123(l): galuhtati/Shutterstock; 123(right, from top to bottom): kai keisuke/Shutterstock; sevenke/ Shutterstock; aomas/Shutterstock; bonchan/Shutterstock; hikaru59/ Shutterstock; 125(l): Tomoharu Awano; 125(r): MeijiShowa/Alamy; 126: Courtesy of Haruki Sato; 129(l): interstid/Shutterstock; 129(r): VTT Studio/Shutterstock; 130: Mizu to Takumi; 131(tl): Mizu to Takumi; 131(bl): Mizu to Takumi; 131(right, from top to bottom): Kritchai7752/ Shutterstock; zepp1969/ Shutterstock; Ermak Oksana/ Shutterstock; yukimco/ Shutterstock; Luba Kuzmicheva/ Shutterstock; 132: Courtesy of Yasuhiro Hikiami; 134:Photour.1904/Shutterstock; 135: Bloomberg/Getty Images;137(t): Lottie Davies for Lonely Planet; 137(b): Courtesy of Kyoto Ippodo Tea Tearoom; 138:Nishihama/Shutterstock; 139(l): Lozzy Squire/Alamy; 139(r):CandyRetriever/ Shutterstock; 141(l): Wissuta.on/ Shutterstock; 141(r):SouthernCrx/ Shutterstock; 142: Bundo Kim/ Unsplash; 143(l): Karl Panganiban/ Shutterstock;143(right, from top to bottom): SOURCENEXT/Alamy; Mironov Vladimir/Shutterstock; skdkzhr/Shutterstock;Shunskee.t/ Getty Images; Daniel Garcia Mendoza/Alamy; 144: Rintaro Kanemoto for Lonely Planet; 145(t):Rintaro Kanemoto for Lonely Planet; 145(b): The Asahi Shimbun/Getty Images;146(l): Darien Robertson for Lonely Planet; 146(r): Jonathan Stokes for Lonely Planet; 147: VTT Studio/ Shutterstock; 148: Various images/ Shutterstock; 149(l): Masayuki Nakaya for Lonely Planet; 149(r): Jonathan Stokes for Lonely Planet; 150: makieni/Shutterstock; 151: Jonathan Stokes for Lonely Planet; 152: Courtesy of Marie Chiba; 155(t): RICHARD A. BROOKS/Getty Images; 155(b): The Asahi Shimbun/Getty Images; 156: The Print Collector /Alamy; 157(l): Rintaro Kanemoto for Lonely Planet; 157(r): Rintaro Kanemoto for Lonely Planet; 158: Courtesy of Shinji Matsunobu; 160: Junichi Miyazaki for Lonely Planet; 161(l): KOHUKU/ Shutterstock; 161(r):yamasan0708/ Shutterstock; 163: Greg Elms for Lonely Planet; 164: ManuelCastro97/Shutterstock; 165: Sergii Rudiuk/Alamy; 166(tl): Philip Lee Harvey for Lonely Planet; 166(bl): marcociannarel/ Shutterstock;166(r): Biodigger/ Shutterstock; 167(l): Teina.F/ Shutterstock; 167 (right, from top to bottom): Philip Lee Harvey for Lonely Planet; Paitoon Keatkeereerut/Shutterstock; 167 Sergii Rudiuk/Alamy; nukopic/ Shutterstock; Samuel Ponce/ Shutterstock; 168: Gift of Mr. and Mrs. Jerome Koizim, 1978/The Metropolitan Museum of Art; 169(t): Tibor Bognar/Alamy; 169(b): Julian Krakowiak; 170: Aflo Co. Ltd./Alamy; 171: Chito Yoshida; 172(l): Tony Evans/ Timelapse Library Ltd./Getty Images; 172(r): steve wanstall/ Getty Images; 173(l): ajisai13/ Shutterstock; 173 (right, from top to bottom): PAUL ATKINSON/ Shutterstock; YA/BOT/Alamy; Courtesy of Tokoname City; Julian Krakowiak; Courtesy of Yuki Ogami; 174: Courtesy of Seiichi Otsuka;176: Kozaru/Shutterstock; 177(t): Yuichi Yamazaki/Getty Images; 177(b): Yuichi Yamazaki/ Getty Images; 178: The Harry G. C. Packard Collection of Asian Art, Gift of Harry G. C. Packard, and Purchase, Fletcher, Rogers, Harris Brisbane Dick, and Louis V. Bell Funds, Joseph Pulitzer Bequest, and The Annenberg Fund Inc. Gift, 1975/The Metropolitan Museum of Art; 179(l): Panithi Utamachant/ Alamy; 179(r): Sepia Times/Getty Images; 180: Tadasu Yamamoto © YAYOI KUSAMA; 181(t): Valentina Cantera/Alamy; 181(b): Kieko Watanabe (Pontic Design Office)/ Kohei Nawa; 182: Jonathan Gregson for Lonely Planet; 183: STR/Getty Images; 184: Courtesy of Ouka;186: RICHARD A. BROOKS/Getty Images; 187(l): Buddhika Weerasinghe/Getty Images; 187(r): Manami Okazaki; 189: Kosuke Yoshino/D-T Inc; 190: LESLIE KEE/SIGNO; 192: Jonathan Gregson for Lonely Planet; 193(l): Jonathan Gregson for Lonely Planet; 193(right, from top to bottom): Olena Antonenko/ Shutterstock; Anna Ivanovska/ Shutterstock; eugenehill/ Shutterstock; FotoKina/ Shutterstock; Pixel-Shot/ Shutterstock; 194: Takamatsu Bonsai no Sato; 195(l): Trevor Williams/Getty Images; 195(right, from top to bottom):BJ Warnick/ Newscom/Alamy; Noa/Alamy; Robert Gilhooly/Alamy; DEA / G. NIMATALLAH/Getty Images; blickwinkel/McPHOTO/I. Schulz/ Alamy; 196: Courtesy of Yusuke Hashimoto;198: Okayama Prefectural Tourism Federation; 199(t): Yuichi Yamazaki/Getty Images; 199(b): Felice Beato/ Gilman Collection, Purchase, Robert Rosenkranz Gift, 2005/The Metropolitan Museum of Art; 200: Historic Collection/Alamy; 201:

kitzcorner/Shutterstock; 202: Bloomberg/Getty Images; 203(l): Onnie A Koski/Getty Images; 203(right, from top to bottom): Toshifumi Kitamura/Getty Images; Onnie A Koski/Getty Images; Fotos593/Shutterstock; Clement Cazottes/Alamy; yajima/Shutterstock; 204: Paul Thompson/FPG/Stringer/Getty Images; 205(t): Sepia Times/Getty Images; 205(b): Carl Court/Getty Images; 206: Manami Okazaki; 207: Manami Okazaki; 209(t): Katsushika Hokusai/The Howard Mansfield Collection, Purchase, Rogers Fund,1936/The Metropolitan Museum of Art; 209(b): Suzuki Harunobu/The Howard Mansfield Collection, Purchase, Rogers Fund, 1936/The Metropolitan Museum of Art; 210(l): Utagawa Hiroshige/The Howard Mansfield Collection, Purchase, Rogers Fund, 1936/The Metropolitan Museum of Art; 210(r): Utagawa Hiroshige/The Howard Mansfield Collection, Purchase, Rogers Fund, 1936/The Metropolitan Museum of Art; 211(t): Jonathan Gregson for Lonely Planet; 211(b): Pictures from History/Getty Images; 212: Bed and Craft; 214: Hachi888/Shutterstock; 217(tl): Makistock / Shutterstock; 217(tr): Kevin Str/Shutterstock; 217(bl): Rintaro Kanemoto for Lonely Planet; 217(br): ESB Professional / Shutterstock; 218(l): Pasakorn Hansetagan/Shutterstock; 218(r): Marcel Hamonic/Shutterstock; 219(t): Malcolm Fairman/Alamy; 219(b): DCrane/Shutterstock; 221: Richard Whitcombe/Shutterstock; 222: Ong.thanaong/Shutterstock; 223(t): structuresxx/Getty Images; 223(b): brize99/Shutterstock; 224: Torsakarin/Getty Images; 225(t): saki kazu/Shutterstock; 225(b): The Asahi Shimbun/Getty Images; 226: f11photo/Shutterstock; 227(t): AsiaTravel/Shutterstock; 227(b): Sergey_Bogomyako/Shutterstock; 228: Amazing Aerial/AirPano/Alamy; 229(t): Rintaro Kanemoto for Lonely Planet; 229(b): PixHound / Shutterstock; 230(l): Matt Munro for Lonely Planet; 230(r): masafarnorth/Getty Images; 231(t): Masayuki Nakaya for Lonely Planet; 231(b): Amazing Aerial/AirPano LLC/ Sergey Semenov/Alamy; 232: Courtesy of Noriko Uchimuro; 234: IBUKI's photograph/Shutterstock; 235(l): Wide Snow/ 500px/Getty Images; 235(r): Bill Raften/Getty Images; 236: Toshi Sasaki/Getty Images; 237: FOTOGRIN/Shutterstock; 238: makieni/Shutterstock; 240: Matjaz Corel/Alamy; 241: Pichit Tongma/Shutterstock; 243(t): Ondrej Prosicky/Shutterstock; 243(bl): 23frogger/Shutterstock; 243(br): Simon Zenger/Shutterstock; 244: BluePacificMedia/Shutterstock; 245: Zoonar GmbH/Noppasin Wongchum/Alamy; 246(l): kitzcorner/Shutterstock; 246(r): Florian Augustin/Shutterstock; 247(t): Blue Planet Archive LLC/Alamy; 247(b): Ippei Naoi/Getty Images; 249(t): Charles Mann/Alamy; 249(b): Kevin Schafer/Getty Images; 250: B.S.P.I./Getty Images; 251: beauty-film/Shutterstock; 252: robertharding/Christopher Rennie/Alamy; 254: Courtesy of Shinobu Sawada; 256: xin.w/Shutterstock; 257(t):The Asahi Shimbun/Getty Images; 257(b): The Print Collector /Alamy; 258: simpletun/Shutterstock; 259(l): Nicolas Datiche/Getty Images; 259(r): paprikaworks/Getty Images; 260: Courtesy of Dr. Nobuko Inaba; 263: Nacho Such/Shutterstock; 264(tl):Toshihiro Nakajima/Getty Images; 264(tr): Ippei Naoi/Getty Images; 264(b): Tupungato/Shutterstock; 266: Naritsorn Hirunon/Shutterstock; 268: Florilegius/Getty Images; 269: Pictures from History/Getty Images; 270(l): Boston Museum of Fine Arts/Wikimedia Commons; 270(r): Michael Ochs Archives/Stringer/Getty Images; 271(l): mikico; 271(right, from top to bottom): Robin Barton; 273(l): cowardlion/Shutterstock; 273(r): Imago/Alamy; 274(l): The Asahi Shimbun/Getty Images; 274(r): MeijiShowa/Alamy; 275(t):Peera_stockfoto / Shutterstock; 275(b): Photo12/7e Art/Toei Animation/Alamy; 276: GRANGER - Historical Picture Archive/Alamy; 277(l): DerekTeo/Shutterstock; 277(right, from top to bottom): BFA/Alamy; Album/Alamy; United Archives GmbH / Alamy; Moviestore Collection Ltd/Alamy; RGR Collection/Alamy; 279(l): Thomas Kyhn/Alamy; 279(r): Vini Brasil/Unsplash; 280: Marc Broussely/Getty Images; 281(t):Michelly Rall/Getty Images; 281(b): Byjeng/Shutterstock; 282: Tomohiro Ohsumi/Getty Images; 283: Ned Snowman/Shutterstock; 284: Courtesy of Tomotaka Takahashi; 286: Behrouz Mehri/Getty Images; 287(l): Supachai Panyaviwat/Shutterstock; 287(right, from top to bottom): Yuichi Yamazaki/Getty Images; icosha/Shutterstock; Nicola_K_photos/Shutterstock; Drazen Zigic/Shutterstock; Zuhri Alka/Shutterstock; 288: Pictures from History/Getty Images; 289: Sakarin Sawasdinaka/Shutterstock; 291(tl): Vassamon Anansukkasem/Shutterstock; 291(tr): The Asahi Shimbun/Getty Images; 291(m): TimeDepot.Twn/Shutterstock; 291(b): Kitinut Jinapuck/Shutterstock; 293(l): Jungmook Lim/Alamy; 293(right, from top to bottom): Sancha Abimanyu/Shutterstock; Pe3k/Shutterstock;ARMOR PROJECT_BIRD STUDIO_SQUARE ENIX; Wachiwit/Shutterstock; Wachiwit/Alamy; 295: f11photo/Shutterstock

Profiles

MARIE CHIBA studied at the National Research Institute of Brewing and trained with producers across Japan. One of the most influential voices in Japan's new sake movement, she owns sake bars Eureka! in Tokyo and Marie in Bangkok, and has authored a sake-themed manga and a book on sake food pairings.
@eureka.sake (tokyo)

SUSUMU HARA is head coach of Aoyama Gakuin University's track and field team, now the most successful in the history of the prestigious Hakone Ekiden race. He has authored several books – including a manga – on running, sharing his coaching philosophy and innovative approach.
hara-susumu.com

YUSUKE HASHIMOTO is a bonsai grower who helped establish Takamatsu Bonsai no Sato, home to one of Japan's largest public bonsai collections. He now promotes bonsai through markets and workshops and runs Sakuya Kobo, focusing on bonsai sales and hands-on learning experiences.
takamatsu-bonsai.com/en/
@bonsai.takamatsu

BENIKO HATSUYANAGI was born in Niigata's Furumachi district, one of Japan's few remaining geisha quarters. An esteemed *geigi* (geisha) and head of the Geigi Association, she helps preserve the refined arts, traditions and hospitality of a profession often associated only with Kyoto.
niigata-cci.or.jp/geigi-en
@ryutoshinko

YASUHIRO HIKIAMI is a *wagashi* chef and fourth-generation owner of renowned Hikiami Kogetsudo in Toyama, specialising in traditional Japanese sweets. His work elevates confectionery into edible art, with each sweet reflecting time, place and the beauty of impermanence.
hikiami.co.jp
@hikiami_kougetsudo

NOBUKO INABA is director of the Mt Fuji World Heritage Centre in Shizuoka, designed by architect Shigeru Ban to commemorate Fuji's designation as a UNESCO World Cultural Heritage Site. The centre explores the volcano's geological, artistic and spiritual significance and offers panoramic views of Japan's most revered peak.
mtfuji-whc.jp

HIROMI ISORI & KEIKO SAITO run Kussharo Factory in Hokkaidō, where together they craft works that embody the spirit and traditions of Ainu culture. Born in a *kotan* (Ainu settlement) on the shores of Lake Kussharo, Hiromi Isori learned woodcarving from his Ainu parents; his partner Keiko Saito practices Ainu embroidery.
visit-teshikaga.com
facebook.com/kussharofactory2007

KAORU KAMO is based in Inami, Toyama – Japan's largest centre of woodcarving – and is a fifth-generation woodcarver and lacquer artist. She also offers hands-on woodblock print workshops at the Bed and Craft boutique hotel in Inami.
en.bedandcraft.com
@bedandcraft

KAZUMI KAYO hails from Okinawa, and founded Yonner Food in Naha in 2007 to preserve and share Ryūkyū culinary wisdom. A qualified nutritionist in Chinese medicine, she teaches Okinawan home cooking, court cuisine and Blue Zone–inspired dishes, passing on the island's food culture to future generations.
yonnerfood.jp
@yonnerfood

FUMIHIKO KONDO is museum director at Daihatsu's Humobility World in Osaka, where displays reveal how Japan's tiny, innovative kei cars became cultural icons shaped by postwar necessity, narrow streets and a national talent for doing more with less.
en.osaka-info.jp/spot/humobility-world

SHINJI MATSUNOBU is a third-generation tea farmer, head of Yamayu Tea Farm in Yame, Fukuoka, and chair of the Yame Tea Division of Japan Agriculture Cooperative. Tea growing in Yame began in 1423, when Zen monk Eirin Shuzui brought tea seeds and cultivation techniques from China and planted the first fields beside the Reigan-ji temple.

HAYATO NAKAMURA was born into one of Japan's most distinguished acting families, and made his stage debut at Tokyo's Kabuki-za aged nine. Acclaimed for revitalising kabuki for younger generations while preserving its elegance, he captivates audiences both in Japan and abroad, alongside work in TV and film.
instagram: @1130_nakamurahayato

KAZUHIRO OTANI is from Nagato Yumoto, Yamaguchi Prefecture's oldest hot-spring town, and is the fifth-generation owner of Otani Sansō ryokan, custodian of Ontō

bathhouse and proprietor of Bettei Otozure, a luxury ryokan awarded a Michelin Key. With the Yudō Association, he works to preserve Japan's bathing culture.
visit.yumotoonsen.com
@yumoto.mirai

SEIICHI OTSUKA runs Daisei Gama, the largest climbing kiln in Mashiko – one of Japan's most renowned pottery towns, known for its earthy stoneware and its enduring influence on Japan's folk-craft Mingei Movement. A seventh-generation potter, his family have been handcrafting ceramics here using wood-ash glazes and traditional methods since 1861.
mashiko-tourism.com

OUKA brings ink art to every corner of Japanese culture – from exhibitions and TV appearances to creating anime characters and titles, corporate logos, product labels, signage and train wraps. Blending traditional calligraphy with creative depictions of *yōkai* (spirits and supernatural beings), she shares her talent through workshops and is an ambassador for Japanese calligraphy.
xxxouka.com
@ouka_yokai

HARUKI SATO is the fourth-generation chef-owner of Dewaya, a Yamagata restaurant famed for its seasonal mountain cuisine. After studying tourism and management in Tokyo, he returned home at 23 to continue his family's legacy; his on-site chef's counter shares the cultural and ecological value of *sansai* (wild mountain vegetables) with a wider audience.
dewaya.com
@sansai_dewaya

SHINOBU SAWADA is editor-in-chief of *Niwa*, Japan's leading garden magazine. Having studied Japanese gardens and environmental design at Kyoto University of the Arts and worked across architecture, interiors and gardening publications, she has deep insight into historical and contemporary Japanese gardens.
niwamag.net
@niwa_mag

TOMOTAKA TAKAHASHI is a robotics creator who was named one of the '33 Persons Who Will Change the Future' by *Popular Science*. Founder and CEO of Robo Garage, visiting professor at Osaka Electro-Communication University and founder of Marine X, his creations include Kirobo, the world's first robot astronaut companion; RoBoHoN, a miniature humanoid smartphone that talks, walks and dances; and energy-efficient Evolta robots.
www.robo-garage.com

NARUKI TAKIMOTO moved to London for a music career, but instead found his calling in sushi. Returning to Japan, he trained for 10 years at prestigious Tokyo sushi restaurants before opening Naruki in 2022. In his hometown of Himi, a fishing port on Toyama Bay, he serves sushi that showcases some of Japan's finest, freshest seafood.
naruki-himi.com
@naruki_himi

TOMOKIYO TANAKA is senior priest at the ancient shrine of Iwashimizu Hachimangū, set atop Otokoyama near Kyoto. He is deeply engaged in interfaith peacebuilding and academic research on the spiritual philosophy of Shintō and its role in fostering harmony.
iwashimizu.or.jp
@iwashimizuhachimangu_grace

NORIKO UCHIMURO was born in Kōbe and moved to Yakushima in 2001 in search of 'a place blessed with sea, mountains, and rivers, where the water and air are delicious.' Now a certified eco-guide, she helps visitors understand the island's deep bond between people and nature.
sangakutaro.com

KENJIRO 'KENNY' UEDA is a 7th-dan master of *Shōrin-ryū* and *Shitō-ryū* karate, and a *kobudō* (traditional martial arts) practitioner with over 40 years of training and worldwide teaching experience. As CEO of Ageshio Japan, he offers specialist karate travel experiences that immerse travellers in the philosophy, culture, and spirit of Okinawan martial arts.
ageshiojapan.com

AYANO UEHARA made history riding in the annual Sōma Nomaoi Festival – a 1000-year-old samurai horseback battle – after rules were amended to permit women over 20. A senior director at Sōma City Hall, she views the festival as essential to preserving her hometown's culture and community spirit.
soma-nomaoi.jp

KOHEI & MANAMI YAMADA are reimagining the ryokan as a cultural salon, blending tradition and innovation in the spirit of Hokuriku-region hospitality. A sixth-generation owner of Hanamurasaki ryokan in Yamanaka Onsen, Ishikawa, Kohei studied art in San Francisco before returning to his hometown.
hana-mura.com
@hanamurasaki_official

NANREI YOKOTA is chief abbot of the Engaku-ji branch of the Rinzai school, president of Hanazono University and director of the Institute for Zen Studies. A Zen master, he guides monks and lay practitioners through sitting Zen, rituals and teachings that connect centuries-old Zen wisdom with the challenges of modern life.
engakuji.or.jp

Love Japan
September 2026
Published by Lonely Planet Global Limited
CRN 554153
www.lonelyplanet.com
10 9 8 7 6 5 4 3 2 1
Printed in Malaysia
ISBN 978 18065 3299 5

Publisher & VP, Print
Piers Pickard
Editorial Director Becca Hunt
Senior Editor Robin Barton
Art Director Emily Dubin
Designer Adrienne Pitts
Editors Polly Thomas, Karyn Noble, Yuriko McLachlan, Craig McLachlan
Print Production
Nigel Longuet

Lonely Planet Global Limited
Digital Depot, Roe Lane (off Thomas St),
Digital Hub, Dublin 8,
D08 TCV4, Ireland
(EU authorised representative)

Stay in touch lonelyplanet.com/contact

Writers Yoko Kawaguchi, Manami Okazaki, Florentyna Leow, Rie Miyoshi, Rob Goss, Simon Richmond, Yuko Tamura, Craig McLachlan, Yuriko McLachlan

Interviews by Kylie Clark

Cover and illustrations Qi Ren

FSC www.fsc.org MIX Paper | Supporting responsible forestry FSC™ C021741

Paper in this book is certified against the Forest Stewardship Council™ standards. FSC™ promotes environmentally responsible, socially beneficial and economically viable management of the world's forests.